Gender and international relations

Gender and international relations

Edited by
REBECCA GRANT AND KATHLEEN NEWLAND

Indiana University Press
BLOOMINGTON AND INDIANAPOLIS

First published 1991 by Open University Press and
Indiana University Press

Manufactured in Great Britain

Library of Congress Cataloging-in-Publication Data

Gender and international relations/edited by Rebecca Grant and
　　Kathleen Newland.
　　　　p.　cm.
　　　ISBN 0–253–32613–3; ISBN 0–253–21265–0 (pbk.)
　　　1. International relations.　2. Sex discrimination against women.
　　3. Feminism.　I. Grant, Rebecca.　II. Newland, Kathleen.
　　JX1391.G46　1991
　　327'.082 – dc20　　　　　　　　　　　　　　　　　　　91–14471

1 2 3 4 5　95 94 93 92 91

To
Lyz Grant Biser
and
Ginny Newland Walther

Contents

List of contributors

Anne Marie Goetz is a research fellow in the Institute of Development Studies at the University of Sussex.

Rebecca Grant is a member of the Political Science Department of the Rand Corporation of Santa Monica, CA.

Fred Halliday is Professor of International Relations at the London School of Economics and Political Science.

Robert O. Keohane is Professor of Government at Harvard University.

Carol Miller is a research student in history at St Hilda's College, Oxford.

Maxine Molyneux is Lecturer in Sociology at the University of Essex.

Caroline O. N. Moser is Lecturer in Social Planning of Developing Countries at the London School of Economics and Political Science.

Kathleen Newland is Lecturer in International Relations at the London School of Economics and Political Science.

J. Ann Tickner is Associate Professor of Political Science at the College of the Holy Cross, Worcester, MA.

Acknowledgements

This book is one of the products of a continuing exploration of gender issues in international relations, which was initiated at the London School of Economics in 1988. Several of the chapters here first appeared in a special issue of *Millennium: Journal of International Studies*, published from the LSE in winter 1988. The special issue grew out of the efforts of several people who had begun to investigate the prospects for research and teaching on women and international relations.

Professor Fred Halliday of the International Relations Department at LSE was the first to suggest the topic to the staff of *Millennium*. In June 1988 the journal joined with the International Relations Department to sponsor a one-day symposium on women and international relations at LSE. Encouraged by the enthusiasm of the participants and the quality of the discussion in the symposium, the editors of *Millennium*, Rebecca Grant and David Long, decided to gather material for a short discussion section to appear in the journal. One of the participants they approached to write an article for the journal was Kathleen Newland. Almost all of those who were asked to write responded positively. The outpourings of articles was such that the editors decided to devote an entire issue of *Millennium* to them.

In January 1989 Fred Halliday, Margot Light and Kathleen Newland introduced a seminar course on women and international relations into the master's degree curriculum of the International Relations Department. The *Millennium* special issue was virtually the only general text specifically on women and international relations available at that time, although there was a great deal of material from other disciplines as well as a growing selection of widely scattered articles. The experience of teaching the course made clear the need for production of a reader. In the meantime scholarly work on gender and international relations was developing a sharper focus. *Millennium* sponsored a panel on the topic at the 1989 joint meeting of the British

International Studies Association and the International Studies Association in London. The summer 1989 issue of *Millennium*, edited by Kathleen Newland, included a discussion section that built upon the special issue.

As editors of this book we are particularly grateful to several *Millennium* staff members. Above all, David Long was instrumental in launching this project. He edited the original versions of several of the chapters reprinted here and has graciously continued to advise us as we compiled the reader. Special thanks also go to the 1988 *Millennium* staff: Hugh C. Dyer, Spyros Economides, Isabelle Grunberg, Fernando Andresen Guimaraes, Mark E. Schaffer, Michael E. Singer and Peter Wilson. The 1990 editors of *Millennium*, Malory Greene and Ian Rowlands, gave us full and cheerful cooperation during the final editing of the manuscript. Ian's technical support and mastery of the electronic mail system was essential, making for much easier transcontinental communication between the editors and a much smoother production of the manuscript. We thank him, too, for moral support and general hand holding.

Among the LSE faculty we are especially indebted, for ideas and encouragement, to Fred Halliday and Margot Light, who co-taught the women and international relations seminar, and to Michael Banks, John Vincent and Philip Windsor. Thanks also to our other colleagues in the International Relations Departments – even the sceptics, who in a most collegial way forced us to sharpen our thinking.

The students who enrolled for the new seminar on women and international relations were both pioneers and guinea-pigs. It was their response to a still evolving course that, above all, convinced us of the value of making gender issues a part of the international relations curriculum, and encouraged us to compile a book that would be useful to them. Their excitement about the subject was infectious; their positive feedback has been the fuel that kept us moving forward. They helped to allay the fears of some colleagues by working hard and distinguishing themselves in university exams and essays. Some have already gone on to publish in this field. As in the best seminars, they were as much teachers as taught.

The article by Caroline Moser first appeared in *World Development* (Vol. 17, No. 11, 1989); we are grateful for her permission and that of Pergamon Press to reprint it here.

Shirley Maltby gave much appreciated help with typing some of the articles under great pressure of time.

We found great pleasure and support in our collaboration with each other and drew heavily on the emotional resources of family and friends. Kathleen would particularly like to thank Jurek Martin for, among many other things, an exemplary working model of non-sexist praxis, personal and professional.

Finally, we would like to thank our authors. A number of them have been involved with us in this process from the very beginning, from the initial symposium at LSE, through the special issue and the ISA panel and into the classroom as guest speakers in the women and international relations seminar. We are enormously grateful to them for their commitment, their encouragement, their stimulation and their friendship. As the exploration of, and debate on, gender issues in international relations is just beginning, we look forward to a continuing collaboration with all of them.

1

Introduction

REBECCA GRANT AND KATHLEEN NEWLAND

International relations is a discipline concerned with the fate of the world; but the world with which it deals is a fragmentary and distorted version of the world in which we live. While we subscribe to the view that no one mind can offer up a whole and true vision of the world as it really is, we do believe that some versions presented of it are less fragmentary and distorted than others and that these can lead to a better understanding of what goes on in the world in that arena cordoned off by our discipline.

International relations, like many other disciplines, has operated with a relatively narrow conception of what is relevant to its subject matter. Excluded from that conception, quite comprehensively, is the experience of most women. This is not only because women are, with rare exceptions absent from the circle of people – the makers of foreign policy – whose direct experience is the stuff of traditional international relations. It is also because international relations theory has, overwhelmingly, been constructed by men working with mental models of human activity and society seen through a male eye and apprehended through a male sensibility. The component ideas of international relations are accordingly gendered, because women and men experience societies and their interactions differently.

The foregoing is an observation that is relevant to all traditional social science; as Sandra Harding has written, it 'has asked only the questions about social life that appear problematical from within the social experiences that are characteristic of men'.[1] This is a particular problem for international relations because theories of international society so often reason from analogy with domestic societies or from a mythic 'state of nature' whose imagined characteristics reflect the gender of the theorist. Knowledge and theory, in other words, are built upon experience. Differences of experience endow fundamental concepts in international relations – such as authority, sovereignty, security, development and power – with different meanings, and with meanings that carry the influence of gender. As long as the discipline excludes all that flows from women's experiences of the world from its field of vision it will continue working with a version of the world that is more partial and distorted than is otherwise possible. Students of international relations cannot fully understand their subject matter until they can evaluate the ways in which gender has shaped both our conceptions of the state and the international system on the one hand, and the methods for analysing them on the other.

Gender constitutes one of the most basic sources of division and definition in political society. Who, for example, is defined as being a citizen and allowed to vote, hold office or go into combat? As a basis of political experience gender has profound implications for the foundations of international relations. Perhaps it is no accident that more international relations scholars have started to take an interest in questions of gender at a time when many are reflecting on the rather narrow philosophical traditions of the discipline. Gender is a topic that points out that the basic units of political experience, the identity of the state and the structure of the international system, have been constructed on an exclusive and sometimes artificial basis. The cumulative process of acquiring knowledge and developing theoretical and practical agendas has drawn on a selective set of sources.

Because women were omitted from most of the classic studies of political theory the discipline of international relations incorporates gender bias in its very definitions and theories of knowledge. As some of the following chapters suggest, part of the challenge is to develop a feminist epistemology for international relations. A feminist epistemology means most simply that gender becomes a prime element in understanding the theory and practice of international relations. At present, gender bias and the exclusion of women's experience in political theory cause doubts about the epistemological basis of the discipline. We look at gender as a methodological and ideological element capable of transforming and enriching our comprehension of international politics.

The process of bringing gender issues to the international relations agenda is not easy, in part because the discipline has adopted epistemological stances based on history and on a positivist conception of social science. From the start international relations has had difficulty drawing the connections between individual citizens – male or female – and the states system. The focus on events and behaviour has not been conducive to feminist thought because the role of women has long been muffled. At the same time the competing influences of realism, idealism, Marxism, behaviourism and so forth have had one particular effect in common. These intellectual concepts which helped define the discipline also gave the appearance of transcending gender issues. This gave international relations the aura of a discipline moving in the most progressive directions, albeit from a narrow starting point. As one scholar has described it:

International Relations started life in a way that was very different from the other social sciences: it was prescriptive, normative and based on a conception of scholarly activity that stressed the immediate policy-relevance of work. This led to the discipline being concerned above all with devising procedures and techniques to assist rational decision-makers to avoid war ... the way the First World War had started loomed large. International Relations developed as a response to events in the real world and defined its purpose as preventing their repetition.[2]

However, international relations has not successfully left behind the basic questions of how political experience is moulded and fitted into the fragmentary vision of the world that we know so well. From the vantage point of the feminist scholar this description highlights both discrimination and opportunity. First, the subject of international relations clearly developed as a product of the twentieth century. Feminist movements, too, were stimulated by the aftermath of the First World War. Yet few links formed between the efforts of the idealist international relations commentators to prescribe world peace and the efforts of women to rally to the same cause. It would be hard not to conclude that international relations as an academic discipline more or less consciously ignored women as actors from the start. It has also ignored the emancipation of women, from the time they won the vote until the time, decades later, when more of them began to win professional stature within governments. Some of the early strands of thinking on international relations were normative, activist, generally well meaning; and yet they were fraught with inherited gender bias. International relations defined its purpose in response to only some of the events of the real world.

For the most part the more recent generations of debate on the substance of the discipline have continued the habit of excluding gender from their thinking. The small collection of academics who write on gender and international relations debate whether dominant currents of thought can be made receptive to gender questions. One of the most disturbing conclusions is that neither realism nor liberalism satisfy the requirements of feminist enquiry, albeit for different reasons. Some scholars have explicitly predicted that reconciliation is impossible. Many others assert that, to some extent, the discipline of international relations must be reconstructed to accommodate research on gender questions.

Despite this assessment a strong sense of opportunity remains. International relations is concerned with affecting policy, clarifying the major struggles of the world, understanding international conflict and assisting decision-makers in national governments and in international institutions. Women belong on this agenda. They have always been a part of relations between states; and many of the most critical problems of the world, in developing and advanced societies, cannot be understood apart from gender politics. To their credit, many scholars and practitioners have recognized that the limited vision of states moving in a system of anarchy does not fulfil the potential of the discipline. However strong the sense of opportunity, what is required is an explicit effort to identify and rectify the gendered construction of international relations.

Women as a category, gender as a topic and the impact of feminism as an ideology are three powerful sources of ideas which can contribute to a new, feminist epistemology of international relations. Even if international relations is interpreted as a sturdy workhorse ploughing toward immediate policy-relevance, its goals will never be attained until it is recognized that women are relevant to policy.

The research embodied in this volume takes special care to point out the difficulties in working with the concepts of women, gender and feminism. As editors we have chosen to title the book *Gender and international relations*; but the choice requires some explanation. Why not substitute women or feminism? We could define the topic of gender and international relations as an examination of women in relation to the state and its international policies. Certainly this is an important component. It has the extra benefit of making clear that women are the subject of the enquiry. However, this approach ultimately could not guarantee that several larger issues would be addressed. It runs the risk of encouraging the view that the subject of women is just one of many possible, optional add-ons to international relations; something akin to an area specialization, having no greater or lesser validity than other points of view. This we want to contradict. We are convinced that the lens of gender offers not just an alternative vision of the world, but one that is more whole and more representative of the spectrum of experience out of which international conflict and cooperation arise. It offers the possibility of an escape from one of the major sources of fragmentation and distortion in our discipline.

Feminism offers a powerful set of criteria for the reconsideration of the field. Like much of international relations it is normative, carrying an implicit agenda for change. In essence, the feminist enquiry is one that gives primacy to women, at the theoretical and practical level. It draws on a diverse body of literature containing many insights for international relations scholars. The terms feminism and feminist theory, however, are neither simple nor well defined. Major divisions separate feminist theorists, and the study of gender and international relations must acknowledge these and indeed welcome them. As international relations scholars we contend that the priority is to accept and admit the differences between radical, liberal or Marxist feminists, not to fight that battle first. The discipline has historically functioned with great diversity in its theoretical foundations. The diversity of feminist thought is no handicap and should not stand in the way of conducting research on the gendered nature of international relations. Several of the chapters that follow touch on some of the controversies in feminist thought.

A major contribution of feminism is that it enables scholars to draw on a coherent body of thought and to formulate hypotheses based on the principles of feminist enquiry. Both criticism and reformulation are included. Feminism calls into question the boundaries of the discipline, particularly those that cordon off the realm of the private from the public affairs that are the 'proper' subject of international relations. In its best known slogan feminism denies the boundary between the personal and the political. A feminist approach to international relations insists not only on the relevance of women's experience but also on its validity as a constitutive element of international relations. It draws attention to the ways in which the exclusion of women from the realm of 'high politics' has legitimized their subordination and oppression.

The limitation of feminist approaches is that they may confine attention to the damage done to *women* by an international system based on patriarchy, when the damage has been more pervasive. The exclusion of women's experience from the conceptualization of international relations has had negative consequences both for the discipline and for male and female inhabitants of the real world. A central hypothesis is that this exclusion has resulted in an academic field excessively focused on conflict and anarchy, and a way of practising statecraft and formulating strategy that is excessively focused on competition and fear. These are problems that go beyond feminism.

The choice of the term gender signifies one further step in the re-examination of the discipline. It carries forward the criteria of feminist thought, including the focus on women, but makes clear that the problematic does not end (though it does begin) with women. We understand gender as 'a systematic social construction of masculinity and femininity that is little, if at all, constrained by biology'.[3]

Using gender as an epistemological starting point promises from the outset that the crucial political problem of the relations between women and men will be thoroughly examined. Relations between women and men in domestic society have coloured the basis of political thought for centuries. The separations and struggles conjured up by the term gender bias reach back to capture the influences that shaped the twentieth century and spawned the subject of international relations in the first place.

To study gender and international relations requires ultimately that the peculiar social construction of masculinity in Western thought be examined and its influence on the theory and conduct of international relations scrutinized. Again, this line of enquiry may be a fruitful one in all the social sciences. It is, however, particularly important in international relations because of the degree of abstraction that results in the conflation of an extreme and exclusive idea of masculinity (the warrior, prince or modern practitioner of *realpolitik*) with the supposedly rational, archetypal human being. The introduction of gender as a consideration breaks down this monolith. It forces a recognition that every archetype emerges from a specific historical context and carries a good deal of baggage from it.

What are scholars of international relations to do with this awareness? For some it seems to threaten an end to theory, as it undercuts all the bases for generalization. For others it promises a truer and more objective international relations, as the horizons of the discipline are systematically expanded. For us it seems to offer at least a more self-conscious and reflective scholarship, an awareness of the sources of assumptions, a healthy degree of humility and a stimulating introduction of new questions. These can only add to the vitality of the discipline.

The divisions among the three ways of broadening the study of international relations are not watertight. Though they have different emphases each has much to contribute. The study of women and international relations is probably the most widely accepted as a legitimate sub-topic of the field, though it is often regarded as marginal. None the less, few would deny that women are involved in distinctive ways in international processes such as migration and development assistance; that transnational phenomena like the changing international division of labour have differential impacts on women and men; or that relations between the sexes are shaped, changed and sometimes distorted by forces external to a particular society. Women's rights have explicitly entered the realm of multilateral diplomacy. Feminism and international relations has a secure niche, though it is even more marginalized at the crossing of two fields of study that have only rarely intersected. Gender and international relations is the formulation most fundamentally challenging to the discipline as traditionally constituted, and therefore the least likely to gain a hearing easily. But it is very much in tune with other currents in the field which are also questioning the assumptions on which traditional scholarship in international relations has been based.

The chapters in this book were selected for one particular reason. All of them represent research specifically on international relations topics. Gender issues raise several new questions and only some of them fit immediately into the current agenda of research on international relations. A great deal more work has been done in other disciplines, much of it relevant to international relations. Numerous books and journal articles have delved into gender issues in domestic politics, philosophy, anthropology and so forth. Historians have reclaimed women's history, much of it interesting to international relations scholars. Studies of women and of feminist movements in different countries have yielded a rich comparative literature. Many of these works will be useful to future work on gender and international relations topics. Our aim in this volume was to spotlight research that has already taken on the task of integration. Also, we wanted to ensure that connections between gender issues and international relations were drawn as clearly and strongly as possible, by scholars well versed in international relations.

Rebecca Grant, in the chapter immediately following this introduction, locates the origins of gender bias in international relations in the foundational theories of political philosophy upon which the discipline draws for some of its most basic concepts. Ann Tickner then provides a model of feminist rethinking of traditional theory as she illuminates the unconscious masculine bias in Hans Morgenthau's six principles of political realism. Robert Keohane comments on a widely used typology of feminist approaches – empiricism, standpoint and post-modernism – and evaluates their potential for contributing to international relations theory.

Maxine Molyneux examines the international influence of socialist states (particularly the Soviet Union) in promoting feminism as an official ideology, and the impact on women's concerns of the collapse of the orthodox communist system. Carol Miller looks farther back in history, to Britain between the two world wars. She investigates the debate on what direct roles women might properly play in international relations, as diplomats and international civil servants.

The role of women in economic development is one of the most prominent areas of international concern for feminist scholars. Caroline Moser analyses the gap between the conceptual awareness of women's important role in development and the actual practice of development planning by international agencies. Kathleen Newland traces the evolution of the non-governmental, transnational movement concerned with the impact of development on women, and looks at how it changed when Women in Development was incorporated within the inter-governmental framework of the United Nations. Anne Marie Goetz examines epistemological issues in feminist writing on women and development, and stresses the importance of situating analysis in the realities of women's specific settings. She also highlights the fundamental problem of different cultural conceptions of feminism, placing it within the setting of post-modernist evaluation.

Finally, Fred Halliday sums up the challenges of incorporating women and international relations into the subject matter of the established academic field. He cautions against expecting the inclusion of a new area of study to revolutionize the teaching and study of international relations as a whole, but argues that it is important for the further development of the discipline.

No one volume can hope to be comprehensive. The diversity of approaches in this volume shows the wealth of ideas that are being generated by the introduction of gender to the study of international relations. Happily, there is now a great deal of work being done. With this collection, we hope to stimulate more.

Notes

1 Sandra Harding, 'Introduction: is there a feminist methodology?', in Sandra Harding (ed.), *Feminism and Methodology* (Milton Keynes: Open University Press, 1987), p. 6.
2 Steve Smith, 'Paradigm dominance in international relations: the development of international relations as a social science', in Hugh D. Dyer and Leon Mangasarian (eds), *The Study of International Relations: The State of the Art* (Basingstoke: Macmillan, 1989), p. 7.
3 Harding, *op. cit.*

2

The sources of gender bias in international relations theory

REBECCA GRANT

Gender issues have been on the research agenda of history, law, philosophy, several of the social sciences and even the natural sciences for the past two decades. International relations has taken on gender questions much more recently. One of the first conclusions was that women were hidden actors in the international system. Women in developing societies often performed much of the labour but received little attention from international aid and development agencies. Yet in the Western world women have been emerging as actors over the last three decades. A handful of women have become generals, ambassadors, middle-level officials in foreign ministries and even prime ministers. Still, the charge that women have nothing to do with relations between states sounds disturbingly plausible. After all, states are not people. Many scholars of international relations may be willing to accept that women constitute a group within societies, and should be taken into account in specific areas of research such as development policy. Very few are comfortable with the idea that women have anything to do with the theory of international relations.

For those who believe women do have something to do with international relations theory (or those who are willing to discuss the matter), the first obstacle is the term women. The real target is gender: not the anatomical difference between the female and the male sex but the complicated aspect of social being known as gender. When tradition teaches that those of the female gender perform certain tasks in society while those of the male gender perform others, the separation is not made between specific, individual women and men. Gender roles are archetypal models of how humans function in society. These roles reflect the way that humans understand their place in the world in intellectual, social and political terms. A gender distinction between who could vote and who could not reflected attitudes toward women at a certain point in history. However, the distinction was based more broadly on how that area of human activity known as politics was defined. Some people and some issues came into the realm of politics; others did not. Reserving the question of gender bias for a moment, it can be seen that much the same thing happened in the realm of international politics. Some concerns and issues became the substance of international relations; others did not.

The gender bias throughout the Western political and philosophical tradition has gone unquestioned in international relations theory. The result is that gender (not to mention women) appears to be an irrelevant question. Yet the whole theoretical approach to international relations rests on a foundation of political concepts, most of which would be far more difficult to hold together coherently were it not for the trick of eliminating women from the prevailing definitions of man as political actor. In the Western tradition men, not women, are the models for political theory. This chapter seeks first to identify some of the sources of gender bias that the academic discipline of international relations has incorporated from the Western tradition.

Sources of gender bias

'Every great scholarly movement has its own lore, its own collectively recalled creation myths, its ritualized understanding of the titanic struggles fought and challenges still to be overcome' in maintaining the distinction between one discipline and another.[1] This is Richard Ashley's warning to beware of the battles that have been fought to define the basic concepts of international relations theory. For each creation myth that has come into the mainstream, others have been rejected. International relations theory depends on conceptions of how the individual functions in society and in the state. Discussions of these concepts in Western political theory have been used as explanations of how states legitimate international action. However, one of the major sources of gender bias in international relations theory is the emphasis on males as citizens and political actors, as seen in several classic concepts of political theory. By adopting these examples without investigating the gender bias in them, international relations theory has duplicated the pattern of bias. At the same time, international relations theory has developed with virtually no tools for assessing gender as a political force.

The state of nature

For most students of international relations theory, a common starting point is the behaviour of man in the 'state of nature'. Like international society, the imagined state of nature lacked a formal, hierarchical social organization. The descriptions of man's pre-social behaviour written by Hobbes or Rousseau are therefore used as guides to the behaviour of states. Hobbes marvels that nature renders man apt to invade and destroy. When 'men live without a common Power to keep them all in awe, they are in that condition that is called Warre'.[2] Whether there is open combat or simply suspicious competition, this view is a basic description of the condition of anarchy between states. Hobbes sees few good qualities in man outside society. Within society, man acquires a sense of justice and injustice and other qualities that moderate his behaviour. Using a few of man's better impulses (or 'Passions', in the words of Hobbes) laws are established to regulate behaviour within society. The reader understands that only society – a society of male actors – confers qualities of justice, law, order and so forth in human relations. Hobbes then moves on from the state of nature to discuss the operation of the Leviathan commonwealth, his real interest.

A limited and selective reading of Hobbes is adopted in international relations theory. This interpretation concentrates on characteristics of behaviour without acknowledging that the only gender role under discussion is the male one. Men dominate the conceptual scheme, leaving no room for the question of how gender relations affect the transition out of the brutish state of nature and into society. Women are invisible in the state of nature. They have no role in the formation of laws in the society that replaces the warlike state of nature. All of Hobbes's analyses of rights, sovereign power and political responsibility appear to pertain only to men. Not surprisingly, analogies drawn from Hobbes do not lend themselves easily to questions about gender roles and their effects on political behaviour. When women are absent from the foundation theories, a source of gender bias is created that extends into international relations theory.

Parables of man in the state of nature claim to be universal models. They aim to define what constitutes the social being, what tendencies he will follow in relations with others. However, the abstract formulation of man in the state of nature has used a male archetype of the individual. Perhaps Hobbes and Rousseau were following Aristotle, the first major thinker to draw an allegedly 'natural' distinction between men and women. To Aristotle, women were physically weaker and therefore intellectually inferior to the male.

The exclusion of women weakens the claims of the model. As Simone de Beauvoir demonstrated in *The Second Sex*,[3] the arguments about the struggle between nature and society can be drawn a different way. She has interpreted the ancient image of man's battle for survival as a struggle against Mother Nature. In this interpretation man pitted himself against the feminine, affective attributes and the capricious power of the state of nature. Women, with their mysterious powers of bringing forth life, were a symbol of the power of nature over mankind. The fertility of the land was compared to a woman's fertility. Both essential processes became the source of superstition as well as need in primitive communities. The aim of society was to achieve greater control over these functions and therefore, at the symbolic level, to assert male dominance over the female. De Beauvoir's no less abstract description suggests something Hobbes does not – that society was founded on gender difference and that any critique of 'man in society' must take this first struggle into account.

Rousseau's version of the state of nature might at first appear to transcend the tangled struggle between male and female. The harmony of Rousseau's state of nature would seem to preclude a struggle against a feminized version of nature. However, Rousseau also used a male archetype. The parable of the stag hunt devised by Rousseau (which will be discussed in a later section) is plain evidence that men are the important actors in the state of nature. His sweeping guide to childraising, *Emile*, makes clear that the female is only an adjunct to the male. Her powers are those of the body not of the mind. (Rousseau himself fathered five children by his mistress and forced her to surrender each child for adoption.) Yet Rousseau is subtle. He acknowledges a certain facility in the female: 'Woman's reign is a reign of gentleness, tact and kindness . . . She should reign in the home as a minister reigns in the state, by contriving to be ordered to do what she wants.'[4] However, Rousseau makes clear that, while women have power in this ambiguous situation, they lack understanding. Women exist naturally in the domain of the senses, and to Rousseau the senses are the snares of reason. Reason and understanding can be attained only by men.[5]

Once again the conception of the state of nature is gender biased. Worse, the assumption that Hobbes and Rousseau present an abstract but universal image of humankind has made it difficult for international relations theory to acknowledge gender difference as a crucial factor in defining political experience.

The concept of the state

The earliest practical source of gender bias in international relations theory dates back to the formation of the state two thousand years ago in ancient Hellas (Greece). The Athenian state represented the first triumph of rationality and social organization. Most international relations scholars accept that the Greek state has been a conceptual model for Western states, particularly for democratic ones. However, the emergence of the *polis* also brought into play a notion of citizenship that relegated women to a private sphere of domestic life.

The formation of the state in ancient Greece marked the transition from societies based on kinship to the dominance of patriarchal units, like the male-headed family. Populations of the city states of the Mediterranean and the Near East were small. Subordinating the labour of women in the family made it possible for the state to concentrate its resources and thereby strengthened the economic power of the state. Spike Peterson has observed that the transition affected the position of women because it was necessary to devalue the processes of reproduction and maintenance of the home. Formation of the state depended on a sexual division of labour to establish and reinforce economic and political structures. These were the grounds for separating women into a private sphere. The married woman did have certain rights in Athenian society but she was barred from political life. Her status under the law was circumscribed and her ability to act on her own will outside the home was negligible. Gender bias in Athenian society was partly the product of the state's requirements in its 'international relations' with other city states.[6]

Seen from the theoretical perspective, two sets of social relations were established, with gender as the most important divider. Female roles in society revolved around the work of the home and the family. Male social relations extended to the duties of citizens and soldiers in a democracy, and in this capacity to relations with other city states. The process of distinction began at the level of relations between the two sexes in the structure of the family. However, the political interpretation of difference rested on gender rather than the anatomical difference of sex. The gendered role of the female in the private sphere is a social construction, not a natural one, just as her absence from the political sphere was based not on physical qualities but on the meaning assigned to them. Men were, of course, part of the family; but their public role as citizens was valued more highly. In the political and philosophical texts the public role of men survives while the private role of women has not.

The unequal status of women in Athenian society has continued to have an enormous influence on Western politics and philosophy; and in the twentieth century, it continues to affect international relations theory. Elisabeth Young-Bruehl reminds us that Greek philosophy was born in this very 'era of transition in the eastern Mediterranean from matriarchal to patriarchal societies, from Earth Goddess religions to religions in which male deities or a male deity dominated'. Recent interpretations of archaeological and literary evidence support this conclusion.[7]

Political theory in the Western philosophical tradition begins with Socrates. The *Phaedo* records that on the day of his death Socrates sent away his weeping wife, Xanthippe. She was banished so that Socrates could discourse with his intellectual, male companions before drinking the hemlock. Socrates assumed that 'the private sphere of women and the family had nothing to do with the public sphere of Man and intellect'.[8]

Xanthippe's exclusion makes a dramatic example of the relegation of women in Athenian society; but it also symbolizes the effect of gender bias on Western thought as it has flowed from its classical sources. As Philip Windsor points out, the relegation of women to the private sphere elevated men to the position of solely responsible moral agents in political society. The public/private split was present at the origin of Western philosophy. It condemned women to a position set apart from the progress that men might make toward philosophical enlightenment.[9] By the same token women had no role in the advancement of political society.

From a sociological perspective the public/private distinction is not so simple. In Athens slaves and foreigners also suffered from discrimination.

Exceptional women on occasion had the power to participate in male dialogues. Likewise, as the all too human tales of the male and female Greek gods reflect, women held considerable power in the domestic realm, enough to influence the lives of men.

The point is that the Western philosophical and political tradition took none of the ambiguity of gender relations into account. Any hint of ongoing struggle was dispatched by the assumption that it was natural for women to fulfil only the domestic role. Plato's Guardians in the *Republic* are imagined as both males and females. But the female Guardians have domestic duties; they are not equal enough to make political decisions. Windsor goes on to say that this distinction dangerously implies 'that private and domestic morality is different in kind from, and works at a level inferior to, that of public choice'.[10] In other words, the public/private split made it possible for the state to adopt a kind of morality that is different from the moral requirements of relations among individuals. In an extreme sense excluding women from the public realm also sets a precedent for applying a different standard of morality to the state's treatment of foreigners. Like Plato's Guardians, the public male citizen soldier and the private woman are images, not real depictions. But philosophy and political theory have employed precisely such abstract images to teach us more about the world in general. Whether the public/private split holds up under sociological or historical analysis is a moot point – so long as it thrives in political philosophy and in turn passes into international relations theory.

Lest the Greek example appear unique, a similar process occurred when the foundations for the modern European state were laid at the time of the Renaissance. Historian Joan Kelly has found that the consolidation of mercantile and manufacturing economies in the city states of Italy sparked a transition in social relations. As in the Athenian model the consolidation adversely affected the position of women in society. 'The status of the feudal noblewoman was high before the rise of the state' because in feudal society 'the family order was [also] the public order of her class; and the scope that familial political power gave women included the Church, where aristocratic women commanded a sphere of their own'.[11] Woman had ruled principalities under the feudal system through their familial rights. France's Salic Law of 1328 symbolized the end to this era. It barred women from inheriting the crown of France, as a few had done in the past.[12]

The division of the domestic and the public order in the Italian city states instituted gender-based inequality. The art and literature of the Renaissance repressed the noblewoman's experience in comparison to the relative latitude found in mediaeval writings. Women were increasingly portrayed as objects in a manner that encouraged the division between man's reasoning mind and the affectivity of the body. 'All the advances of Renaissance Italy . . . worked to mold the noblewoman into an aesthetic object: decorous, chaste, and doubly dependent – on her husband as well as the prince', according to Kelly.[13]

Again, the division of women from political life gave rise to the idea that women were symbols of virtue and human qualities which men could not match. Men protected and sheltered women; women were the 'beautiful souls'[14] who personified the highest ideals of the state. The way that male society viewed women was full of ambiguity. None the less, women were firmly shut off from the functions of the state. Women experienced the effects of wars and other manifestations of state conduct. But it was left to the men – the citizens of the state – to formulate policy for dealing with other states. If the public–private barrier was sometimes eroded in domestic society, this rarely happened at the level of international relations.

The myths and practices of state formation in ancient Greece and Renaissance Italy have given international relations theory a particular, gender-biased understanding of what constitutes the state and how it functions. Separating women from the public realm has led to suspicion about the very understanding of history and philosophy used in international relations theory. There are two consequences of this. First, the concept of the state is open to criticism. The social relations on which the state is based are not pure types; they are products in part of gender bias. Second, it casts shadows on the ability of the Western tradition to give an accurate picture of human relations.

The security dilemma

The combination of classical sources and twentieth-century interpretations has been especially significant in the sectors of international relations theory that deal with the concepts of security and anarchy. The concept of the security dilemma marks an important transition from the role of gender difference in domestic political society, to gender bias in international theory.

Robert Jervis has defined the security dilemma as the problem that 'most of the ways in which a country seeks to increase its security have the unintended effect of decreasing the security of others'.[15] The origins of the security dilemma can be traced back to ancient Greece – particularly to Thucydides, soldier author of *The Peloponnesian Wars*. 'What made war inevitable was the growth of Athenian power and the fear which this caused in Sparta', Jervis illustrates.[16] Jervis implies that the security dilemma is both a classical feature and a constant problem of international relations, springing from human nature and political organization. The need to constitute a state to consolidate economic power led to the state becoming a threat to other states.

However, the origins of the security dilemma also spring from a selective definition of gender roles in political society. The contrast between the roles of males and females crystallized around the problem of defending the state. Men served as soldiers and this strengthened their claim on the exclusive right of citizenship. Women had no role in conflict and therefore they had no role in the 'international' relations between the Greek city states. The distinction between private morality and public action was duplicated and transmitted to international relations. The study of warfare between the Greek city states has added another layer of gender bias.

First, Thucydides himself exemplifies the selective interpretation of experience that is part of the origin of gender bias. In the case of Thucydides it is acceptable to use the writings and perspectives of an individual to draw inferences about the nature of state security. He was both a soldier and a citizen; like other men of his time he accepted the political distinctions between gender roles. Thucydides was able to use his personal experiences to enrich his political observations and the tales of the ancient battlefield. An Athenian woman writing on the Peloponnesian wars might have had very different recollections. Perhaps she would have placed emphasis on the economic hardships of war and the loss of her sons in battle. With Thucydides, these private and domestic concerns are subordinate to the greater cause of waging war to defend the state. Certainly privation and casualties are important to the attitude of domestic society toward the war. As a problem of international relations these concerns are subjugated by the will of the state. In Thucydides' world the public morality of war was supported to a degree by relegating alternative views to the private sphere of women's concerns.

The definition of the security dilemma continues to be a source of gender bias. In the security dilemma, international relations theory seeks an abstract representation of the state which can be manipulated as a generic model of a rational actor. Women have been left out of this model because the division between public and private has been enshrined in political theory. An example is Rousseau's parable of the stag hunt, which reappeared in Kenneth Waltz's *Man, The State and War*.[17] Most recently, the parable has been mentioned in discussions of cooperation within the security dilemma. The stag hunt takes place in the state of nature. The ideal is for the hunters to cooperate in pursuing the stag, a quarry which will benefit them all. But each hunter is independent; the group has banded together temporarily in pursuit of a common goal. There is a constant risk that one or more hunters may defect in order to chase a rabbit that would feed their families but, of course, make it harder for the group to kill the stag.

As readers, we hear little about the competing needs and values that influence the hunters. The parable implies that the stag hunt is the exceptional event in the social relations of this group. While the hunters are away testing their mettle and cohesion, the women and children of their society remain behind to forage for other foods and do the other tasks necessary to the existence of the group. The choices of individual hunters are probably directly affected by the situation of the family; one hunter may have a greater need than another to settle for a rabbit on a particular day. By defecting that hunter is acknowledging the contextual relations that bind him to family concerns. In this sense, the controlled anarchy of the hunting group is a condition created for specific purposes and in reference to one interpretation (hunting the stag is best) of domestic requirements. The stag hunt makes a poor analogy for the behaviour of states because it cannot easily demonstrate the range of choices and values that motivate the hunters.

What if women were the leaders? Perhaps there would be little difference in their perception of the security dilemma. Boadicea, the Celtic warrior queen; the virginal Elizabeth I rallying England to face the Spanish Armada in 1588; and Margaret Thatcher's leadership of Britain during the Falklands War belie the generality of peaceable female leadership. However, these examples are of individual and exceptional women. The real question is whether the concept of the female gender role offers insight into ways to reduce the tensions of the security dilemma.

A study of playground activity conducted by Carol Gilligan illustrates a theoretical difference. Boys tended to continue a competitive game to the point of conflict between the players. Girls were more likely to break off the game before it reached conflict in order to preserve the relationship among the players. Girls also tended to choose games like skipping a rope, in which one player's success did not derive from another player's loss.[18] One can draw a loose analogy, but an intriguing one. Could states likewise manage their relations so as to manoeuvre short of conflict? Gilligan's example raises the theoretical possibility that the overall interdependent relationship among the actors in a game is important enough to encourage management of potential conflict. Once this example is drawn there is no need to wonder whether all national leaders will have to be women before the model could be tested. The point is that the feminist analysis delivers another aspect of potential human behaviour. Like Hobbes's thoughts on the state of nature, Gilligan's example hints at a different set of 'natural' rules.

These examples suggest that the definition of what constitutes security for a state does not necessarily reflect the concerns of all the state's population. Second, the epistemological parameters of what we know as international relations have been severely limited. The line between domestic and international politics is often unclear. Yet little has been done to account for this in international relations theory. The classical examples suggest that international politics is that which in no way involves the affective, individual morality associated with women. Perhaps the Achilles' heel of international relations theory is that it cannot easily account for the differences between the private human being and his or her public face.

The implications of gender bias at the root of the concept of the security dilemma are particularly important. Gender bias in issues of war and security has been the source of much of the gender bias in international relations theory. International relations theory is, of course, particularly concerned with war and with how states seek security. When international relations began to take shape as an academic subject, war and war prevention were issues that clearly separated international relations from other areas in politics. The study of international law and its ability to settle disputes peaceably was one of the origins of the subject of international relations in the late nineteenth and early twentieth centuries. The classic divide between realism and idealism grew out of attempts to improve understanding of international conflict in the aftermath of the First World War. Thus, as the subject of international relations emerged, there was no room for a feminist perspective without a re-evaluation of the whole basis of the discipline.

Since Thucydides, according to Jervis, international relations have been shaped by the anarchical context.[19] Certainly international relations theory has centred on this concept. As Hedley Bull wrote in the 1970s, states inhabit an anarchical society. However, the origins of anarchy go back to the process of state formation in ancient Greece and to the security dilemma. It is much easier to think of anarchy as part of a world where the relationship between nature and human society had changed dramatically.[20] Societies operate in anarchy if each is seen to have a similar dependence on nature. The dominance of men over women was based on the effort of men – as leaders of human societies – to dominate nature. The economic structure and organization of labour required for this feat gave rise to the unequal political ties of the state. The state was then personified as an entity unto itself, subject to no higher authority. Only another state, or empire, could subjugate the state. Nature no longer had the power to do so, and hence there were no prescribed bonds between states, only anarchy.

Robert Gilpin describes this phenomenon. In a defence of realism, he mentions that 'loyalty to the tribe for most of us ranks above all other loyalties other than that of the family'.[21] Unfortunately Gilpin did not pursue this revealing contention, but discussed the competition of tribes in anarchy as a central problem of international relations. He might as easily have taken the highest loyalty to the family as a metaphor for a 'family of states'. He did not; that would have required a reversal of fundamental realist assumptions. From the realist perspective anarchy is the obvious backdrop for international relations and anything to do with women and the family is still confined to domestic society.

Critical theory rebels

The traditional sources of gender bias have persisted even in the most current offerings of international relations theorists. While Jervis and Gilpin were defending realism in the 1980s, other international relations theorists were challenging the established traditions of thought. Radical critiques by Richard Ashley and others have explored many of the avenues used by feminist theorists working in other disciplines. More attention has been given to social relations, to the hegemony imposed by Enlightenment rationality, to the ambiguous relationship between domestic politics and conceptions of international society. The critical theorists and post-modernists of many a different stripe have especially criticized the concept of the state. Despite the extent of the rebellion, gender issues have not been widely considered. The interactions between the image of man in society and the theory of relations between states have been intricately dissected. Theorists may now be more aware of the historical problem of gender bias; but with the foundations of international relations theory already established in classic texts, it has been difficult indeed to bring in gender questions. Western thought has left so many other windmills to joust with that the problem of gender bias at the origins of that tradition has gone unexamined. In fact, much of the newest work in international relations theory almost seems to have steered away from examining the sources of gender bias.

Ashley's contributions to the attack on neorealism make a good example of how hard it is to focus on gender bias even in a sweeping critique of the Western political tradition. The scope of Ashley's critique is impressive. It involves the position of the body politic in the state, a major source of gender bias. The concept of anarchy is thoroughly dissected and the way that the state legitimizes violence also comes under heavy fire. Conveniently, Ashley directed part of his criticism toward Gilpin and Jervis, among others.

Ashley uses the images of sovereign man and man in society to highlight the reliance on symbolism in the constitution of both the idea of the state and in turn, of international relations. He criticizes the image of man in society as a representation imposed by 'arbitrary practices of exclusion' and repeatedly reinforced by historical practice. The image of sovereign man is necessary to the idea of the state. Through this image the state begins to dominate the 'anarchy' of competing ideas and desires. The anarchy which Ashley refers to may first describe the triumph of the state over nature; and it goes on to refer to the inherent competition of national interests and ideas in anarchical, international society. To Ashley, the 'unproblematic figure of "sovereign man" [*sic*] at the center of one domestic society' allows the different activities of another state's domestic societies to look like external dangers. Foreigners must remain foreign. The slippages must be 'excluded, arrested or controlled' or else the first society will sacrifice its unique identity as a state and the ability to compete and make war in international society.[22] This barricade of difference, however, can become a source of conflict as well as of state identity.

What Ashley does not go on to say – though it leaps from his work – is that the exclusion of women is a necessary part of the unproblematic figure of 'sovereign man'. The male role of the warrior is the strongest underpinning of authority implicit in the image of sovereign man. Man is the rational, choice making citizen; but the power of the image of sovereign man comes from his ability to legitimate violence. Sovereign man has the power to separate public morality from private morality. Ashley mentions the problem of the state and its ability to legitimate war as perhaps the most crucial flaw in the discourse of international relations. However, the legitimation of violence by the state is an extension of the process of excluding female-associated traits (private morality) from public and political life.

How, Ashley asks, did the domestic society of sovereign men come into being not as 'an arbitrary representation' but as a source of original truth and meaning and the real basis of the state?[23] To Ashley this was no accident.

International relations theory simply dares not answer the question because it would unravel the premises of state action. That would also make it very difficult to maintain the separation between domestic and international politics, and to continue to theorize about states as actors. Or, as Ashley phrases it, the question must be

> endlessly deferred because to ask it is to render problematic and political what must be taken to be unproblematic and beyond politics if discourses of state are to secure legitimacy through the claim to represent an unquestioned ground: the will of a domestic population of 'reasoning men . . .'[24]

The work of Ashley and other post-modernist theorists responds to problems with the way that the Western tradition of political thought has been used in international relations theory. However, unless the post-modernists move to an explicit investigation of gender issues, their revisions of international relations theory repeat many of the habits of gender bias. Their attempt to contribute to what is called a critical theory of international relations aims to ferret out biases but gives no special place to gender bias.

As an illustration, part of the problem is that, like earlier theory based on Hobbes or Rousseau, critical theory also draws on political and philosophical texts that contain gender bias. In the case of critical theory it is mainly twentieth-century texts (except for Marx). Critical theory does not even have the fig leaf of dating from classical Greece or the European Enlightenment, when the exclusion of women was the norm. The feminist movements of the twentieth century have gone largely unnoticed. That is all the more disheartening because of what critical theory stands for. As Marx defined it in 1843, critical theory is 'the self-clarification of the struggles and wishes of the age'.[25] In the twentieth-century writings of figures like Habermas, this should include feminism – but generally it does not. Since Habermas appears to have influenced Ashley's work on international relations theory, the modern problem is worth brief consideration.

Perhaps the problem that now plagues critical theory began with Marx's view of gender. Marx tended to see reproduction as a natural and ahistorical phenomenon.[26] If that sounds gentle and accurate, remember that for Marx, ahistorical was very nearly a synonym for unimportant. Ironically this implies that the ahistorical task of reproduction as carried out by women had little to do with the things that most concerned Marx – the evolution of consciousness in human societies and, ultimately, the impending triumph of class consciousness in resistance to capitalism. More will be said of Marxism and international relations in a later section. The issue here is that Habermas has been accused of gender blindness and that some of Ashley's work on international relations theory has followed concepts developed by Habermas.

One example is particularly striking. When Habermas focuses on late welfare capitalism he draws the distinction between the mechanism of the state and what he calls the 'life-world', the realm of private and social interaction. Habermas attempts to get at the ways the state intrudes into the life-world of its citizens. He defines four roles as reference points: the worker, the consumer, the citizen and the client. Roles like childbearer or others associated with the female gender are omitted entirely.[27] Each of the four roles reflects a male image, although they clearly are intended to apply to men and women. Habermas duplicates the public–private split; he ruins the claim to universality because of the different ways his four types would apply to women and men. As Fraser says, the 'gender blindness of the model occludes important features of the arrangements he wants to understand'.[28] Habermas wants to criticize male dominance but his diagnostic categories deflect attention elsewhere. Fraser's conclusion on Habermas is relevant to the critical theorists of international relations and their efforts to tear down the realist model. As long as the category of gender bias is not made explicit, there is nothing in critical theory to suggest that it will be tackled.

Another feature of Habermas's work has been adapted to the context of international relations. This is what Ashley calls the model of the dialogue.[29] For Habermas the dialogue is a model of reason. Reason comes not from a single, unitary source (as philosophy from Athens to the Enlightenment contended) but from a communicative process. In his eagerness to eliminate the synthetic unity of reason, Habermas must retain a commitment to impartiality.[30] Many voices can engage in dialogue and act as a source of knowledge and reason. Instead of the monologue of Reason there takes place what is best described as ongoing conversation. No one interpretation can dominate others. Interests and ideas that have been marginalized should be able to have an equal share because each is recognized as a valid interpretation of the world.

Ashley finds Habermas's concept useful in two ways. First, it undermines the idea that anarchy produces a single dictation of how international relations functions. To Ashley, the model of the dialogue produces a more accurate picture of how states relate. International relations is like a conversation, where the interaction is best understood as a vocal *mélange* of trade, diplomacy, competition, alliances. There is no single way to model this interaction by relying on an image of 'states in the anarchical context'. Second, the model of the dialogue has useful implications for a much more constructive dialogue among states, an aim espoused by the critical theory advocates. Under these conditions, no one theoretical interpretation of international relations can impose hegemony.[31]

Thus far the critical theory approach seems like a good thing indeed for weeding out gender bias and developing gender-sensitive theory. This may be so. But as in Habermas, the commitment to impartiality is the problem. The terms of the dialogue are to engage in discussion 'under conditions that neutralise all motives except that of cooperatively seeking truth'.[32] Nothing in critical theory insists on corrections of gender bias. Critical theory gives no special place to feminist thinking. Given the weight of gender bias in the foundations of international relations theory, that may place the feminist motive in jeopardy. 'A feminist study is a study whose objective is to explain the situation of women', wrote Christine Delphy. Theoretical premises which do not include this acknowledgement of the feminist premise can be used only at the risk of incoherence.[33] As the examples show, critical theory can leave out feminist struggles and wishes.

Finally, critical theory is silent on the issue of whether or not it is an evolutionary mode of thought – in addition to being a corrective. For international relations theory and for feminist thought, this is a crucial point. Ultimately, the purpose of gender critique is to produce a better understanding of the range of human interaction that affects international relations. Identifying gender bias is not enough. A gender-sensitive theory of international relations must fulfil the condition of being 'world constitutive'. A critical theory approach to international relations may not be up to that mark and it certainly gives no guarantee of where the feminist voice will fit in. In sum, the newest international relations theory is radical – but it comes with no guarantee of being feminist.

The bottom line: is gender theory world-constitutive?

Gender bias exists in international relations theory for a variety of reasons and has thrived on the flaws of the Western tradition. However, the bottom line is that the gender factor resurrects a debilitating choice between what is private and moral, and what is public and can be legitimized in the national interest. The study of international relations theory has attempted to produce explanations of public, international action without fully confronting the precarious structure of thought that separates domestic politics from international action. Under the traditional requirements international relations theory has two tasks. First, it must present a schema of the international context, defining who the actors are and how they interact. Next, the theory must demonstrate some ability to explain what motivates action and how the international context operates. Under the first requirement women found no place in the international context. In the second case the political theory which was used to explain motivations came from gender-biased sources and the exclusion was repeated. Hence, women appear to have no role in a discussion of how the international context operates – the topic that is the final objective of major theories of international relations. Men, states and wars were the bases of theory, not women.

A gender-neutral theory of international relations must seek to define and explain the international system if it is to gain acceptance as a major theory. That is no easy task. Feminist scholarship in other disciplines has been able to focus more on reconstruction and on including women as subjects of research. Joan Kelly has encapsulated the process in her statement that introducing gender as a category of social thought changes the conceptual foundations of history. The history of patriarchy, of relations between the sexes, the changes in family organization and its relation to society, and of course the investigation of particular women in history, have all made a significant contribution. In Kelly's work gender, class and race were all fundamental categories. She was concerned with how gender roles and symbolism in societies maintained or challenged the social order. Ultimately the most exciting task would be to study how men and women were initially socialized into their respective gender roles, for this would indicate how the social structure affected the evolution of human consciousness. As a historian, Kelly was able to direct her work toward the position of the individual within the societal context. The importance of gender roles emerged clearly and with a mandate to alter overall conceptions of history, although, as Kelly said, it was difficult for the professional historian to accept gender roles as a category for analysis.[34]

International relations theory has simply not been able to make similar progress. In part this is because international relations has not been too concerned with the individual in society. But the example of anthropology shows how making progress at first depends on other things, too. One method is to ensure that the feminist agenda asks the kind of questions that scholars in the discipline can grasp quickly, and relate to their more familiar areas of study. According to Marilyn Strathern the study of gender has become a field of its own right in anthropology and would seem to provide an 'unparalleled position from which to scrutinize Western assumptions'. Feminist scholarship in anthropology asks how systems of inequality arise, how ideology contributes to social identity and whether categories like 'the domestic' are useful. A number of other features are commendable and enviable from the standpoint of international relations theorists. Anthropologists employ cross-cultural data and insist that what happens to women cannot be considered in isolation from what happens to men and women and indeed, society as a whole.[35] These are good guidelines for international relations theorists, too. But as Strathern concludes, the initial momentum of feminist scholarship in anthropology came from the fact that by addressing issues of bias, the feminist scholars were actually giving their colleagues good anthropological advice, not just shaking the foundations.[36]

From the perspective of the main schools of international relations theory neither the approach of historians nor anthropologists will be very helpful. It is extremely difficult to introduce gender as a category of thought in international relations as long as the discipline is ensnared by the trap of dividing the domestic and the international. To date few of the questions raised by feminist scholarship have hit the mark and identified places for methodological correction, as they did to an extent in anthropology. In international relations the challenge put forward by identifying sources of gender bias is complete. The most fundamental concepts of human behaviour, the composition of the state, and the workings of anarchy and the security dilemma must be substantially revised or even reformulated. To some feminist scholars of international relations, there is little hope for anything less than radical transformation of the subject matter of the discipline. They argue that the reconciliation of feminism and international relations should be preempted if it is going to amount to nothing more than suddenly including women without analysing their global subordination.[37]

The final irony is that the problem of gender bias in international relations practically defies history. International relations is a newcomer among academic disciplines. This should be kept in mind because it is not feasible to claim that, like philosophy, international relations was first developed as a subject when prejudice against women was the norm. Women in Britain and America have had the vote longer than most universities have had faculties teaching international relations. While many of the examples used in this chapter reach back to the Enlightenment or to texts from antiquity, it is important to remember that international relations theory is not that old. Most of the common paradigms in international relations theory were drawn from earlier works but assembled during the twentieth century. Many came to the fore after 1945, as part of the increased attention in universities to the subject of 'international relations'. One might think that feminism would have made some impact from the start, since Western societies have made strides in recognizing the equality of women and reducing gender bias in the public sphere. However, theorists writing in the 1930s, the 1950s and even the 1980s have continued to draw on a foundation fraught with gender bias.

Indeed, the process of identifying gender bias reaches a difficult point here. Because international relations theory attaches less weight to the position of the individual in society than does history or anthropology it is hard to know where to begin. Somehow the influence of gender roles has to be lifted out of the complex mesh of public and private identity in the state. Then work must be done to establish that gender theory does carry the qualities necessary to create a 'world constitutive' picture of the international context and of relations between states and institutions within it. However, there are a few avenues to explore.

Avenues for gender theory

As more women teach and write in the discipline of international relations the awareness of the problems of gender bias has increased. No excuses remain for an uncritical acceptance in international relations theory of the gender bias inherited from the classic political and philosophical texts. But developing a theory of international relations that is free from gender bias depends on introducing theoretical premises which vary considerably from the systemic tendencies of current theories. Gender theory is at heart a theory of social relationship. It is also a theory based in human experience. Every human experience – even that of international politics – has gender content because gender is one of humanity's major socializing forces. Already it is clear that development of gender theory in international relations will push first toward a different definition of the international context. The image of an anarchical society does little to account for the subordination of women in many societies or to explain how domestic publics continue to sanction international violence.

In other ways international relations theory has opened avenues revealing different conceptions of the international context. Marxist theories have frequently been marginalized; but part of their emphasis on structural relations and dependency theory has stuck. This suggests that a different view of the individual's relationship to international society can be established. In this case the emphasis is on labour, and looking at women's labour in the international context is one avenue. Another quite distinct path is normative theory, a product in part of the idealist approach to international relations. Normative theory introduces the possibility that international relations theory can focus on the values behind the norms of international conduct. Under this umbrella normative theory can also be prescriptive. These are encouraging possibilities for gender theory because they recognize the need for fundamental re-evaluation.

However, in the long run the potential for gender theory may be even greater. This can proceed on two levels: a working understanding of gender in the international system; and a grasp of gender as a source of political philosophy intimately bound up with the state of the world.

First, how can international relations scholars draw on the wealth of gender theory in feminist scholarship? To date, only a minor share of feminist writings have focused on the international context. Most of the theoretical work on gender and feminism has addressed core questions of how concepts are represented and how the male tradition relates to feminist consciousness. However, at this level it is not necessary for international relations theorists to settle all the questions raised by gender theory. Nor must all the possible sources of bias be aired, nor all the representations of male and female in language and political symbols be identified. What is necessary, and indispensable, is that international relations theorists account for women as actors and subjects.

Beyond that task, international relations theory may have much to learn from feminism in all its forms. As the twentieth century draws to a close the sources of contemporary political theory and philosophy grow more pessimistic about man's place in the world. His ability to understand the political substance of international relations, to answer long held questions about social being, seems more in doubt. The critical theorists have by and large abandoned 'reason', as a tool man cannot use effectively. While these are developments in political philosophy, much of the panic has been a reaction to international events, particularly the two world wars. Man – whether he is defined by the state of nature, by his wealth, his education or his labour – is a being with an infinite capacity for danger. As political philosophy abandons faith in the concepts of Man and Reason the alternative is to emphasize the 'many voices' envisaged by critical theory. Put simply, it is safer to welcome plurality and give up the Enlightenment's monolithic ideas of truth and progress.

There is a choice. Feminism (in the broadest sense as an intellectual form based on the issue of gender) offers the chance to reconstruct the definitions of the human as a social being, to revise the criteria for theory and explanation. The feminist movement of the 1960s and 1970s was not, as some critical theorists saw it, a fragment of emancipation on a par with student movements or other valuable but non-universal roads to greater freedom for certain groups. By now, Western society is laden with prejudices based on gender, race and other factors and is in need of some deflation. However, it is gender which is most fundamental and which provides a basis for new sources of theory and understanding without sinking to frightened abandonment of the good parts of the Western tradition.

What does this mean for international relations theory? Theorists should work to establish an awareness of gender bias. From this basis it will be possible to include gender issues. Finally, the sources of gender bias surveyed in this chapter demonstrate both a weakness in current theory and an opportunity for new theoretical work. As Heraclitus said when the problem was just beginning: 'The unlike is joined together and from difference results the most beautiful harmony, and all things take place by strife.'

Notes

1 Richard Ashley, 'The poverty of neorealism', *International Organization* (Vol. 38, No. 2, Spring 1984).
2 Thomas Hobbes, *Leviathan* (New York: Washington Square Press, 1964), p. 84.
3 Simone de Beauvoir, *The Second Sex* (New York: Alfred A. Knopf, 1952).
4 Jean-Jacques Rousseau, *Emile* (New York: Everyman, 1974), p. 370.
5 *Ibid.*, pp. 306, 364.
6 V. Spike Peterson, 'Sex and the sovereign state: what's at stake in taking feminism seriously?', Unpublished manuscript, December 1989.
7 Elisabeth Young-Bruehl, 'The education of women as Philosophers', *Signs: Journal of Women in Culture and Society* (Vol. 12, No. 2, Winter 1987), p. 212.
8 Philip Windsor, 'Women and international relations: what's the problem?', *Millennium: Journal of International Studies* (Vol. 17, No. 3, Winter 1988), p. 452.
9 *Ibid.*
10 *Ibid.*
11 Joan Kelly, *Women, History and Theory* (Chicago, IL: University of Chicago Press, 1984), p. 4.
12 Joan Kelly, 'The querelle des femmes', in *ibid.*, p. 84.
13 Joan Kelly, 'Did women have a Renaissance?', in *ibid.*, p. 46.
14 The term 'beautiful souls' is used by Jean Bethke Elshtain in her book *Women and War* (Brighton: Wheatsheaf, 1987).
15 Robert Jervis, 'Realism, game theory, and cooperation', *World Politics* (Vol. 40, No. 3, April 1988).
16 *Ibid.*
17 The example is found in Carol Gilligan, *In a Different Voice: Psychological*

Theory and Women's Development (Cambridge, MA: Harvard University Press, 1982).

18 Kenneth Waltz, *Man, the State and War* (Lexington, MA: Addison-Wesley, 1979).

19 Jervis, *op. cit.*

20 Simone de Beauvoir was the first to advance this argument.

21 Robert Gilpin, 'Political realism's richness', *International Organization* (Vol. 38, No. 2, Spring 1984).

22 Richard K. Ashley, 'Untying the sovereign state: a double reading of the anarchy problematique', *Millennium: Journal of International Studies* (Vol. 17, No. 2, 1988), pp. 256–7.

23 *Ibid.*

24 *Ibid.*

25 Marx's definition of critical theory is quoted in Nancy Fraser, 'What's critical about critical theory?', in Seyla Benhabib and Crucilla Cornell (eds), *Feminism as Critique* (Cambridge: Polity Press, 1986).

26 Linda Nicholson, 'Feminism and Marx: integrating kinship with the economic', in *ibid.*, pp. 25, 28–9.

27 Fraser, *op. cit.*, pp. 35–41.

28 *Ibid.*, p. 45.

29 Ashley, *op. cit.*

30 Iris Marion Young, 'Impartiality and the civic public', in Benhabib and Cornell, *op. cit.*, p. 66.

31 Ashley, *op. cit.*

32 Young, *op. cit.*

33 Christine Delphy, quoted in Sarah Brown, 'Feminism, international theory and international relations of gender inequality', *Millennium: Journal of International Studies* (Vol. 17, No. 3 Winter 1988), n. 31.

34 Kelly, 'Did Women have a Renaissance?' *op. cit.*

35 Marilyn Strathern, 'An awkward relationship: the case of feminism and anthropology', *Signs: Journal of Women in Culture and Society* (Vol. 12, No. 2, Winter 1987), pp. 278–9.

36 *Ibid.*

37 Brown, *op. cit.*, p. 462.

3

Hans Morgenthau's principles of political realism: a feminist reformulation

J. ANN TICKNER

> It is not in giving life but in risking life that man is raised above the
> animal: that is why superiority has been accorded in humanity not to the
> sex that brings forth but to that which kills
>
> Simone de Beauvoir[1]

International politics is a man's world, a world of power and conflict in which warfare is a privileged activity. Traditionally, diplomacy, military service and the science of international politics have been largely male domains. In the past women have rarely been included in the ranks of professional diplomats or the military; of the relatively few women who specialize in the academic discipline of international relations, few are security specialists. Women political scientists who do study international relations tend to focus on areas such as international political economy, North–South relations and matters of distributive justice.

Today, in the United States, where women are entering the military and the foreign service in greater numbers than ever before, they are rarely to be found in positions of military leadership or at the top of the foreign policy establishment.[2] One notable exception, Jeane Kirkpatrick, who was US ambassador to the United Nations in the early 1980s, has described herself as 'a mouse in a man's world'; for, in spite of her authoritative and forceful public style and strong conservative credentials, Kirkpatrick maintains that she failed to win the respect or attention of her male colleagues on matters of foreign policy.[3]

Kirkpatrick's story could serve to illustrate the discrimination that women often encounter when they rise to high political office. However, the doubts as to whether a woman would be strong enough to press the nuclear button, (an issue raised when a tearful Patricia Schroeder was pictured sobbing on her husband's shoulder as she bowed out of the 1988 US presidential race) suggest that there may be an even more fundamental barrier to women's entry into the highest ranks of the military or of foreign policy making. Nuclear strategy, with its vocabulary of power, threat, force and deterrence, has a distinctly masculine ring;[4] moreover, women are stereotypically judged to be lacking in qualities which these terms evoke. It has also been suggested that, although more women are entering the world of public policy, they are more comfortable dealing with domestic issues such as social welfare that are more compatible with their nurturing skills. Yet the large number of women in the ranks of the peace movement suggests that women are not uninterested in issues of war and peace, although their frequent dissent from national security policy has often branded them as naive, uninformed or even unpatriotic.

In this chapter I propose to explore the question of why international politics is perceived as a man's world and why women remain so under-represented in the higher echelons of the foreign policy establishment, the military and the academic discipline of international relations. Since I believe that there is something about this field that renders it particularly inhospi-table and unattractive to women, I intend to focus on the nature of the discipline itself rather than on possible strategies to remove barriers to women's access to high policy positions. As I have already suggested, the issues that are given priority in foreign policy are issues with which men have had a special affinity. Moreover, if it is primarily men who are describing these issues and constructing theories to explain the workings of the international system, might we not expect to find a masculine perspective in the academic discipline also? If this were so then it could be argued that the exclusion of women has operated not only at the level of discrimination but also through a process of self-selection which begins with the way in which we are taught about international relations.

In order to investigate this claim that the discipline of international re-lations, as it has traditionally been defined by realism, is based on a masculine world view, I propose to examine the six principles of political realism formu-lated by Hans Morgenthau in his classic work *Politics Among Nations*. I shall use some ideas from feminist theory to show that the way in which Mor-genthau describes and explains international politics, and the prescriptions that ensue are embedded in a masculine perspective. Then I shall suggest some ways in which feminist theory might help us begin to conceptualize a world view from a feminine perspective and to formulate a feminist epistemology of international relations. Drawing on these observations I shall conclude with a reformulation of Morgenthau's six principles. Male critics of contemporary realism have already raised many of the same questions about realism that I shall address. However, in undertaking this exercise, I hope to make a link between a growing critical perspective on international relations theory and feminist writers interested in global issues. Adding a feminist perspective to its discourse could also help to make the field of international relations more accessible to women scholars and practitioners.

Hans Morgenthau's principles of political realism: a masculine perspective?

I have chosen to focus on Hans Morgenthau's six principles of political realism because they represent one of the most important statements of contemporary realism from which several generations of scholars and practitioners of international relations in the United States have been nourished. Although Morgenthau has frequently been criticized for his lack of scientific rigour and ambiguous use of language, these six principles have significantly framed the way in which the majority of international relations scholars and practitioners in the West have thought about international politics since 1945.[5]

Morgenthau's principles of political realism can be summarized as follows:

1 Politics, like society in general, is governed by objective laws that have their roots in human nature, which is unchanging: therefore it is possible to develop a rational theory that reflects these objective laws.
2 The main signpost of political realism is the concept of interest defined in terms of power which infuses rational order into the subject matter of politics, and thus makes the theoretical understanding of politics possible. Political realism stresses the rational, objective and unemotional.
3 Realism assumes that interest defined as power is an objective category which is universally valid but not with a meaning that is fixed once and for all. Power is the control of man over man.
4 Political realism is aware of the moral significance of political action. It is also aware of the tension between the moral command and the requirements of successful political action.
5 Political realism refuses to identify the moral aspirations of a particular nation with the moral laws that govern the universe. It is the concept of interest defined in terms of power that saves us from moral excess and political folly.
6 The political realist maintains the autonomy of the political sphere; he asks 'How does this policy affect the power of the nation?' Political realism is based on a pluralistic conception of human nature. A man who was nothing but 'political man' would be a beast, for he would be completely lacking in moral restraints. But, in order to develop an autonomous theory of political behaviour, 'political man' must be abstracted from other aspects of human nature.[6]

I am not going to argue that Morgenthau is incorrect in his portrayal of the international system. I do believe, however, that it is a partial description of international politics because it is based on assumptions about human nature that are partial and that privilege masculinity. First, it is necessary to define masculinity and femininity. According to almost all feminist theorists, masculinity and femininity refer to a set of socially constructed categories, which vary in time and place, rather than to biological determinants. In the

West, conceptual dichotomies such as objectivity vs subjectivity, reason vs emotion, mind vs body, culture vs nature, self vs other or autonomy vs relatedness, knowing vs being and public vs private have typically been used to describe male/female differences by feminists and non-feminists alike.[7] In the United States, psychological tests conducted across different socio-economic groups confirm that individuals perceive these dichotomies as masculine and feminine and also that the characteristics associated with masculinity are more highly valued by men and women alike.[8] It is important to stress, however, that these characteristics are stereotypical; they do not necessarily describe individual men or women, who can exhibit characteristics and modes of thought associated with the opposite sex.

Using a vocabulary that contains many of the words associated with masculinity as I have identified it, Morgenthau asserts that it is possible to develop a rational (and unemotional) theory of international politics based on objective laws that have their roots in human nature. Since Morgenthau wrote the first edition of *Politics Among Nations* in 1948, this search for an objective science of international politics based on the model of the natural sciences has been an important part of the realist and neorealist agenda. In her feminist critique of the natural sciences, Evelyn Fox Keller points out that most scientific communities share the 'assumption that the universe they study is directly accessible, represented by concepts and shaped not by language but only by the demands of logic and experiment'.[9] The laws of nature, according to this view of science, are 'beyond the relativity of language'. Like most feminists, Keller rejects this view of science which, she asserts, imposes a coercive, hierarchical and conformist pattern on scientific inquiry. Feminists in general are sceptical about the possibility of finding a universal and objective foundation for knowledge, which Morgenthau claims is possible. Most share the belief that knowledge is socially constructed: since it is language that transmits knowledge, the use of language and its claims to objectivity must continually be questioned.

Keller argues that objectivity, as it is usually defined in our culture, is associated with masculinity. She identifies it as 'a network of interactions between gender development, a belief system that equates objectivity with masculinity, and a set of cultural values that simultaneously (and cojointly) elevates what is defined as scientific and what is defined as masculine'.[10] Keller links the separation of self from other, an important stage of masculine gender development, with this notion of objectivity. Translated into scientific inquiry this becomes the striving for the separation of subject and object, an important goal of modern science and one which, Keller asserts, is based on the need for control; hence objectivity becomes associated with power and domination.

The need for control has been an important motivating force for modern realism. To begin his search for an objective, rational theory of international politics, which could impose order on a chaotic and conflictual world, Morgenthau constructs an abstraction which he calls political man, a beast completely lacking in moral restraints. Morgenthau is deeply aware that real men, like real states, are both moral and bestial but, because states do not live up to the universal moral laws that govern the universe, those who behave morally in international politics are doomed to failure because of the immoral actions of others. To solve this tension Morgenthau postulates a realm of international politics in which the amoral behaviour of political man is not only permissible but prudent. It is a Hobbesian world, separate and distinct from the world of domestic order. In it, states may act like beasts, for survival depends on a maximization of power and a willingness to fight.

Having long argued that the personal is political, most feminist theory would reject the validity of constructing an autonomous political sphere around which boundaries of permissible modes of conduct have been drawn. As Keller maintains, 'the demarcation between public and private not only defines and defends the boundaries of the political but also helps form its content and style'.[11] Morgenthau's political man is a social construct based on a partial representation of human nature. One might well ask where the women were in Hobbes's state of nature; presumably they must have been involved in reproduction and childrearing, rather than warfare, if life was to go on for more than one generation.[12] Morgenthau's emphasis on the conflictual aspects of the international system contributes to a tendency, shared by other realists, to de-emphasize elements of cooperation and regeneration which are also aspects of international relations.[13]

Morgenthau's construction of an amoral realm of international power politics is an attempt to resolve what he sees as a fundamental tension between the moral laws that govern the universe and the requirements of successful political action in a world where states use morality as a cloak to justify the pursuit of their own national interests. Morgenthau's universalistic morality postulates the highest form of morality as an abstract ideal, similar to the Golden Rule, to which states seldom adhere: the morality of states, by contrast, is an instrumental morality guided by self-interest.

Morgenthau's hierarchical ordering of morality contains parallels with the work of psychologist Lawrence Kohlberg. Based on a study of the moral development of 84 American boys, Kohlberg concludes that the highest stage of human moral development (which he calls stage 6) is the ability to recognize abstract universal principles of justice; lower on the scale (stage 2) is an instrumental morality concerned with serving one's own interests while recognizing that others have interests too. Between these two is an interpersonal morality which is contextual and characterized by sensitivity to the needs of others (stage 3).[14]

In her critique of Kohlberg's stages of moral development, Carol Gilligan argues that they are based on a masculine conception of morality. On Kohlberg's scale women rarely rise above the third or contextual stage. Gilligan claims that this is not a sign of inferiority but of difference. Since women are socialized into a mode of thinking which is contextual and narrative, rather than formal and abstract, they tend to see issues in contextual rather than in abstract terms.[15] In international relations the tendency to think about morality either in terms of abstract, universal and unattainable standards or as purely instrumental, as Morgenthau does, detracts from our ability to tolerate cultural differences and to seek potential for building community in spite of these differences.

Using examples from feminist literature I have suggested that Morgenthau's attempt to construct an objective, universal theory of international politics is rooted in assumptions about human nature and morality that, in modern Western culture, are associated with masculinity. Further evidence that Morgenthau's principles are not the basis for a universalistic and objective theory is contained in his frequent references to the failure of what he calls the 'legalistic–moralistic' or idealist approach to world politics which he claims was largely responsible for both the world wars. Having laid the blame for the Second World War on the misguided morality of appeasement, Morgenthau's *realpolitik* prescriptions for successful political action appear as prescriptions for avoiding the mistakes of the 1930s rather than as prescriptions with timeless applicability.

If Morgenthau's world view is embedded in the traumas of the Second World War, are his prescriptions still valid as we move further away from this event? I share with other critics of realism the view that, in a rapidly changing world, we must begin to search for modes of behaviour different from those prescribed by Morgenthau. Given that any war between the major powers is likely to be nuclear, increasing security by increasing power could be suicidal.[16] Moreover, the nation state, the primary constitutive element of the international system for Morgenthau and other realists, is no longer able to deal with an increasingly pluralistic array of problems ranging from economic interdependence to environmental degradation. Could feminist theory make a contribution to international relations theory by constructing an alternative, feminist perspective on international politics that might help us to search for more appropriate solutions?

A feminist perspective on international relations?

If the way in which we describe reality has an effect on the ways we perceive and act upon our environment, new perspectives might lead us to consider alternative courses of action. With this in mind I shall first examine two important concepts in international relations, power and security, from a feminist perspective and then discuss some feminist approaches to conflict resolution.

Morgenthau's definition of power, the control of man over man, is typical of the way power is usually defined in international relations. Nancy Hartsock argues that this type of power-as-domination has always been associated with masculinity, since the exercise of power has generally been a masculine activity: rarely have women exercised legitimized power in the public domain. When women write about power they stress energy, capacity and potential, says Hartsock. She notes that women theorists, even when they have little else in common, offer similar definitions of power which differ substantially from the understanding of power as domination.[17]

Hannah Arendt, frequently cited by feminists writing about power, defines power as the human ability to act in concert, or to take action in connection with others who share similar concerns.[18] This definition of power is similar to that of psychologist David McClelland's portrayal of female power, which he describes as shared rather than assertive.[19] Jane Jaquette argues that, since women have had less access to the instruments of coercion, they have been more apt to rely on power as persuasion; she compares women's domestic activities to coalition building.[20]

All of these writers are portraying power as a relationship of mutual enablement. Tying her definition of female power to international relations, Jaquette see similarities between female strategies of persuasion and strategies of small states operating from a position of weakness in the international system. There are also examples of states' behaviour that contain elements of the female strategy of coalition building. One such example is the Southern African Development Coordination Conference (SADCC), which is designed to build regional infrastructure based on mutual cooperation and collective self-reliance in order to decrease dependence on the South African economy. Another is the European Community, which has had considerable success in building mutual cooperation in an area of the world whose history would not predict such a course of events.[21] It is rare, however, that cooperative outcomes in international relations are described in these terms, although Karl Deutsch's notion of pluralistic security communities might be one such example where power is associated with building community.[22] I am not denying that power as domination is a pervasive reality in international relations. However, there are also instances of cooperation in inter-state relations, which tend to be obscured when power is seen solely as domination. Thinking about power in this multidimensional sense may help us to think constructively about the potential for cooperation as well as conflict, an aspect of international relations generally played down by realism.

Redefining national security is another way in which feminist theory could contribute to new thinking about international relations.[23] Traditionally in the West, the concept of national security has been tied to military strength and its role in the physical protection of the nation state from external threats. Morgenthau's notion of defending the national interest in terms of power is consistent with this definition. But this traditional definition of national security is partial at best in today's world.[24] The technologically advanced states are highly interdependent, and rely on weapons whose effects would be equally devastating to winners and losers alike. For them to defend national security by relying on war as the last resort no longer appears very useful. Moreover, if one thinks of security in North–South rather than East–West terms, for a large portion of the world's population security has as much to do with the satisfaction of basic material needs as with military threats. According to Johan Galtung's notion of structural violence, to suffer a lower life expectancy by virtue of one's place of birth is a form of violence whose effects can be as devastating as war.[25]

Basic needs satisfaction has a great deal to do with women, but only recently have women's roles as providers of basic needs, and in development more generally, become visible as important components in development strategies.[26] Traditionally the development literature has focused on aspects of the development process that are in the public sphere, are technologically complex and are usually undertaken by men. Thinking about the role of women in development and the way in which we can define development and basic needs satisfaction to be inclusive of women's roles and needs are topics that deserve higher priority on the international agenda. Typically, however, this is an area about which traditional international relations theory, with the priority it gives to order over justice, has had very little to say.

A further threat to national security, more broadly defined, which has also been missing from the agenda of traditional international relations, concerns the environment. Carolyn Merchant argues that a mechanistic view of nature, contained in modern science, has helped to guide an industrial and technological development which has resulted in environmental damage that has now become a matter of global concern. In the introduction to her book *The Death of Nature*, Merchant suggests that, 'Women and nature have an age-old association – an affiliation that has persisted throughout culture, language, and history.'[27] Hence she maintains that the ecology movement, which is growing up in response to environmental threats, and the women's movement are deeply interconnected. Both stress living in equilibrium with nature rather than dominating it, both see nature as a living non-hierarchical entity in which each part is mutually dependent on the whole. Ecologists, as well as many feminists, are now suggesting that only such a fundamental change of world view will allow the human species to survive the damage it is inflicting on the environment.

Thinking about military, economic and environmental security in interdependent terms suggests the need for new methods of conflict resolution that seek to achieve mutually beneficial, rather than zero sum, outcomes. One such method comes from Sara Ruddick's work on 'maternal thinking'.[28] Ruddick describes maternal thinking as focused on the preservation of life and the growth of children. To foster a domestic environment conducive to these goals, tranquillity must be preserved by avoiding conflict where possible, engaging in it non-violently and restoring community when it is over. In such an environment the ends for which disputes are fought are subordinate to the means by which they are resolved. This method of conflict resolution involves making contextual judgements rather than appealing to absolute standards and thus has much in common with Gilligan's definition of female morality.

While non-violent resolution of conflict in the domestic sphere is a widely accepted norm, passive resistance in the public realm is regarded as deviant. But, as Ruddick argues, the peaceful resolution of conflict by mothers does not usually extend to the children of one's enemies, an important reason why women have been ready to support men's wars.[29] The question for Ruddick then becomes how to get maternal thinking, a mode of thinking which she believes can be found in men as well as women, out into the public realm. Ruddick believes that finding a common humanity among one's opponents has become a condition of survival in the nuclear age when the notion of winners and losers has become questionable.[30] Portraying the adversary as less than human has all too often been a technique of the nation state to command loyalty and to increase its legitimacy in the eyes of its citizens. Such behaviour in an age of weapons of mass destruction may be self-defeating.

We might also look to Gilligan's work for a feminist perspective on conflict resolution. Reporting on a study of playground behaviour of American boys and girls, Gilligan argues that girls are less able to tolerate high levels of conflict, and more likely than boys to play games that involve taking turns and in which the success of one does not depend on the failure of another.[31] While Gilligan's study does not take into account attitudes toward other groups (racial, ethnic, economic or national), it does suggest the validity of investigating whether girls are socialized to use different modes of problem solving when dealing with conflict, and whether such behaviour might be useful in thinking about international conflict resolution.

Toward a feminist epistemology of international relations

I am deeply aware that there is no *one* feminist approach but many, which come out of various disciplines and intellectual traditions. Yet there are common themes in the different feminist literatures that I have reviewed which could help us to begin to formulate a feminist epistemology of international relations. Morgenthau encourages us to try to stand back from the world and to think about theory building in terms of constructing a rational outline or map that has universal applications. In contrast, the feminist literature reviewed here emphasizes connection and contingency. Keller argues for a form of knowledge, which she calls 'dynamic objectivity', 'that grants to the world around us its independent integrity, but does so in a way that remains cognizant of, indeed relies on, our connectivity with that world'.[32] Keller illustrates this mode of thinking in her study of Barbara McClintock, whose work on genetic transposition won her a Nobel prize after many years of marginalization by the scientific community.[33] McClintock, Keller argues, was a scientist with a respect for complexity, diversity and individual difference whose methodology allowed her data to speak rather than imposing explanations on it.

Keller's portrayal of McClintock's science contains parallels with what Sandra Harding calls an African world view.[34] Harding tells us that the

Western liberal notion of rational economic man, an individualist and a welfare maximizer, similar to the image of rational political man on which realism has based its theoretical investigations, does not make any sense in the African world view where the individual is seen as part of the social order acting within that order rather than upon it. Harding believes that this view of human behaviour has much in common with a feminist perspective. If we combine this view of human behaviour with Merchant's holistic perspective which stresses the interconnectedness of all things, including nature, it may help us to begin to think from a more global perspective. Such a perspective appreciates cultural diversity but at the same time recognizes a growing interdependence, which makes anachronistic the exclusionary thinking fostered by the nation state system.

Keller's dynamic objectivity, Harding's African world view and Merchant's ecological thinking all point us in the direction of an appreciation of the 'other' as a subject whose views are as legitimate as our own, a way of thinking that has been sadly lacking in the history of international relations. Just as Keller cautions us against the construction of a feminist science which could perpetuate similar exclusionary attitudes, Harding warns us against schema that contrast people by race, gender or class and that originate within projects of social domination. Feminist thinkers generally dislike dichotomization and the distancing of subject from object that goes with abstract thinking, both of which, they believe, encourage a we/they attitude characteristic of international relations. Instead, feminist literature urges us to construct epistemologies that value ambiguity and difference. These qualities could stand us in good stead as we begin to build a human or ungendered theory of international relations which contains elements of both masculine and feminine modes of thought.

Morgenthau's principles of political realism: a feminist reformulation

The first part of this paper used feminist theory to develop a critique of Morgenthau's principles of political realism in order to demonstrate how the theory and practice of international relations may exhibit a masculine bias. The second part suggested some contributions that feminist theory might make to reconceptualizing some important elements in international relations and to thinking about a feminist epistemology. Drawing on these observations, this conclusion will present a feminist reformulation of Morgenthau's six principles of political realism, outlined earlier in this paper, which might help us to begin to think differently about international relations. I shall not use the term realism since feminists believe that there are multiple realities: a truly realistic picture of international politics must recognize elements of cooperation as well as conflict, morality as well as *realpolitik*, and the strivings for justice as well as order.[35] This reformulation may help us to think in these multidimensional terms.

1 A feminist perspective believes that objectivity, as it is culturally defined, is associated with masculinity. Therefore, supposedly 'objective' laws of human nature are based on a partial, masculine view of human nature. Human nature is both masculine and feminine; it contains elements of social reproduction and development as well as political domination. Dynamic objectivity offers us a more connected view of objectivity with less potential for domination.

2 A feminist perspective believes that the national interest is multidimensional and contextually contingent. Therefore, it cannot be defined solely in terms of power. In the contemporary world the national interest demands cooperative rather than zero sum solutions to a set of interdependent global problems which include nuclear war, economic well-being and environmental degradation.

3 Power cannot be infused with meaning that is universally valid. Power as domination and control privileges masculinity and ignores the possibility of collective empowerment, another aspect of power often associated with femininity.

4 A feminist perspective rejects the possibility of separating moral command from political action. All political action has moral significance. The realist agenda for maximizing order through power and control gives priority to the moral command of order over those of justice and the satisfaction of basic needs necessary to ensure social reproduction.

5 While recognizing that the moral aspirations of particular nations cannot be equated with universal moral principles, a feminist perspective seeks to find common moral elements in human aspirations which could become the basis for de-escalating international conflict and building international community.

6 A feminist perspective denies the autonomy of the political. Since autonomy is associated with masculinity in Western culture, disciplinary efforts to construct a world view which does not rest on a pluralistic conception of human nature are partial and masculine. Building boundaries around a narrowly defined political realm defines political in a way that excludes the concerns and contributions of women.

To construct this feminist alternative is not to deny the validity of Morgenthau's work. But adding a feminist perspective to the epistemology of international relations is a stage through which we must pass if we are to think about constructing an ungendered or human science of international politics which is sensitive to, but goes beyond, both masculine and feminine perspectives. Such inclusionary thinking, as Simone de Beauvoir tells us, values the bringing forth of life as much as the risking of life; it is becoming imperative in a world in which the technology of war and a fragile natural environment threaten human existence. An ungendered, or human, discourse becomes possible only when women are adequately represented in the discipline and when there is equal respect for the contributions of women and men alike.

Notes

An earlier version of this paper was presented at a symposium on Gender and International Relations at the London School of Economics in June 1988. I would like to thank the editors of *Millennium*, who organized this symposium, for encouraging me to undertake this rewriting. I am also grateful to Hayward Alker Jr and Susan Okin for their careful reading of the manuscript and helpful suggestions.

1 Quoted in Sandra Harding, *The Science Question in Feminism* (Ithaca, NY: Cornell University Press, 1986), p. 148.

2 In 1987 only 4.8 per cent of the top career Foreign Service employees were women. Statement of Patricia Schroeder before the Committee on Foreign Affairs, US House of Representatives, p. 4; *Women's Perspectives on US Foreign Policy: A Compilation of Views* (Washington, DC: US Government Printing Office, 1988). For an analysis of women's roles in the American military, see Cynthia Enloe, *Does Khaki Become You? The Militarisation of Women's Lives* (London: Pluto Press, 1983).

3 Edward P. Crapol (ed.), *Women and American Foreign Policy* (Westport, CT: Greenwood Press, 1987), p. 167.

4 For an analysis of the role of masculine language in shaping strategic thinking see Carol Cohn, 'Sex and death in the rational world of defense intellectuals', *Signs: Journal of Women in Culture and Society* (Vol. 12, No. 4, Summer 1987).

5 The claim for the dominance of the realist paradigm is supported by John A. Vasquez, 'Colouring it Morgenthau: new evidence for an old thesis on quantitative international studies', *British Journal of International Studies* (Vol. 3, No. 5, October 1979), pp. 210–28. For a critique of Morgenthau's ambiguous use of language see Inis L. Claude Jr, *Power and International Relations* (New York: Random House, 1962), especially pp. 25–37.

6 These are drawn from Hans Morgenthau, *Politics Among Nations: The Struggle for Power and Peace,* 5th revised edition (New York: Alfred Knopf, 1973), pp. 4–15. I am aware that these principles embody only a partial statement of Morgenthau's very rich study of international politics, a study which deserves a much more detailed analysis than I can give here.

7 This list is a composite of the male/female dichotomies which appear in Evelyn Fox Keller's *Reflections on Gender and Science* (New Haven, CT: Yale University Press, 1985) and Harding, *op. cit.*

8 Inge K. Broverman, Susan R. Vogel, Donald M. Broverman, Frank E. Clarkson and Paul S. Rosenkranz, 'Sex-role stereotypes: a current appraisal', *Journal of Social Issues* (Vol. 28, No. 2, 1972), pp. 59–78. Replication of this research in the 1980s confirms that these perceptions still hold.

9 Keller, *op. cit.*, p. 130.

10 *Ibid.*, p. 89.

11 *Ibid.*, p. 9.

12 Sara Ann Ketchum, 'Female culture, woman culture and conceptual change: toward a philosophy of women's studies', *Social Theory and Practice* (Vol. 6, No. 2, Summer 1980).

13 Others have questioned whether Hobbes's state of nature provides an accurate description of the international system. See for example Charles Beitz, *Political Theory and International Relations* (Princeton, NJ: Princeton University Press, 1979), pp. 35–50 and Stanley Hoffmann, *Duties Beyond Borders* (Syracuse, NY: Syracuse University Press, 1981), Chapter 1.

14 Kohlberg's stages of moral development are described and discussed in Robert

Kegan, *The Evolving Self: Problem and Process in Human Development* (Cambridge, MA: Harvard University Press, 1982), Chapter 2.

15 Carol Gilligan, *In a Different Voice: Psychological Theory and Women's Development* (Cambridge, MA: Harvard University Press, 1982). See Chapter 1 for Gilligan's critique of Kohlberg.

16 There is evidence that, toward the end of his life, Morgenthau himself was aware that his own prescriptions were becoming anachronistic. In a seminar presentation in 1978 he suggested that power politics as the guiding principle for the conduct of international relations had become fatally defective. For a description of this seminar presentation see Francis Anthony Boyle, *World Politics and International Law* (Durham, NC: Duke University Press, 1985), pp. 70–4.

17 Nancy C. M. Hartsock, *Money, Sex and Power: Toward a Feminist Historical Materialism* (Boston, MA: Northeastern University Press, 1983), p. 210.

18 Hannah Arendt, *On Violence* (New York: Harcourt, Brace and World, 1969), p. 44. Arendt's definition of power, as it relates to international relations, is discussed more extensively in Jean Bethke Elshtain's 'Reflections on war and political discourse: realism, just war, and feminism in a nuclear age', *Political Theory* (Vol. 13, No. 1, February 1985), pp. 39–57.

19 David McClelland, 'Power and the feminine role', in David McClelland, *Power, The Inner Experience* (New York: Wiley, 1975).

20 Jane S. Jaquette, 'Power as ideology: a feminist analysis', in Judith H. Stiehm (ed.), *Women's Views of the Political World of Men* (Dobbs Ferry, NY: Transnational Publishers, 1984).

21 These examples are cited by Christine Sylvester, 'The emperor's theories and transformations: looking at the field through feminist lenses', in Dennis Pirages and Christine Sylvester (eds), *Transformations in the Global Political Economy* (Basingstoke: Macmillan, 1989).

22 Karl W. Deutsch *et al.*, *Political Community and the North Atlantic Area* (Princeton, NJ: Princeton University Press, 1957).

23 New thinking is a term that is also being used in the Soviet Union to describe foreign policy reformulations under Gorbachev. There are indications that the Soviets are beginning to conceptualize security in the multidimensional terms described here. See Margot Light, *The Soviet Theory of International Relations* (New York: St Martin's Press, 1988), Chapter 10.

24 This is the argument made by Edward Azar and Chung-in Moon, 'Third World national security: toward a new conceptual framework', *International Interactions* (Vol. 11, No. 2, 1984), pp. 103–35.

25 Johan Galtung, 'Violence, peace, and peace research', in Galtung, *Essays in Peace Research*, Vol. I (Copenhagen: Christian Ejlers, 1975).

26 See, for example, Gita Sen and Caren Grown, *Development, Crises and Alternative Visions: Third World Women's Perspectives* (New York: Monthly Review Press, 1987). This is an example of a growing literature on women and development which deserves more attention from the international relations community.

27 Carolyn Merchant, *The Death of Nature: Women, Ecology and the Scientific Revolution* (New York: Harper and Row, 1982), p. xv.

28 Sara Ruddick, 'Maternal thinking' and 'Preservative love and military destruction: some reflections on mothering and peace', in Joyce Treblicot, *Mothering: Essays in Feminist Theory* (Totowa, NJ: Rowman and Allenhead, 1984).

29 For a more extensive analysis of this issue see Jean Bethke Elshtain, *Women and War* (New York: Basic Books, 1987).

30 This type of conflict resolution contains similarities with the problem solving

approach of Edward Azar, John Burton and Herbert Kelman. See, for example, Edward E. Azar and John W. Burton, *International Conflict Resolution: Theory and Practice* (Brighton: Wheatsheaf, 1986) and Herbert C. Kelman, 'Interactive problem solving: a social-psychological approach to conflict resolution', in W. Klassen (ed.), *Dialogue Toward Inter-Faith Understanding* (Tantur/Jerusalem: Ecumenical Institute for Theoretical Research, 1986), pp. 293–314.

31 Gilligan, *op. cit.*, pp. 9–10.

32 Keller, *op. cit.*, p. 117.

33 Evelyn Fox Keller, *A Feeling for the Organism: The Life and Work of Barbara McClintock* (New York: Freeman, 1983).

34 Harding, *op. cit.*, Chapter 7.

35 'Utopia and reality are . . . the two facets of political science. Sound political thought and sound political life will be found only where both have their place': E.H. Carr, *The Twenty Years Crisis: 1919–1939* (New York: Harper and Row, 1964), p. 10.

4

International relations theory: contributions of a feminist standpoint

ROBERT O. KEOHANE

In a recent paper Christine Sylvester applied an interesting typology of feminist theory to international relations. Sylvester employs Sandra Harding's useful distinction in *The Science Question in Feminism*[1] among feminist ways of looking at society to examine international relations:

1 Feminist empiricism observes that states and the inter-state system have been fundamentally gendered structures of domination and interaction. Feminist empiricism asks 'whether it is accurate to focus on states and worldwide capitalist processes and not also examine the social attitudes and structures which impart a gender to international relations'.[2]

2 Feminist standpoint theories argue that women's experiences at the margins of political life have given them perspectives on social issues that provide valid insights into world politics. From her vantage-point at the periphery, the feminist theorist offers a critique of theories constructed by men who put themselves in the position of policy-makers (or, as in Morgenthau, look 'over his shoulder'). Instead, feminists critically examine international relations from the standpoint of people who have been systematically excluded from power.[3] The feminist standpoint conception as I use it does not imply that feminist perspectives are necessarily superior in an absolute sense to traditional views – only that they contain valid insights into the complex realities of world politics.

3 Feminist post-modernism is a difficult term to define, and seems to cover a variety of tendencies; but for Harding and Sylvester its essence appears to be a resistance to the conception of 'one true story' and to à 'falsely universalising perspective' such as that of white men. As Harding says, 'this creates a powerful internal tension: the standpoint epistemologies appear committed to trying to tell the "one true story" about ourselves and

the world around us that the postmodernist epistemologies regard as a dangerous fiction'.[4]

My argument in this commentary is that despite the post-modernist criticisms, the conception of a feminist standpoint provides a particularly promising starting-point for the development of feminist international relations theory. In the first instance, the insights of a feminist standpoint would be *conceptual*, criticizing the implicit biases in our thinking about international relations. Beginning but not ending with an analysis of the words and symbols used in international relations discourse this analysis would seek to improve our understanding of existing international relations practice by examining how core concepts of international relations are affected by the gendered structure of international society. How have distinctively male values, and social structures in which male values are given priority, affected the concepts developed in international society? That is, to what extent have the concepts of international relations been androcentric? Having re-examined key concepts of international relations, such work from a feminist standpoint would facilitate deeper feminist empirical analysis of world politics.

The feminist standpoint on power, sovereignty, reciprocity

It seems to me that a feminist analysis will have to re-analyse key concepts such as power, sovereignty and reciprocity. It will ask whether male constructions of these concepts have affected how we think about international relations, and how our thinking might be changed by reflecting on the concepts.

Consider, for example, the concept of power. Morgenthau defines power rather crudely as 'man's control over the minds and actions of other men'.[5] Kenneth N. Waltz views power not as a relationship but as the 'old and simple notion that an agent is powerful to the extent that he affects others more than they affect him'.[6] More common now is the conception of power as a characteristic of a relationship between A and B in which A has the ability 'to get B to do what he would otherwise not do'.[7]

As David Baldwin has pointed out, any definition of power as control, to be meaningful, must specify the scope and domain of power. Such a definition therefore refers to the 'ability of one actor to influence another actor *with respect to certain outcomes*'. Nevertheless, emphasis on power as control can obscure the end of having power – to affect one's environment consistently with one's preferences. Furthermore, it omits the order creating function of power, which Hannah Arendt has referred to as 'the human ability not just to act but to act in concert'.[8] As Jean Bethke Elshtain has observed,

> the 'high politics' emergent from received readings of these texts [Thucydides, Machiavelli, *et al.*] is, in [Joan] Scott's words, a 'gendered concept', for it establishes its crucial importance and public power, the

reasons for and the fact of its highest authority, precisely in its exclusion of women from its work.[9]

Emphasizing power as the ability to act in concert would call attention to areas of world politics in which human beings seek to collaborate to cope with collective problems, such as those arising from ecological and economic interdependence. It would more easily be recognized that world politics is far from a zero sum game in which one side's gain is the other's loss, and that the amount of power in the international system can vary over time. Effective international institutions create 'the ability to act in concert', which may not exist in the absence of such institutions.

Redefining power may help us to rethink the notion of sovereignty. Hedley Bull defines sovereignty in classic power-as-control terms: 'internal sovereignty means supremacy over all other authorities within [a given] territory and population', while 'external sovereignty' means 'not supremacy but independence of outside authorities'.[10] Similarly, for F.H. Hinsley, the original idea of sovereignty was 'the idea that there is a final and absolute political authority in the political community', and that 'no final and absolute authority exists elsewhere'.[11]

Phrased thus, sovereignty seems to reflect traditionally male thinking, with its emphasis on control and its penchant for absolute and dichotomous categories. From this perspective it would be worthwhile to ask whether the concept of territorial sovereignty, so fundamental to the modern state system, has anything to do with gender. Such a question could be fundamental to a feminist standpoint analysis of world politics. It is important, however, not to prejudge the answer. After all, the modern doctrine of sovereignty itself arose in opposition to that most patriarchal of all institutions, the Papacy.[12] Furthermore, the conception of the 'sovereignty of the people', as articulated by James Wilson and other American Federalists, can be viewed as an expression of the conception of power as the ability to act in concert. In order to act in concert, 'the people, as the fountain of government' can delegate sovereignty, 'in such proportions, to such bodies, on such terms, and under such limitations, as they think proper'.[13] In the United States, national sovereignty and its corollary, national citizenship, were used in the nineteenth century as weapons by anti-slavery forces and therefore had a progressive character.[14] Critical conceptual analysis must be aware of the complexity of established concepts such as sovereignty and the multiple uses to which they have been put. Indeed, a feminist standpoint might help to distinguish between notions of sovereignty based on power-as-control and those based on power-as-action-in-concert, and to reinvigorate the latter conception, which has recently been obscured by statist and realist thought.

Sovereignty is closely related to reciprocity. As Martin Wight has argued,

> it would be impossible to have a society of sovereign states unless each state, while claiming sovereignty for itself, recognized that every other

state had the right to claim and enjoy its own sovereignty as well. This reciprocity was inherent in the Western conception of sovereignty.[15]

Such specific reciprocity is based on individualistic and egoistic premises: it is a procedure for coexistence based on 'tit for tat'.[16] What I have elsewhere called diffuse reciprocity, on the other hand, is based on social norms and a widespread pattern of obligation. The norms on which diffuse reciprocity rests may reflect empathy of people toward one another, and could therefore be consistent with what Carol Gilligan refers to as 'an ethic of care' and what Joan Tronto discusses as a conception of identity describable as 'the connected self'.[17] The emphasis of many feminist thinkers on a way of thinking that identifies with others rather than differentiating oneself from others could therefore be an important insight into conceptualizing a form of reciprocity that is norm conditioned and empathetic rather than individualistic and egoistic.

Beyond specific analysis of concepts such as power, sovereignty and reciprocity, a feminist analysis would be critical of overly objectivist or reductionist models such as are found in neorealism.[18] It would emphasize the role of purposeful human action and subjectivity in creating new conditions of life, and the need for what Evelyn Fox Keller calls 'dynamic objectivity' in studying international relations – 'a form of knowledge that grants to the world around us its independent integrity but does so in a way that remains cognizant of, indeed relies on, our connectivity with that world'. Dynamic objectivity uses 'consciousness of self in the interests of a more effective objectivity'.[19] Along with the concept of empathy, that of dynamic objectivity could be particularly relevant to an understanding of reciprocity in terms other than rationalistic tit for tat.

Another appropriate target of feminist thinking would be dichotomous thinking in general and in particular the dichotomy between hierarchy and markets as modes of organization. The inadequacy of such a dichotomy is a theme of contemporary network theory in sociology,[20] which also seems related to the emphasis of feminist theory on networks and the feminist opposition to dichotomies. Feminist theories stress networks of family ties and links between these networks and the state. The analysis may also be applicable to transnational networks.

A feminist theory of international relations could help to articulate an institutional vision of international relations – a network view, emphasizing how institutions could promote lateral cooperation among organized entities, states or otherwise. Such an analysis would go beyond the question of who is able to control whom, under what conditions. Such a question is still relevant to crucial issues of international relations, but it does not capture well much of what is important in the contemporary world, particularly in so far as states seek collectively to cope with the consequences of interdependence. A feminist–institutionalist theory also asks under what conditions are human beings able to act in concert, across state boundaries, to create networks that achieve common purposes.

Feminist empiricism and post-modernism

Feminist empiricism takes a fundamentally sociological approach, investigating how gender (the institutionalization of sex differences) affects the modern inter-state system. Feminist empiricism emphasizes that women have been victims of patriarchal states and that both major aspects of modern international relations – its institutionalization of warfare and its reinforcement of state sovereignty – have had harmful, and often disastrous, effects on women's lives. It is often pointed out, for instance, that Third World development has been male dominated and that women have often suffered from the form that development has taken. Recognition of these often over-looked facts is an important contribution of feminist empiricism.

Nevertheless, emphasizing the victimization of women by 'the patriarchal state' or 'the interstate system' provides only limited insights into international relations. Some analysts succumb to the temptation to discuss, in sweeping terms, 'the patriarchal state' or 'the war system' without making distinctions among states or international systems. To do so commits the analytical error of reifying a stylized 'patriarchal state' or 'war system'. Furthermore, excoriating universal repression seems to lead more toward moralizing about its iniquity than toward the analysis of sources of variation in its incidence.

At a descriptive level, a valuable contribution of feminist empiricism would be to document the extent to which the inter-state system depends on the under-rewarded labour of women or on gendered structures of society that disadvantage women. One can ask, as Cynthia Enloe has started to do, to what extent the inter-state system is dependent on gendered roles (diplomat, soldier) that sharply differentiate, by gender, public and private realms.[21] More ambitiously, feminist empiricism could seek to explore the conditions under which repression of women is more or less severe: what types of states and international systems have more adverse consequences for women's lives than others?

To make a major impact on thinking about international relations, however, it will not be sufficient explicitly to point out that women have been marginalized in the state and in inter-state politics. This reality is well known, even if conventional international relations theory has tended to ignore it. Feminist empiricism will be most significant, it seems to me, if used in conjunction with feminist standpoint reconceptualizations to re-examine central concepts of international relations theory by asking about their values for empirical research. Feminist empiricism, guided by feminist reconceptualization, could go beyond the question of 'the role of women in international relations' to a critical analysis of the extent to which contemporary international relations theory helps us to understand what is happening in world politics today.

As indicated above, post-modernism is a puzzling label that seems to denote a variety of positions. One version of it, however, denies the possibility of having a single epistemology, even one with slightly different variants. As Mary E. Hawkesworth puts it, 'postmodernist insights counsel that Truth be abandoned because it is a hegemonic and, hence, destructive illusion'.[22] According to these post-modernists, 'feminist empiricism is committed to untenable beliefs about the nature of knowledge and process of knowing' and feminist standpoint theories 'remain committed to an overly simplistic model of knowledge that tends to assume a "collective singular subject"'.[23] In this view, we cannot agree on an epistemological basis for substantive discussions: that is, on standards against which we can evaluate knowledge claims.

It seems to me that this post-modernist project is a dead end in the study of international relations – and that it would be disastrous for feminist international relations theory to pursue this path. Of course I am aware that social knowledge is always value laden and that objectivity is an aspiration rather than an accomplishment. But I object to the notion that because social science cannot attain any perfectly reliable knowledge, it is justifiable for students of society to 'obliterate the validity of reality'.[24] I also object to the notion that we should happily accept the existence of multiple incommensurable epistemologies, each equally valid. Such a view seems to me to lead away from our knowledge of the external world and ultimately to a sort of nihilism. Hawkesworth argues that 'the world is more than a text' and that feminists should avoid 'the postmodernist tendency to reject all reasons'.[25] I would go further and say that agreement on epistemological essentials constitutes a valuable scientific asset that should not be discarded lightly. With such agreement, people with different commensurable terms can perhaps come to an agreement with the aid of evidence. As philosophers of science such as Imre Lakatos have argued, the invalidity of naive falsificationism does not destroy the possibility of establishing standards for scientific research: participants in the process apply criteria having to do with resolution of anomalies, discovery of new facts, and what Lakatos calls 'the requirement of continuous growth'.[26]

A major aim of science, even social science, is to provide us with a common set of epistemological tools, in a discipline, for ascertaining the nature of reality and therefore testing the adequacy of our theories. This is not to pretend that any knowledge is perfectly 'objective': clearly our values, our upbringing, our bodily experiences and our positions in society – gender, class, culture, race – all affect what we believe. But science has the value of narrowing gaps in belief by providing common standards to test beliefs, and therefore disciplining our minds, protecting us to some extent from bias. The very difficulty of achieving social scientific knowledge is an argument for cherishing rather than discarding social science and the aspiration for a more or less unified epistemology.

I fear that many feminist theorists of international relations may follow the currently fashionable path of fragmenting epistemology, denying the possibility of social science. But I think this would be an intellectual and moral disaster. As Linda Alcoff points out, 'post-structuralist critiques of subjectivity pertain to the construction of all subjects or they pertain to none. . . . Nominalism threatens to wipe out feminism itself.'[27] That is, feminist theory cannot be without a positive standpoint – it cannot be *only* adversarial. Retreating to post-modern adversarial analysis would foreclose the relations that could be regarded as valuable by people outside the feminist circle. Scientifically, it would lead away from what I think feminist theory should do: generate novel hypotheses that could then be evaluated with evidence, in a way that could lead to convincing results. Politically, as Hawkesworth declares,

> should postmodernism's seductive text gain ascendancy, it will not be an accident that power remains in the hands of the white males who currently possess it. In a world of radical inequality, relativist resignation reinforces the status quo.[28]

Conclusion

What I am calling for in these comments is an *alliance* between two complementary critiques of neorealism: first, what I call 'neoliberal institutionalism' and, second, an emerging feminist standpoint theory of international relations. Neoliberal institutionalism seeks, like neorealism, to understand state behaviour as far as possible through an analysis of the nature of the international system. Unlike neorealism, however, it argues that institutions – 'persistent and connected sets of rules (formal and informal) that prescribe behavioural roles, constrain activity, and shape expectations' – are as important as the distribution of power in affecting state behaviour.[29] Feminist standpoint thinkers should find intellectual affinities with the institutionalist view of international relations, since it emphasizes power as ability to act in concert, diffuse as well as specific reciprocity, and the role of networks as well as hierarchies. The feminist perspective should, for its part, be able to give theories of complex interdependence and institutional change a richer, more gender-conscious formulation, and also to criticize the gender bias to be found in conceptions of interdependence and institutionalization created by men.

From a normative standpoint the feminist emphasis on connectedness can also make a major contribution. Suppose we begin with connectedness as a given, rather than separateness: suppose planet earth were the primary affiliation rather than the separate nation state? This is not helpful for positive analysis but might provide a normative grounding for prescription.[30] An extension of the work of Tronto and others into the international sphere could therefore make a major contribution. In addition to offering a critique of mainstream theories of international relations, feminist standpoint theories may reinforce an emerging trend away from the fragmentation and atomization inherent in traditional conceptions of international relations, toward a network-oriented, institutionalized approach that is truer to the emerging reality. Feminist theories may also contribute to a normative conception stressing connectedness and obligations to other inhabitants of planet earth. This would represent a radical break with the contractual morality of our previous conceptions.

Notes

These comments on the feminist standpoint in international relations theory were originally prepared for a panel on Gender and International Relations organized by Ann Tickner of The College of the Holy Cross at the International Studies Association/British International Studies Association Joint Convention in London, March–April 1989. These remarks are highly tentative and are not as thoroughly grounded in feminist analysis as they should be. Readers are asked to view them as contributions to an emerging conversation, rather than as a definitive statement of my views. In revising my comments, I had the benefit of a conference on Gender and International Relations held at the University of Southern California in April 1989, organized by Jane Jaquette and V. Spike Peterson. I am indebted to Mary F. Katzenstein, Nannerl O. Keohane, and Susan Moller Okin for conversations about my preliminary ideas on this subject, and to Donna Gregory for some very helpful criticisms of my treatment of post-modernism.

1 Sandra Harding, *The Science Question in Feminism* (Ithaca, NY: Cornell University Press, 1986). See Christine Sylvester, 'The emperor's theories and transformations: looking at the field through feminist lenses', in Dennis Pirages and Christine Sylvester (eds), *Transformations in the Global Political Economy* (Basingstoke: Macmillan, 1989).
2 *Ibid.*, p. 16.
3 See J. Ann Tickner, 'Hans Morgenthau's principles of political realism: a feminist reformulation', *Millennium: Journal of International Studies* (Vol. 17, No. 3, Winter 1988).
4 Harding, *op. cit.*, p. 195.
5 Hans J. Morgenthau, *Politics Among Nations* (New York: Knopf, 1967), p. 26.
6 Kenneth N. Waltz, *Theory of International Politics* (Reading, MA: Addison-Wesley, 1979), p. 192.
7 David A. Baldwin, 'Power analysis and world politics', *World Politics* (Vol. 31, No. 2, January 1979), p. 179.
8 Quoted in Nancy C.M. Hartsock, *Money, Sex and Power: Toward a Feminist Historical Materialism* (New York: Longman, 1983), p. 219. Also see Tickner, *op. cit.*, p. 434.
9 Jean Bethke Elshtain, 'Feminist themes and international relations discourse', paper presented at the International Studies Association/British International Studies Association joint convention, London, 28 March–7 April, 1989, p. 6.
10 Hedley Bull, *The Anarchical Society: A Study of Order in World Politics* (New York: Columbia University Press, 1977), p. 8.
11 F.H. Hinsley, *Sovereignty* (London: C.A. Watts, 1966).
12 See Martin Wight, *Systems of States* (Leicester: Leicester University Press, 1977).
13 James Wilson, quoted in Gordon S. Wood, *The Creation of the American*

Republic, 1776–1787 (Chapel Hill, NC: University of North Carolina Press, 1969), p. 530. Wood points out that the Federalists appropriated the absolutist concept of sovereignty – the notion there must be only one 'final, indivisible and incontestable authority in every state to which all other authorities must be ultimately subordinate' – to their purposes by creating the fiction of 'popular sovereignty'. In another vein, however, Madison once admitted that if sovereignty could not be divided, 'the political system of the United States is a chimera, mocking the vain pretensions of human wisdom'. See Charles E. Merriman, *A History of American Political Theories* (New York: Macmillan, 1903), p. 259, citing an 1865 edition of Madison's Works, Volume 4, p. 61.

14 James H. Kettner, *The Development of American Citizenship, 1608–1870* (Chapel Hill, NC: University of North Carolina Press, 1978).

15 Martin Wight, *op. cit.*, p. 135.

16 Robert Axelrod, *The Evolution of Cooperation* (New York: Basic Books, 1984); Robert O. Keohane, 'Reciprocity in international relations', *International Organization* (Vol. 40, No. 1, Winter 1986), pp. 1–27.

17 Carol Gilligan, *In a Different Voice: Psychological Theory and Women's Development* (Cambridge, MA: Harvard University Press, 1982); Joan C. Tronto, 'Beyond gender difference to a theory of care', *Signs: Journal of Women in Culture and Society* (Vol. 12, No. 4, Summer 1967), pp. 644–63. This point is also indebted to a talk by Joan Tronto at a conference on Gender and International Relations at the Center for International Studies, University of Southern California, 28–9 April 1989. For a discussion of empathy as a factor in international cooperation, see Robert O. Keohane, *After Hegemony: Cooperation and Discord in the World Political Economy* (Princeton, NJ: Princeton University Press, 1984), Chapter 7.

18 Since I have often been misunderstood on this point, let me emphasize that I do not identify with neorealism, understood as 'an attempt to systematize political realism into a rigorous, deductive systemic theory of international politics'. Robert O. Keohane, 'Realism, neorealism and the study of world politics', in Robert O. Keohane (ed.), *Neorealism and Its Critics* (New York: Columbia University Press, 1986), p. 15 and n. 7 on p. 25; and Robert O. Keohane, *International Institutions and State Power* (Boulder, CO: Westview, 1989), pp. 7–9.

19 Evelyn Fox Keller, *Gender and Science* (New Haven, CT: Yale University Press, 1985), p. 117.

20 I am indebted for this point to discussions with, and unpublished papers by, Walter Powell.

21 Some of this perspective is reflected in Cynthia Enloe, *Does Khaki Become You? The Militarization of Women's Lives* (London: Pluto Press, 1983); I am also indebted for this point to conversations with Professor Enloe.

22 Mary E. Hawkesworth, 'Knowers, knowing, known: feminist theory and claims of truth', *Signs: Journal of Women in Culture and Society* (Vol. 14, No. 3, Spring 1989), p. 554.

23 *Ibid.*, p. 553.

24 I owe this remark to Joan Tronto, who made it in the course of a critique of post-modernist international relations thinking at the Gender and International Relations conference, University of Southern California, cited above. ·

25 Hawkesworth, *op. cit.*, p. 556.

26 Imre Lakatos, 'Falsification and the methodology of scientific research programs', in Imre Lakatos and Alan Musgrave (eds), *Criticism and the Growth of Knowledge* (Cambridge: Cambridge University Press, 1970), p. 175.

27 Linda Alcoff, 'Cultural feminism versus post-structuralism: the identity crisis in feminist theory', *Signs: Journal of Women in Culture and Society* (Vol. 13, No. 3, Spring 1988), p. 419.
28 Hawkesworth, *op. cit.*, p. 557.
29 Robert O. Keohane, *International Institutions, op. cit.*, pp. 3, 9.
30 See Robert O. Keohane, 'Closing the fairness–practice gap', *Ethics and International Affairs* (Vol. 3, 1989), pp. 101–16.

5

Marxism, feminism and the demise of the Soviet model

MAXINE MOLYNEUX

Recent discussion of the relationship between issues of gender and international relations has considered how policies of states towards women are conditioned by international factors. These factors include the most obvious – wars, economic trends, legal changes, nationalist upsurges. They may also include less overt or recognized mechanisms through which supranational and transnational influences may affect both policies and the socio-economic position of women within specific societies. The comments that follow introduce into this discussion a hitherto absent group of states, those that were ruled by communist parties. It suggests some less obvious ways of thinking about the international dimension in relation to the policy making process, especially with respect to policies on women. This international dimension is relevant both to the period of undisputed communist party control and to the more recent dissolution of the orthodox communist system.

That these 'socialist'[1] states had something that could be identified as state policy on women is undeniable, and this indeed distinguished them from most Western capitalist states: they proclaimed themselves to be committed to the equality of women and men and sought, for a variety of ideological and economic reasons, to mobilize women into public life. To recognize that they failed to emancipate women even in terms of generally held feminist criteria, should not obscure the degree to which they implemented quite radical policies which had significant effects on women's legal, social, political and economic status.[2]

The point emphasized here is that these policies cannot be analysed without bringing international factors into account because, in the first place the social and economic policies that socialist states adopted were, despite local variations, initially derived from an international example – the Soviet experience. This was especially true of policies concerning women and the family. Indeed, one of the hallmarks of orthodox socialist policy on women was its implacable anti-particularism, its insistence on the universal character of gender inequality and on the possibility of generalizing the measures needed to resolve it. Second, the international dimension acquired a special significance because the pace and direction of policy regarding women reflected overall state priorities, which were themselves to a considerable extent a product of these states' competitive and conflictual position in the international arena. This international impact was equally clear in the phase of *perestroika* and rethinking, when socialist states began the attempt to revitalize their economies and societies; this process was one that promised multiple, and contradictory, implications for gender relations.

To sketch in this relationship between policies on women, international factors and socialist states involves not only the introduction of a relatively new dimension into the discussion, but also a recognition of a number of gaps in the literature on gender relations in socialist states. It is not surprising that there emerged no body of literature which aimed to theorize the international dimension of the women/state relation with respect to the socialist bloc. The key elements of any such analysis – the 'socialist' state and 'the international' – were themselves undertheorized. While there is a substantial literature on women in socialist societies, it none the less remained very much outside the mainstream theoretical debates about gender relations and the state as a whole. The international dimension itself only recently began to enter analyses of gender inequality, but the socialist states had little presence in these analyses, even when the impact of the world economic order on women's socio-economic status and on policy making was recognized.[3]

In the absence, then, of any very advanced debates on this issue, the following remarks are intended merely as a starting point for further discussion. They address but do not attempt a full answer to the question of how state policy in the socialist bloc with respect to women was influenced by international factors. Implicit in them is a consideration of what the study of socialist policy on women can contribute to the broader evaluation of international determinants of gender relations. With all the differences and specificities of socialist as distinct from capitalist states, there is much in their history and evolution that is of relevance to a broader analysis of 'the international' and women.

The 'woman question' and the policy response

Despite the commitment of principle that socialist states made to the emancipation of women, itself an inheritance of the radical liberal and classical Marxist ideas of the nineteenth century, the policies adopted ostensibly to further this end owed at least as much to the practical considerations of revolutionary states. Such states sought to mobilize women and transform their social position as part of the planned reorganization of society: policy on women was to a considerable degree derivative of other, more general goals.[4] A starting point in most analyses of the impact of international influences on policy is the world economy: socialist states always had to define their economic policies in relation to it, whether these were premised on autarchic separation or measured integration. Socialist states were clearly far from immune from the effects of world market competition, dependency, price trends and the like. Their policies on women were to a considerable degree a reflection of the macroeconomic policies they pursued to advance their position at the international economic level. The wider international arena, both politically and economically, provided a range of initial conditioning factors which directly affected state policy, including land reforms, five-year plans, great leaps forward and the like. All these policies implied major social transformations, which affected women's social and economic position. The policies were formulated as responses to a perceived need to pursue an international rivalry against the antagonistic, capitalist world beyond.

The effects on policy of inter-state rivalry – ranging from economic competition to a desire to catch up with the more advanced states to outright conditions of war – all had implications for the way women were perceived by planners. Women could be mobilized en masse as paid or unpaid workers into the 'development effort' or drafted into the militia. Another, more sensitive area was population policy: the prospects for economic growth were considered by planners to be conditional on higher (e.g. USSR, Hungary, Mongolia) or lower (e.g. China, Vietnam) birth rates. Policies of intervention, sometimes of a starkly repressive kind, were implemented accordingly.

The pressure from outside, which the socialist states tried hard to resist, did not diminish with time. On the contrary it increased, and internal pressures for reform within the socialist countries were fed by comparisons with their more prosperous (and democratic) rivals, so that the political and economic reforms introduced in all but a handful of socialist states were to some extent precipitated by the concern to catch up with the capitalist world.

There is perhaps no need to elaborate further upon the central importance of the economy for policy making. An issue which is much less examined in relation to policy formation is the role of, for want of a better word, ideology. All public policies contain ideological elements which have a role in the formulation of the goals and strategies of states. Ideology also makes an important contribution to the efforts of states to legitimize their rule and their policies. Two important ideological influences on policy formation with respect to women in the socialist states can be singled out, both of which have a well defined international dimension: the communist tradition and the impact of feminism.[5] These can be considered as much currents of thought as social movements, through which ideology is produced and disseminated as a result of political practice. These two separate (and clearly unequal) influences may be considered as examples of two different kinds of inputs into policy: input 'from above', i.e. through the state as in the case of communist party theory, and input 'from below', largely through non-state channels including internal opposition forces, as in the case of feminism.

The communist tradition and Marxist theory

A selective and official version of Marxism was always a very important constituent of policy making with respect to women, and more broadly, throughout the countries ruled by communist parties. Although each party sought to define its policies in relation to specific local conditions and circumstances, when it came to addressing 'the woman question' there was a surprising degree of uniformity in the legal provisions and in the social policies that were adopted to secure state goals with respect to women. For the countries within the Soviet sphere of influence, the guiding principles behind policies claimed inspiration from the teachings of Marx, Engels and Lenin. The policies themselves had their origins in an orthodox codification of their teachings: the early proclamations on women of the Bolshevik Party, agreed to at the second congress of the Comintern in 1920.[6] This embodied the principles of a programme designed to improve the socio-economic and political position of women, while at the same time seeking to draw them into the process of social and economic transformation. The theoretical basis on which the policies were based was Engels's argument that women's subordination was linked to the rise of private property and class society; it could only be overcome through the revolutionary transformation of social relations and the ending of women's marginalization in production and entrapment within the domestic sphere. The 1920 resolutions therefore called for socialized child care, the mobilization of women into productive and wage earning activity, and the equalization of rights in the family. Later, in 1936, these principles were incorporated into the first Constitution of the Soviet Union. With relatively minor revisions, this 'basic law' was adopted by all of the 'states of socialist orientation', from Albania to Vietnam.[7]

This international diffusion of the 'scientific' socialist policy package took place through state to state and Party to Party relations. More concretely, it was effected through practical cooperation between the Communist Party of the Soviet Union (or of other more established socialist states such as the German Democratic Republic (GDR)) and those of the newly emerging socialist states who relied on the former for advice and expertise.[8] In this way the basic framework of policy on women within the socialist bloc was itself internationalized: it was not just imposed from above but also, it could be argued, from outside.

Feminism

The second international influence is of a very different kind and represented a growing challenge to the orthodox socialist account of gender inequalities. As an influence on policy making, feminism poses more analytic problems as its impact was more diffuse and less easily traced. It is none the less important to consider in any discussion of policy making with respect to women, even in countries generally considered impermeable to such influences.

As a social movement as much as a body of ideas, feminism always existed in an uneasy relation with socialism. As far as the socialist states themselves were concerned, it represented views which were regarded as inappropriate and (ironically, perhaps, given Marxism's 'alien' origins) were often seen as unwelcome 'foreign' intrusions with little application in the socialist countries themselves. For its part feminism as it developed in the post-war period, and especially in the 1970s, increasingly took issue with socialism's claim adequately to represent women's interests. Its adherents criticized the policy initiatives that were adopted to 'emancipate women' on the grounds that they did not go far enough and did not challenge the bases of men's power and privileges embodied in the distribution of political power and in the sexual division of labour at home and at work.

From the mid-nineteenth century onwards feminists had rejected the orthodox socialist view that women's subordination was explicable in class terms and would wither away, like the state, with the abolition of class relations. Feminists before, during and after the Russian Revolution argued for women's organizations with some independence from the party line, through which women's interests could be more effectively identified and advanced. Despite some initial alliances, Bolshevism had, by the mid-1920s, turned against feminism and sought to suppress it.

As feminist movements in a variety of different countries gained momentum during the early 1970s, 'scientific' socialist parties and states reaffirmed their rejection of what they identified as a specifically Western phenomenon, branding it (as they did most other unorthodox radical ideas from the West) as heterodox and subversive. Many were the speeches made by leaders of official women's organizations in socialist countries denouncing feminism as a 'bourgeois' and even 'imperialist' tendency, which threatened to divide men and women and divert them from the common struggle. Most feminist groups that did emerge in the 1970s were discouraged and suppressed. In Hungary in 1973 protesters against new restrictions on abortion presented a petition containing 1,553 signatures; the organizers, mostly students, were prevented from finishing their studies.[9] In the USSR in 1979 the feminist dissident publishers of the *Almanac* associated with Tatiana Monomova were hounded by the secret police; some were sent into exile.[10]

But despite the gulf which separated feminism from orthodox socialist positions, it became increasingly difficult during the second half of the 1970s for the latter to insulate itself from the former's growing international presence. This was so for three main reasons. First, feminism began to gain support among socialists and to lose its exclusive identification with the West and with the claims of those who were seen as relatively privileged women. Its demands began to have meaning for both Third World women and for

socialists dissatisfied with the political and theoretical limitations of orthodox interpretations of Marxism. As the dynamic of both women's movements and feminist ideas spread to the Third World, national liberation
movements and socialist parties found themselves in dialogue with local
interpretations and applications of feminist principles.[11] This encounter
between a radicalized feminism and a more open and revisionist socialism
was also taking place in most of the European communist and socialist
parties, most notably in the Italian communist party. In the process feminism
acquired a certain, albeit still conditional, legitimacy for socialists which it
had lacked before. In this context, ruling communist parties could not as
easily cling to the old certainties or get away with their mechanical dismissals
of feminist ideas and social movements.

A second dimension of the impact of feminism was evident in the growing
debate within planning circles and aid agencies in the 1970s about women
and development. This was stimulated by the need to assess the deteriorating
economic situation in most parts of the Third World; the feminization of
poverty and other trends disadvantageous to women were on the agenda for
discussion. In 1976 the UN Decade for Women opened an international
forum for debate of these issues and placed resources in the hands of
governments and NGOs to help to improve the situation of women,
especially among the rural poor. The participation of delegates from the
socialist states in the work and meetings of the Decade opened up a number of
new opportunities for research, for collaboration and networking. At the
same time it exposed individuals from those countries (often members of their
women's organizations) to a variety of different feminisms from all regions of
the world. Initially the public encounter between orthodox socialist and
feminist positions was as mutually antagonistic as that between Western and
Third World feminists. However, in both cases the eventual outcome of a
decade of debate, cooperation and struggle for resources against often cynical
governments was more positive. In many cases a greater understanding and
appreciation of the differences among those concerned to seek improvements
in women's situation emerged, and this was so whether the individuals
involved chose to define themselves as feminists or not.

Third, the Decade produced its own literature on gender inequalities, some
of which dealt with the socialist states. This yielded some valuable
comparative data which hitherto did not exist.[12] In the same period feminist
criticisms of socialism's failures with respect to women received some
confirmation from the sociological literature emerging from within the
socialist states themselves. It was reinforced by growing evidence of women's
discontent. It was clear that women were not emancipated in any real sense in
these societies, and that in many ways the theoretically emancipated (i.e.
working) women carried an even heavier workload (domestic and waged)
than in the West. Survey after survey showed that women were bearing the
major responsibility for domestic work and for children, while other studies
documented the obstacles impeding women's attainment of equality at work.

By the 1970s in many of the socialist states (e.g. Hungary, the USSR, China, Cuba, the GDR), policy debates about women's place in society were well under way, while discontent among women was surfacing in the media and was beginning to be noticed and taken into account.[13] Few heads of state were now prepared to claim that women were 'emancipated' and many agreed with Brezhnev and, later, with Gorbachev that something had to be done to improve women's situation. Meanwhile, within this general context of public debate and discussion of 'women's problematic place in society', feminist interest groups were making a hesitant appearance in some of the socialist states, and, despite official disapproval, had begun to engage in the debates over policy. Some of these groups identified themselves as neofeminist, to distinguish themselves from earlier feminists as well as from other currents of feminism with which they disagreed. A Yugoslav feminist wrote of a 'new wave of feminist activity' appearing in the late 1970s and of the emergence of feminist groups which 'promoted public discussions and lectures on many previously unquestionable matters. Many of their members have written articles for newspapers and magazines and statements for the radio and television, thus helping to raise the consciousness of men and women.'[14] These groups or others like them continued to campaign on issues of feminist concern such as abortion, rape, incest and inequalities embodied in legislation and social provision. They had some successes. Similar groups appeared in other socialist states and challenged government assumptions about gender roles and the policies based on them.[15]

A different kind of feminist response emerged in the GDR during the early 1980s. A group of women organized themselves into a protest movement around peace issues, following a proposal to extend conscription to women in times of national emergency. Several hundred women petitioned the government, and small peace demonstrations of the 'women in black' were held. The protesters declared their opposition to 'all forms of violence as a mode of conflict resolution'.[16] Although they were threatened and detained by the security police no further action against them was taken. Indeed, their protest met with some success, as call up procedures planned to accompany a new deployment of nuclear weapons in 1983 were abandoned. This movement emerged in a context where debate was influenced by feminist writers such as Christa Wolf, who had developed an analysis which linked peace issues with a general critique of contemporary society as lacking in human values and in need of the qualities historically (but not inherently) associated with women's 'nurturing' roles.[17]

Reforms and transformations

While there are reasons to doubt that feminism of whatever variety could have had a major influence in the socialist states while the old power structures remained in place, it became more difficult to silence its various voices in the conditions of greater public debate which accompanied political and economic changes in the USSR and Central and Eastern Europe since 1985. Broadly, what was at stake in the turmoil of the reform process was the creation of new definitions and understandings of citizenship. Feminists began to play a part in defining the terms of the debate for women. Here the wheel came full circle and the two strands of international influence and determination were conjoined: the opening up of socialist societies induced by international ideological competition created the possibility for other international ideological currents to gain a foothold. As with the earlier transformative policies, this new phase of social and political change was to a considerable extent a function of the international position of the socialist states – in this case their evident inability to compete with the capitalist world – fuelled by growing discontent from below.

Throughout the socialist and formerly socialist countries the opening up of political life had at least two consequences for women. On the one hand, it meant that feminist ideas and views critical of official policies could be expressed more openly than ever before. Feminist groups began a dialogue with feminists in other countries including those from the West. This discussion was made all the more possible by the climate of critical debate and greater information in general on social questions. On the other hand, the official international ideology of Marxism began to lose its privileged position within state discourses (and even within Communist Parties), and was widely rejected by the populations of these states. Ideas of 'women's emancipation', so long part of official ideology, were all too readily associated with the dead hand of an authoritarian bureaucracy imposing reforms from above, and with its largely moribund official women's unions. Some of the new opposition groups (a number of which were dominated by nationalist and religious ideas) were quick to turn the widespread dislike of the former state and its policies into a general disparagement of feminist concerns.[18]

Solidarity's hostility to legalized abortion was an obvious case of how, in the rejection of the authoritarian socialist state, some of women's legislative gains of the past could be threatened. At the same time the place vacated by official ideology was in part filled by new conceptions of freedom and modernity associated with an admired, often idealized, Western way of life. The appearance in Eastern Europe and the USSR of innumerable beauty contests and the sudden availability of pornography were for many feminists among the less savoury features of the post-communist era. Again, the restraint exercised by Communist Parties over such matters was now seen as part of their lack of sophistication, deriving from a dictatorial puritanism that was contrasted with the free sensuality of liberal capitalism. It is interesting in this respect that one of the first things that the new liberalized Polish and East German communist youth magazines did was to institute a regular photograph of a female nude as a sign of their new freedom from orthodoxy. Yet in a context where sex and eroticism were previously seen as pornography and perpetrators were punished severely, it is little wonder that notions of sexual freedom were sometimes crudely fashioned, and feminist critiques were dismissed as yet another form of censorship.[19]

The key issue is what impact the new, internationally encouraged openness in these states, and the collapse of communist party rule, will have on policies regarding women. It is too early in the process to be able to say with any certainty what the various outcomes will be; but there are indications that more traditional views of women's place in society may gain ascendancy. Throughout Eastern Europe and the Soviet Union concern has been growing about the effects of what is seen as 'social decomposition', evidenced by high divorce rates, alcoholism, juvenile alienation and crime. Attention has focused on the family and on the role of women within it, with the view commonly expressed that many of these problems result from women's inability, through overwork, to put enough time into childcare and home-making. A parallel concern is the low birthrate which most governments would like to see rise. As a result they have debated (and in some cases implemented) policy measures designed to encourage women to have fewer abortions and more children. These measures include allowing women with children under five years more time away from work, and payments of the 'mother's allowance' variety for women to stay at home with their infants for up to two years.

Gorbachev has repeatedly emphasized the need to strengthen the family as a stabilizing element in society, and this has been interpreted as reaffirming women's central place within it. The draft programme of the Communist Party of the Soviet Union (CPSU) published in October 1985 stressed the need to improve 'care for the family' to make it more 'durable' and 'spiritually and morally healthy'. In his address to the February 1986 Party Congress Gorbachev spoke of introducing changes which would enable women to combine 'their maternal duties' with involvement in economic activity. Measures were proposed which would shorten women's working week or allow them to work at home; pre-school day care would be extended as would paid leave for mothers of infants under 18 months of age. Some of Gorbachev's closest advisers on social issues have even spoken of the need to introduce higher wages for men so that married women could afford to leave the workforce. They argued that this redomestication of women would take care of several problems at once. It would alleviate the pressures on women who had to combine paid work with domestic responsibilities. It would boost the birth rate, long a subject of concern in planning circles in the Russian Republic. And it might cushion the effect of female unemployment, an expected byproduct of the rationalization of industry (and the elimination of a range of unnecessary jobs which were created when full employment was a state goal and all citizens were obliged by law to work).

Official and popular attitudes have converged in a common denunciation of women's double day and of the burdens women bear as a result of trying to combine paid work with continuing responsibilities in the home. The language of these criticisms contained appeals for the restoration of a more 'natural' state of affairs where 'women were women and men were men'.[20] But taken together, the new social provisions and dynamics of reform promised a deepening of the already considerable divide between the sexes in terms of their social roles, responsibilities and rewards. In general, the eventual outcome for women of the collapse of the old policies will depend not only on what specific policies – political, economic and social – the new governments will adopt, but on how far women are able and willing to mobilize and influence policy making. But as far as organized politics in the USSR are concerned the picture is not promising.

In 1986 Gorbachev gave support to greater female participation in political life when he called for a revival of women's Soviets and of the women's movement in general, as well as greater female representation in public bodies. Yet as Soviet commentators were soon to point out, the work of the *zhensovieti* presupposed a broader willingness on the part of Party and employment officials to listen to what they said. From the information available, this broader context was far from favourable. The call for women to be promoted to positions of authority was double edged, not least because the decreasing power of the state meant that Gorbachev's appeals did not necessarily materialize into action. This was evident in the fate of women within the parliament of the USSR itself; in the elections of the Supreme Soviet of March 1989 the proportion of women elected fell by over half – from 34.5 per cent to 15.3 per cent. A similar result occurred the previous year in Poland, with a fall from 20.2 per cent to 13.3 per cent in the January 1988 elections. Gorbachev showed that he could and would act in areas under leadership control, such as in the promotion of women to more senior posts: in September 1988, for the first time in 28 years, a woman, Alexandra Biriukova, was appointed a candidate member of the CPSU Politburo, a post she held until the re-shuffle of July 1990. But amidst widespread indifference, and hostility to what was seen as the traditional authoritarian imposition of quotas from above, the success of this kind of promotion of female representation must be doubtful.

Overall, the new climate of political liberalism did not immediately produce any strong feminist political presence in the post-socialist states. Feminist groupings, networks and currents were active in most countries but continued to face formidable obstacles, not so much (as in the past) from the state but, this time, from forces within civil society. In the USSR after 1985, amid an eruption of political debate, it was striking how, in the plethora of forces new and old, gender issues appeared to have had such a small role. The religious and nationalist groups paid scant attention to them beyond denouncing state interference in family life and women's 'involuntary emancipation'. The 'informal political forces' were little better; in the People's Front that grew up in 1989, women's issues were not given any prominence and women speakers seemed few and far between in the liberalized political atmosphere. Only five women out of 1,256 delegates spoke at the June 1988 party conference, and only one of these raised issues pertaining to women.[21] The ironic conclusion seemed to be that socialist state policy on women, which had not achieved their emancipation, succeeded only in alienating much of the population from any serious commitment to improving women's socio-economic position.

At the social level, in most of these countries there were a number of elements that conspired against the emergence of significant support for feminist ideas at least in the medium term. Leaving aside a fairly general dislike of what was imagined to be feminism, the harsh conditions of life and the coercive character of public institutions may have led to a romanticization of the family and private life, something which undermined women's aspirations for alternatives to traditional female roles. If this was so, then it was likely that the kinds of policies suggested by Gorbachev would find more resonance within the female population than more radical demands from feminists for changes in male–female relations. Nevertheless, it must be said that women do not have uniform interests, and the new feminist groups which emerged in the USSR and in Eastern and Central Europe in the 1980s could find a response within certain sectors of the population.

To conclude, it is evident that the conjunction of two important international factors – inter-state competition with its impact on socio-economic policies and international ideological trends and their reception within socialist states – has been responsible for shaping much of socialist policy and thinking with respect to women in the earlier, orthodox phase. It has also played a role in precipitating the collapse of communist governments or policies. The impact of this collapse on women has been contradictory, opening new opportunities for women to organize but also fomenting forces that may be hostile to any feminist agenda. In the new political conjuncture which has opened up in the post-communist world, external ideological influences will no doubt continue to play a significant part in shaping policy options, but the composition of those elements has altered irreversibly. Marxist-Leninism can no longer constitute the basis of official ideology as communist parties distance themselves from their past or, increasingly are displaced by other political forces. What will take its place is not yet clear. Feminism, on the other hand, has a future of some kind to look forward to in most of these states. Its conflictual history with official orthodoxy, its diverse and constantly evolving character as a political ideology and potentially greater ability to respond to the needs and wishes of its constituency, may protect it from losing the small foothold it has gained over the years. Whether it succeeds in building on that base in the widely differing political conditions of the 'post-communist bloc' will depend upon the success of each of the states concerned in establishing societies that are committed not just to democracy but to principles of social justice as well. Whatever the outcomes, the one thing these trends do not confirm is the view, implicit in most international relations writing and in much of the literature on women, that the domains of gender and 'the international' do not intersect.

Notes

This chapter is based on a panel presentation at the International Studies Association/ British International Studies Association joint convention, London, 28 March–1 April 1989. It is part of a larger study of the impact on gender divisions of the end of communist party rule published by UNRISD (Geneva) during 1990.

1 'Socialist' is used here as a shorthand for states ruled by Communist Parties. Rudolph Bahro's term 'existing socialist', coined in the 1970s, was perhaps more appropriate in that it recognized the very partial nature of the socialism that had evolved. It referred to those states which broadly adhered to Marxist doctrine and which had socialized a substantial proportion of the economy, while effecting policies of social redistribution. They had not, however, introduced measures to democratize political power, and were therefore not 'socialist' in the full sense. The term 'existing' is now anachronistic. (See Rudolph Bahro, *The Alternative in Eastern Europe* (London: New Left Books, 1978).)

2 See Barbara Wolf Jancar, *Women Under Communism* (Baltimore, MD: Johns Hopkins University Press, 1978); Gail Lapidus, *Women in Soviet Society* (Los Angeles, CA: University of California Press, 1978); Sonia Kruks *et al.*, *Promissory Notes* (New York: Monthly Review Press, 1989).

3 Gita Sen and Karen Grown, for instance, recognized the importance of including the socialist states in their analysis, and promised to do so in the next stage of their work. See Gita Sen and Karen Grown, *Development, Crises and Alternative Visions* (New York: Monthly Review Press, 1987).

4 More elaborated discussions of these points can be found in Maxine Molyneux, 'Women's emancipation under socialism: a model for the Third World?', *World Development* (Nos. 9/10, 1981) and Maxine Molyneux, 'Mobilisation without emancipation? women's interests, state and revolution in Nicaragua', *Feminist Studies* (Vol. 11, No. 2, Summer 1985).

5 I am using a broad definition of feminism here which encompasses campaigns for equal rights as well as struggles against gender-based forms of subordination and domination. In the socialist countries the term 'feminist' is often (but not always) avoided by those who would be so described by most definitions of the term.

6 The guidelines laid down by the 1920 resolutions included bringing women out of the home and into the economy; reorganizing peasant households that 'kept women in subservient positions'; developing communal services to alleviate domestic work and childcare; providing equal opportunities for women; mobilizing women into political work and into government administration; and providing protective legislation 'to safeguard women's reproductive activities'. See Jancar *op. cit.*

7 See William Butler, *Soviet Law* (London: Butterworth, 1983).

8 For instance, the Constitution of the People's Democratic Republic of Yemen was drawn up with the help of East European jurists. See R. Stookey, *South Yemen: A Marxist Republic in Arabia* (London: Croom Helm/Westview, 1982) and Maxine Molyneux, 'Legal reform and socialist revolution in democratic Yemen: women and the family', *International Journal of the Sociology of Law* (Vol. 13, 1985), pp. 147–72.

9 Cited in Chris Corrin, 'The situation of women in Hungarian society', unpublished paper, Leeds University, 1988.

10 For an account of the *Almanac* collective, see Alix Holt, 'The first Russian feminists', in Barbara Holland (ed.), *Soviet Sisterhood* (London: Fourth Estate, 1985). See also Mary Buckley, 'Soviet ideology and female roles', in Stephen

White and Alex Pravda (eds), *Ideology and Soviet Politics* (London: Macmillan, 1988), pp. 159–79.

11 For an interesting discussion of this phenomenon, see Gail Omvedt, *Women in Popular Movements: India and Thailand during the Decade of Women* (Geneva: UNRISD, 1986).

12 See, for example, V. Bodrova and R. Anker, *Working Women in Socialist Countries: The Fertility Connection* (Geneva: ILO 1985); *World Survey on the Role of Women in Development* (New York: United Nations, 1986); Ruth Legar Sivard, *Women: A World Survey* (Washington DC: World Priorities, 1985).

13 For a discussion of these issues in the Soviet context see Mary Buckley (ed.), *Soviet Social Scientists Talking: An Official Debate about Women* (London: Macmillan, 1986).

14 Rada Ivekovic and Slavenka Drakulic, 'Yugoslavia: neo-feminism – and its Six Mortal Sins', in Robin Morgan (ed.), *Sisterhood is Powerful* (Harmondsworth: Penguin Books, 1984); and author's conversation with Yugoslav writer and feminist activist Slavenka Drakulic, 1989.

15 In Nicaragua, for example, feminist interest groups were effective in influencing a number of government policy initiatives; in 1982, they protested at being excluded from the draft and gained acceptance into the army on a volunteer basis; and they were active in campaigns for legalized abortion. For details, see Maxine Molyneux, 'The politics of abortion in Nicaragua', *Feminist Review* (No. 29, Spring 1988) and 'Female collective action, socialist states and revolutions' (forthcoming). It is relevant to note that a Cuban delegation of four and a Nicaraguan delegation of 40 attended the fourth Latin American Feminist Conference (*Encuentro*) in Mexico in 1987 and participated in the debates over feminist issues.

16 For a fuller discussion, see Barbara Einhorn, 'Socialist emancipation: the women's movement in the GDR', in Jan Bradshaw (ed.), *The Women's Liberation Movement: Europe and North America* (London: Pergamon, 1982).

17 Barbara Einhorn, 'Sisters across the curtain: women speak out in East and West Europe', *END: Journal of European Nuclear Disarmament* (No. 8, February–March 1984), pp. 26–9.

18 The statement of the bloc of Russian Public Patriotic Movements welcomes 'modernization' as 'the way to free woman from involuntary emancipation and return her to the family, where she fills the role of mother, keeper of the hearth and bulwark of the nation'. *The Current Digest of the Soviet Press* (Vol. 42, No.1, February 1990).

19 Victor Erofeev points out 'This was not an abstract threat. In the early 1980s the caricaturist Wacheslav Sysoyev who had incurred official displeasure mainly for political reasons, spent two years in northern prison camps . . . because some erotic drawings had been found . . . [in] . . . his home'. *Liber* (Vol. 2, No. 1, February 1990) in *Times Literary Supplement* (23 February–1 March 1990).

20 See Mary Buckley, *Women and Ideology in the Soviet Union* (Brighton: Harvester, Wheatsheaf, 1989).

21 Larisa Vasilyeva wrote in *Pravda* (24 June 1989) 'When a woman ran against a man she usually lost. And although there were some women at the Congress, they didn't represent the "living female soul". They were mainly functionaries or excitable sorts who didn't get a chance to speak anyway': *Current Digest of the Soviet Press* (Vol. 42, No. 25, 1989).

6

Women in international relations? The debate in inter-war Britain

CAROL MILLER

The topic of women and international relations, which quite recently has become a field of scholarly inquiry, was an area of extended debate in Britain during the inter-war years. The debate turned on the question of how far women, having just been granted the vote,[1] should be integrated into the arena of foreign affairs via the Diplomatic Service and the League of Nations.[2] In theory, at least, the question was settled early. In 1919 the Covenant of the League of Nations was ratified, with Article 7 stipulating that 'all positions under and in connection with the League, including the Secretariat, shall be open to men and women'. And in 1921, under the authority of what was titled, rather inappropriately, the Sex Disqualification (Removal) Act of 1919, the Foreign Secretary reserved to men all posts in the Diplomatic and Consular Services. However, throughout the inter-war years the question of the role of women in international affairs was discussed and debated by the League Assembly, the House of Commons, the Foreign Office, various government commissions and the press, as well as by dozens of national and international women's organizations.

This chapter will emphasize the way in which certain political institutions – the League of Nations and the British Foreign Office – viewed the role of women in international politics. An institutional approach has its shortcomings, in that it places less emphasis on the way women perceived their role in international affairs than on the official view of that role. Nevertheless, there are two important reasons for taking such an approach. The first is that women's participation in international affairs was delimited by the official perception of what exactly the role of women should be. Second, there was a prolonged debate between members of these institutions and women's organizations during the inter-war years concerning the role in international affairs which will be traced in this chapter, and which reveals conflicting views on the question.

Research on women and international politics during the inter-war years reveals that there were certain assumptions about the role of women in international politics which both informed the nature of their contribution in this area, and which made it difficult for women to enter fully into this political sphere on a similar footing to men.[3] To understand these assumptions and to elucidate how they sometimes worked for, sometimes against, the efforts to broaden women's sphere of political activity to include official positions in the international arena, it must be recognized that the word women denotes not just a biological group but also a heavily loaded social category to which is attached a variety of sometimes contradictory character-istics, interests and values.[4] Thus, whenever the themes of women and international affairs or women and the League of Nations were raised for discussion, there was brought into play an elaborate set of assumptions about the category of women.

During the inter-war years the contribution of women was severely circumscribed because claims made for the greater participation of women at the level of international politics could not break free from the association of the category women with specific political space[5] or policy areas rooted in traditional ideas about women's nature and women's spheres of activity. This was true despite the fact that these claims were most often voiced on the basis of equal citizenship: that is, women had been deemed to be equal citizens when they won the right to vote and to hold public office, and there was no reason why their civic responsibilities should not extend to the international sphere.[6] In this chapter I will attempt to demonstrate that the arena of international politics during the inter-war years was a profoundly gendered environment and, as a consequence, the study of the role of women in international affairs brings one face to face with the intractable workings of gender.

Despite Article 7's provision that all League positions would be open equally to men and women, the status actually achieved by women at Geneva was a great disappointment to interested observers. Women were never appointed as members of the League Council. Very few women were selected by their governments as delegates to the Assembly. At the first meeting of the Assembly in 1920 there were two women as substitute delegates. By 1929 the representation of women in the Assembly had grown to one woman as full delegate, with 11 as substitute delegates. This was certainly an improvement but hardly significant given the fact that these 12 delegates came from a possible total of 250. By contrast, in the League Secretariat, the civil service of the League of Nations, women held the majority of posts. Nevertheless, if examined more closely it appears that women's experience was one of ghettoization. Only one woman ever held a position as head of section, Dame Rachel Crowdy, who was chief of the Social Section from 1919 to 1930.

Apart from a handful of women in the first division, the top administrative rank of the Secretariat, most women were part of the second division, which was responsible for the secretarial and routine administrative duties, or the third division, as telephone operators or office keepers.

The proportion of women to men in the first division never reached 10 per cent, and in most instances was well below this level. In 1921 there were four women members of the first division. The number peaked in 1930 at 13, after which it gradually declined, so that by 1939, the last year of the League's regular activities, there were only 8 women members. Only 9 nationalities were ever represented by women in the first division; at any one time, as many as half of the posts were held by British women.[7] Women's organizations consistently urged the Secretary General to improve the representation of women in the Secretariat, stating that they felt the 'narrow ideas as to the value and possibilities of women's work . . . are being perpetuated in the League to the detriment of women' and, further, they ventured that 'the administrative methods of the League might justly be expected to lead, rather than to keep pace with, those of the less progressive nations'.[8] Much was made by the women's organizations in the 1920s of the fact that Dame Rachel Crowdy was called Chief of Section, while other section heads held the title of 'Director', and that she received a lower salary than the directors, who were all male. Dame Rachel herself was of the opinion that she had the disadvantage of her sex against her; in 1926 she wrote, 'women in the Secretariat have an equal opportunity for work with men, though not necessarily an equal opportunity for the position which should go with the work'.[9]

The League appears to have taken some interest in the position of women in the Secretariat, although with little positive effect. For instance in 1930 the Committee of Thirteen, reviewing the organization of the Secretariat, noted the fact that despite Article 7 very few women were present in the higher grades of the Secretariat. This was explained by the nationality quotas which had to be met in the Secretariat, but also by the rarity of requisite qualifications in women candidates. The only positive action taken by the Committee was to recommend that 'the Secretary-General shall continue, when recruiting staff, to adhere strictly to this provision of the Covenant'.[10] Yet, according to Wertheimer, a senior member of the Secretariat for ten years, when the reins of the Secretariat passed from an English to a French Secretary General in 1933, 'the administrative role and importance of women officials deteriorated slowly but steadily' despite the recommendation of the Committee of Thirteen.[11]

Nevertheless, documenting the low representation of women at Geneva is perhaps less meaningful than exploring the role attributed to women in international affairs. Brian Harrison's research on the participation of women in the House of Commons between 1919 and 1945 led him to conclude that women MPs encountered the widely held idea that men and women should concern themselves with different areas of policy.[12] Women's political space was identified with issues specially concerning women and their families, such as family allowances, equal pay, education, housing and public health. In the field of foreign affairs women's contribution was confined largely to humanitarian issues such as refugees' and sailors' welfare or international peace. In connection with the League of Nations it would appear that women's participation was also delimited by a conception that women's special space was that of social and humanitarian issues. This conclusion is based on the way in which the League assessed women's role in international affairs and is reinforced by the view women themselves took of their work in the League and in international affairs in general.

In the early years of the League a pattern emerged which was to be followed throughout the inter-war period. Women were infrequently appointed by their governments, or by the League, to sit on committees except those of social and humanitarian questions. One woman, if that, as compared with 12 to 18 men was the recognized ratio on most permanent League committees, like those dealing with mandates, opium traffic, health or economic and financial questions. On committees concerned with the protection and welfare of children or the traffic in women and children, however, there was usually a more equal ratio. In fact, the League even invited delegates from the international women's organizations to sit as assessors on the Advisory Committee on the Traffic in Women and on the Child Welfare Committee. When at its yearly meetings the Assembly broke up into committees to discuss specific questions, women delegates were most frequently appointed to the Fifth Committee which considered social and general questions including the traffic in women and children, child welfare, opium traffic, intellectual cooperation and refugee questions.[13] In the highest divisions of the Secretariat women were not evenly distributed throughout the various sections but were clustered in the Social Section, the library, the precis-writing department and the interpreting and translating department.[14] Women were never represented in the first division posts of the Financial and Economic Section, Legal Section, Mandates Section or Minorities Questions Section. It is significant, too, that the only woman as head of section in the Secretariat was head of the Social Section.

That League representatives were of the opinion that there were separate places for men and women in the activities of the League is vividly illustrated in an anecdote recounted by Mrs Moss, a substitute delegate for Australia in 1927. Mrs Moss found herself in the position of full delegate on the occasion of the absence of one of her male colleagues. As she took her place among the 49 'amazed and horrified' men on the Fourth Committee, which dealt with finance, budgets and the codification of international law, the Chairman was said to have asked politely, 'Have you lost your way Madam?'[15]

Helena Swanwick, editor of *Foreign Affairs* and several times a member of the British delegation to the League, found the distinctions between men and women prevalent at the League Assembly particularly objectionable. A specialist on disarmament and political questions, she despaired at the fate which awaited her at the Fifth Assembly in 1924, saying:

> I knew that, as a woman, I was predestined for the Fifth Committee, a sort of rag-bag of miseries and forlorn hopes . . . A woman, it appeared, was assumed to be well-informed about Opium, Refugees, Protection of Children, Relief after Earthquakes, Prison Reform, Municipal Co-operation, Alcoholism, Traffic in Women. I did know something about this last, but of the other questions I was as ignorant as – the rest of the delegation.[16]

One of the subjects which came before the Fifth Committee in 1924 was a scheme drawn up by Senator Ciraolo, President of the Italian Red Cross, proposing that the members of the League should form a federation for the purpose of rendering aid to countries which had been victims of great disasters. When Ciraolo closed the debate he made a tearful appeal to the women 'to leave to men the task of stating practical objections and to let your mother-hearts be moved by suffering'.[17]

Swanwick thought the scheme unworkable and she was roused to speak. She deprecated the implications of the distinctions between men who were supposed to be 'business-like' and women with their 'mother-hearts', suggesting that such appeals were injurious to the work of the Fifth Committee which was popularly known at Geneva as *La Commission Sentimentale*. She feared that if they were presumed to be sentimentalists who passed a number of resolutions without any serious intention of implementing them, they would lose all credibility.[18]

In her defiance of the expectation that as a woman she would support any humanitarian scheme however impracticable, Mrs Swanwick was aware that she had 'upset the apple cart'.[19] Her behaviour was considered by many delegates as 'unwomanly' and another female delegate smote her with the words 'Je déteste ces hommes-femmes.'[20] Although the majority of the women delegates did not in fact support the Ciraolo scheme, the incident is just one example of how women were perceived to have a specific, that is, supportive, role to play in the social and humanitarian work of the League.

The issue of women and the League of Nations was placed officially on the Assembly agenda in 1931 by the Disarmament Committee discussions in relation to the Disarmament Conference.[21] The Committee submitted to the Assembly a draft resolution introduced by the Spanish delegation requesting the Council to consider 'means of associating feminine action and feminine feeling with the work of the League of Nations by an effective and direct collaboration'.[22] Intended only to encourage greater unofficial support from women and women's organizations, the Spanish resolution engaged the League in a debate concerning the official collaboration of women in the work of the League which some years later resulted in a League-sponsored inquiry into the legal status of women.[23] However, the Spanish resolution represents another example of the way in which gender stereotypes informed ideas about the role of women in international affairs. The committee argued that 'in view of the importance of the educative and moral role played by women, and of their influence in the formation of public opinion' the League could benefit from furthering their cooperation with women.[24] It was stated, too, that 'it was impossible in questions of peace and disarmament not to appeal to the women and mothers' and that 'means should be found at the Disarmament Conference to give women a part worthy of their high pacifist mission'.[25] It is worth noting that no one appears to have taken up the Finnish delegate's protestation that the Spanish resolution 'gave the impression that it was solely the fault of men if there was not an international spirit free from all prejudice'.[26] However, despite the emphasis on the important contribution of women to creating the 'moral atmosphere' necessary for the League's principal aim of establishing international peace, women were rarely given an opportunity to participate in the decision making processes of the League Council of the Disarmament Committee. In fact, it was considered by women's organizations to be a major achievement when in 1929 a women delegate to the Assembly was appointed to sit on the Disarmament Committee.

League representatives appear to have been of the opinion that the influence women could wield in the international arena as individuals on League committees was negligible compared with what they could do for social and humanitarian problems or world peace as members of women's organizations, or indeed, simply by being women. That the League saw women's organizations as having an important role to play influencing public opinion in favour of the League and League policies was demonstrated by the attention paid to these organizations by the Secretariat.[27] Secretariat members regularly represented the League at the annual meetings of these associations. The Secretariat was sensitive to the opinions of the more influential of these organizations, often soliciting their views on various topics of relevance to the League's work. For example, Dame Rachel Crowdy advised the Secretary General in 1923 that the League would do well to reconsider its position on the Commission of Enquiry for the Protection of Women and Children in the Near East as 'there is already a strong feeling among certain International and National Women's Organizations that the Secretariat is not making sufficient effort to continue this work'.[28]

Women, in part, tended to reinforce the rather narrow interpretation of their role in the international arena. The lobby efforts of women's groups appear to have been specifically focused; the League files contain regular correspondence from these organizations on issues such as refugees, traffic in women and children, health questions, education issues, the welfare of children, nationality of women and other questions concerning the status of women.[29] This is not to say that women absolutely accepted their limited role in the League or the League's view of the proper areas of women's international work – quite the contrary, as Mrs Swanwick's comments suggest. There was also a persistent protest by a number of prominent women and women's organizations against the dumping of skilled and intelligent women on the Fifth Committee, and the labelling of some of the social and humanitarian activities as women's questions.

Both the London-based Council for the Representation of Women in the League of Nations and the Geneva-based Joint Standing Committee of Women's International Organizations lobbied national governments as well as the League to improve the position of women in the League. For example, they compiled lists of women who were, in their view, qualified to serve on all League committees, not just those dealing with social and humanitarian issues, and distributed these lists to appropriate government departments and to the League of Nations. They protested against the fact that no more than a handful of women were ever included on official government delegations to the League or sat on League committees. Further, they drew attention to the fact that women's experience both on Assembly committees and in the Secretariat was one of ghettoization. One observer drew the conclusion that the status of women at the League was 'another indication of the survival in men's minds of the idea that women are not in the full sense political beings' and that women were thought specially suited to only one class of international questions, 'those that concern children and the home'.[30] Even at the level of international politics it would appear that there was a division between things political and things social, and women were seen to have a special contribution to make to the social.

Still, despite efforts to promote the representation of women at the League on the basis of equal citizenship there seems to have been as much effort expended to reinforce the view that women were different from men, and that there was a distinct contribution for women to make in the arena of international politics. One argument often put forward as a reason for the need for the greater participation of women was to allow women 'to contribute their own special point of view, their own share of constructive thought to the solution of the World's Problems as they are presented at Geneva'.[31] For instance, in 1921 the Council for the Representation of Women in the League of Nations protested against the government's failure to send a woman delegate to a conference on the traffic in women and children, stating that this area was 'a tragedy which is supremely woman's' and that more could have been achieved at the conference if more women had been included.[32] And in 1928 Gabrielle Radziwill, representing the League at the Congress of the International Woman Suffrage Alliance, reported that it was felt that the League should make greater use of 'the special knowledge of women'.[33]

This tension between demands for equality as citizens and special representation as women underlies much of the debate concerning the role of women in international affairs. Helena Swanwick often remarked that there was no such thing as a woman's point of view or a specific woman's role in international politics; nevertheless, on at least one occasion she asserted that women were the 'most formidable contingent' in the formation of public opinion for the cause of peace.[34] And in 1927 Dame Rachel Crowdy replied to a request from an organizer of an Armistice Day bazaar for a message from women at the League that 'we do not work as women in the Secretariat but as individuals – therefore it would be difficult to send any special message from the women here'.[35] Nevertheless, Dame Rachel was of the opinion that the League's work could benefit from the greater participation of women and women's organizations. Dame Rachel gave numerous lectures on the topic of women's work at the League and she saw herself as a liaison between the League and women's organizations, often even taking up their causes.[36] She frequently pressed for the representation of women on League committees as, for instance, in 1928 when she sought representation of women on the Mandates Committee.[37]

Even among organizations that were orientated towards equal citizenship there was little challenge to the assumption that women had a special role to play in creating the proper 'moral atmosphere' for the peace work of the League or in work of a social and humanitarian nature; instead, there seems to have been a belief that if equal citizenship were realized at the international level, women's special contribution could be more effective. According to an article written in 1929 for *Woman's Leader*, the journal of the National Union of Societies for Equal Citizenship, women delegates at the League had a double responsibility:

> it certainly is as humans and as citizens, and not just as women, that women wish to be present at the League . . . but as the world is still suffering from being 'man-made', there are problems which both particularly affect women and also towards the right solution of which women's special experience – accentuated by the 'man-madeness' of the world – can largely contribute.[38]

In the same vein, Helena Swanwick often puzzled over 'how women were to make effective use of their experience and of the specifically womanly bent of their temperament, to complete the government of the world, still so overwhelmingly manly'.[39] Thus, although claims for the greater participation of women in the work of the League were often expressed in terms of women's rights to equal participation on the basis of equal citizenship, as much emphasis seems to have been placed on the idea that women had special experiences and special capacities which made them particularly capable for work in certain areas – social and humanitarian issues and peace work.[40] The fact that the League seemed to share the view that women had a special contribution to make both strengthened the role of women in these areas, and at the same time confined them to these areas despite efforts to have the participation of women extended to broader concerns.

In contrast to the generally positive, albeit limited, view of women's role in the international arena which informed the League's position, the British Foreign Office quite firmly maintained that there was no place for women in the Foreign Service.[41] Yet the refusal of the Foreign Office to open the

Diplomatic and Consular Services to women may have had as much to do with the assumptions they shared with the League on the role of women in this sphere of politics as with the official view, which read that women had no contribution to make in this field at all.

The arguments against the admission of women ranged from well reasoned practical considerations to unabashed anti-feminism. Against the claim that women's inexperience was one of the greatest liabilities the Foreign Office had to consider, those in favour of the admission of women were quick to argue that women now possessed the same educational opportunities as men for acquiring the knowledge requisite for posts in international politics – specialization in modern history, languages, economics and international relations. All they needed now was a chance to prove themselves.[42] As in other fields, it was the necessities of war which gave women this chance when the shortage of qualified male candidates during the Second World War opened up opportunities for women in overseas posts.[43]

The fact that it was not until 1946 that women were finally admitted to the Diplomatic Service may be tied to the entrenched assumptions about women held by members of the Foreign Office. The question of the admission of women to the Diplomatic Service was first discussed by the Royal Commission on the Civil Service, 1929-31. The Commission made no definite decision except that the question should be re-examined at a later date.[44] In 1934 an Interdepartmental committee on the Admission of Women to the Diplomatic and Consular Services was appointed by the Foreign Secretary to review the question. The committee was composed of representatives of the Foreign Office, the Treasury and the Civil Service Commission, including two women civil servants of senior rank. The committee reported in 1936, and though opinion was so strongly divided that no majority decision could be reached the government preferred to support the position of the Foreign Office against the admission of women. One of the committee members wrote of 'the obscurantism of the Foreign Office in all matters – the institution is still under the impression that Metternich is still alive – naturally makes its members impervious to ideas . . . '.[45]

In 1930 the Under-Secretary for Foreign Affairs stated quite bluntly that it was not in the public interest to appoint women to diplomatic posts as they were simply not capable of the work. In his view women would find it difficult to discuss questions connected with politics, commercial and economic matters, 'a great deal of that being done over tete-a-tete meals and in clubs and on occasions of that sort'.[46] At one inquiry it was stated that

> the contribution which women are particularly fitted to make to the general work of a diplomatic mission abroad, in connection, for instance, with social and philanthropic duties and the observance of women's movements, is now adequately performed by wives and daughters of members of the Service without any cost to the State.[47]

Another concern often voiced at the inquiry was the question of the role of husbands of women diplomats, as it was argued that they would have difficulties finding suitable employment, and it was apparently not imagined that they could provide the same functions performed by wives of diplomats. Further, a unique problem would have existed in cases where nationality laws demanded that a British woman, upon marriage to a foreigner, take the nationality of her husband. Another factor which was considered a serious obstacle to the employment of women in the Diplomatic Service was the belief that women were unable to bear the strain of working in hot and unhealthy climates.

· Certainly there were some difficulties which had to be considered if women were to be admitted to the Foreign Service. The status of women in most countries throughout the world had not advanced to that held by British women, and there were obvious problems involved with sending women diplomats to work in countries where women had absolutely no political rights and where the existence of sex prejudice was so strong that it would, in turn, prejudice the possibility of women effectively carrying out their diplomatic work. And, as it would be impractical to place women only in the countries more advanced where women's rights were concerned and which, incidentally, were also some of the most important seats of diplomacy during this period, the argument was that it was best not to have women at all.

However, the failure of women to gain admission to the Diplomatic Service during the inter-war years must be considered in the political context. For instance, the fact that the 1934–36 Interdepartmental Inquiry coincided with the Abyssinian crisis, Germany's reoccupation of the Rhineland and the realization that collective security through the League was a bankrupt concept, may help to explain the intransigence of the Foreign Office. Also, the government White Paper of 1935, *Statement Relating to Defence*, if interpreted as the beginning of a policy of rearmament, may have influenced the Foreign Office against the admission of women who were seen to be closely connected with disarmament and the peace movement, as will be discussed below.[48]

The final official word on the subject during the inter-war years was the government's decision in 1936 that 'the time had not yet arrived when women could be employed either in the Consular Service or in the Diplomatic Service with advantage to the State or with profit to women'.[49] The government did not consider that any injustice was being done to women by their continued exclusion from the Diplomatic Service because it 'is, to say the least, doubtful whether women are suited to this work owing to the conditions prevailing; it is equally doubtful whether the admission of women would contribute any special advantage to the State'.[50] That the government deemed women not only to be unsuited to diplomatic work, but also insisted that their admission would not contribute any 'special advantage' demonstrates the kind of dilemma which faced advocates of women's admission.[51] The implication of the government's position was that women were not considered to be equal citizens, nor was it seen that their difference could be of advantage to the state in international politics, as was the case with the League.

Certainly advocates of women's admission made demands on the grounds of equal citizenship, drawing support from the work done by women in connection with the League, as well as the precedent set by the 20 countries which had in some way opened the doors of their foreign services to women. In a refrain echoed throughout the period, it was argued that there had never been a time when Britain had more need of the best brains available, and that the admission of the most gifted and intelligent women could only benefit the state.[52] Still, much of the debate hinged on the question of whether or not women had a special role to play in the arena of international affairs. When giving evidence before the 1931 Civil Service Inquiry, the Equal Rights Commission said that 'it was not in the general interest that these avenues should be closed to women . . . as their employment could not but lead to better international understanding'.[53] Winfred Holtby, journalist and writer, wrote in 1934 that the diplomatic services were infused with outmoded, even dangerous, phraseology and standards: 'prestige, power, precedence, sovereignty, strategic advantage and subtle methods of facesaving'. The benefit of the admission of women, according to Holtby, was that 'women are not handicapped by a great burden of outworn ritual; they care, desperately, earnestly, with an urgency which increases monthly for peace throughout the world'.[54]

The decision to refuse the admission of women to the Foreign Service may have been influenced by the perception that women's contribution to international affairs related more to the supposedly vague and sentimental issue of international peace than the calculations of strategic planning and international diplomacy. Even if the Foreign Office supported the general aims of the League,[55] it is more than likely that it was not so impressed by women's record in peace work.

The idea that women cared 'desperately' and 'earnestly' for peace, echoed in the League Assembly and repeatedly by the press and by women's organizations during the inter-war years, reinforced the view that women had a special role to play in international affairs in the area of peace work. This was reconfirmed in women's debating contribution on foreign affairs in the House of Commons where they avoided debate on issues like foreign policy and defence and spoke more frequently on humanitarian concerns or peace questions. Members of the Foreign Office must have been aware of the views of women MPs, as for instance, Nancy Astor, who said that peace was 'particularly a woman's question' and Edith Summerskill who saw the War Office as a 'traditionally masculine' area.[56] In debates on foreign policy and defence women rarely spoke except when it was to make a humanitarian appeal against war, as in the debates over international arbitration in 1930.[57] Further, the visibility of women like Vera Brittain in the pacifist Peace Pledge Union and the activities of women in connection with the Peace Ballot would have reinforced an association between women and peace.[58]

It is difficult to know whether or not there were a disproportionate number of women supporters of the League of Nations, disarmament or of the policy of appeasement. Whatever the case, there was certainly a perception that women had an important contribution to make to world peace. However, to men still operating with a more traditional approach to diplomacy, words like 'desperately' and 'earnestly' could be interpreted as naively and sentimentally. Newspaper articles from the period reflect a fear that 'the cranks, sentimentalists and pacifists' might be reinforced by women's entrance into the Foreign Service.[59] The view that women were too emotional, too sympathetic, relying more on intuition than rational thought in decision making, was a common argument against the admission of women found in the press at the time and even though such ideas do not appear in the official reports they must have been shared by at least some of the members of the Foreign Office.

Harold Nicolson, diplomat and author of several books on diplomacy, insisted that the three specifically feminine qualities of 'zeal, sympathy and intuition . . . unless kept under the firmest control, are dangerous qualities in international affairs'.[60] According to Nicolson, 'the ideal diplomatist should be impartial, imperturbable and a trifle inhuman', qualities which he designates as 'male qualities'.[61] Certainly, the Foreign Office would not have appreciated the view put forward by enthusiasts that 'if women handled international negotiations there would be no more war'.[62] On one occasion the Foreign Office received a memorandum from the League of Nations concerning the collaboration of women in the organization of peace and it was noted by a member of the Foreign Office that the recommendations were for the attention of the disarmament conference 'which will doubtless find them very tiresome'.[63]

The role which the Foreign Office attributed to women at the League may have much to do with the view the Foreign Office took of the League itself. Popular opinion in Britain placed a large part of the blame for the outbreak of war in 1914 on the pre-war system of conducting international relations. The new or open diplomacy heralded by the creation of the League was intended to bring an end to the dangers attributed to old or secret diplomacy. The Foreign Office was placed in the awkward position of outwardly supporting the ideals of the League while at the same time essentially carrying on business as usual or at least, in the words of one Foreign Secretary, using 'a judicious mixture of the new League methods and "old diplomacy"'.[64] Indeed, it was felt by those against the admission of women to the Diplomatic Service that 'the good work performed by women in connection with the League of Nations' in no way demonstrates

any true criterion of their ability to carry out the duties of a diplomatic officer, seeing that the atmosphere and conditions of work at Geneva differ in a marked degree from those obtaining in ordinary diplomatic posts.[65]

Wary of the new diplomacy, the Foreign Office were probably equally as wary of the women who, in their enthusiasm over the League and in their involvement with the peace movement, publicly demonstrated their support for new diplomacy.

Nevertheless, the Foreign Office claimed to support the principle put forward by Article 7 of the Covenant. A Foreign Office memo in 1932 states that it had been for some time the policy of the Foreign Office to encourage the collaboration of women in the work of the League by appointing women to League delegations. Further, it noted that 'H[is] M[ajesty's] G[overnment] are in sympathy with the policy of the League of Nations of appointing a number of women to responsible positions in the Secretariat of the League'.[66] As the selection of Assembly delegates and committee members was carried out, in part, through the Foreign Office, it holds some responsibility for the patterns of appointment which emerged. For instance, commenting on a letter from the National Union of Societies for Equal Citizenship concerning the representation of women on the Child Welfare Committee, a Foreign Office official wrote that 'if there is anything on which women should be represented, I should have thought that it was any body concerned with child welfare'.[67]

However, the Foreign Office was sometimes less than sympathetic with women's international work in social and humanitarian areas, both in voluntary organizations and in connection with the League. For example, in response to a request for British support of the League's proposed inquiry on the status of women, the Foreign Secretary wrote to the President of the Council for the Representation of Women in the League of Nations that, in his view, 'it was the province of each country to decide for itself what status it gave its women and no resolution in favour of such an inquiry would be sponsored by the British government'.[68] The League itself often came under fire when aspects of its social and humanitarian work infringed upon areas which the Foreign Office deemed to be of national rather than international domain.[69] As Foreign Secretary, Austen Chamberlain ruffled feathers which the social section spent many anxious months attempting to unruffle when his report to the League Council in 1926 stated that child welfare 'is not primarily a matter for international action'.[70] As women were often associated with work of this nature, it is possible that the Foreign Office may have considered them responsible for encouraging the League to expand its activities into areas of domestic concern. In 1930 a member of the Home Office advised Mr Cadogan of the Foreign Office of

> a noticeable tendency on the part of women's organisations in various countries to regard the [Child Welfare] Committee – naturally enough – as a useful vehicle for bringing up questions of special interest to women but not directly connected with Child Welfare . . . [u]nless this tendency is checked the Committee will be led far beyond the confines of its proper work.[71]

One final reason for the failure of women to gain admission to the Diplomatic Service might have been the view of the Diplomatic Service as a masculine sanctum. It was bound by traditions and rituals which reinforced its male-dominated, club-like atmosphere, hence the concern that women would not fit in. Even the executive of the League of Nations Union, for whom the work of women in connection with the aims of the League was important, saw the Diplomatic Service as off limits to women.[72] In the arguments against the admission of women to the Diplomatic Service there are references to the fact that the presence of women would upset the decorum of official ceremonies, especially in countries where affairs of state excluded the presence of women. As late as 1962, for instance, the Foreign Office apparently was still attempting to solve questions of etiquette on the point of whether or not a woman ambassador, appointed to the Court of St James from Costa Rica, should be requested to leave the dinner table when the port was served.[73] These entrenched male rituals probably made it even more difficult for the Foreign Office to conceive of the admission of women to its ranks as diplomats.

Thus the arguments concerning women's lack of experience, even if placed against the turbulent international scene, do not completely explain the continued exclusion of women from the diplomatic service during the inter-war years. Gender must be introduced into the equation. A thread which runs through the debate is the pitting of masculine versus feminine, political versus social, rational versus emotional, war versus peace – all aligned in terms of a male/female dichotomy. The assumptions about the category 'women' which kept women out of the diplomatic service were probably summed up most succinctly by Harold Nicolson, when he said that 'the special virtues of women' – intuition and sympathy – are 'singularly ill-adapted to diplomatic life'.[74]

In conclusion, the role of British women in international politics during the inter-war years must be understood in the context of gender roles and relationships which pervaded the whole of society. In the League the official participation of women was theoretically provided for, while their unofficial cooperation both as members of voluntary organizations and as individual citizens was regularly solicited and highly praised. Even so, women's contribution was circumscribed by pre-existing assumptions about the interests and capacities of women. In contrast, in the Foreign Office, these same assumptions about women may have worked completely against the admission of women to the ranks of the Diplomatic Service. It is difficult to ascertain whether arguments made by women for a greater official role in international politics based on the idea that they had a special contribution to make were purely reactive or a conscious strategy when the equality argument failed. Whatever the case, the persistence of the idea that women had a special role in international affairs opened some doors but, with few exceptions, kept the more important ones firmly shut.

Notes

1 The Representation of the People Act of 1918 gave the vote to women householders and wives of householders over 30, and The Parliament (Qualification of Powers) Act, again of 1918, granted women the right to sit in Parliament. In 1928 the Representation of the People Act gave women suffrage on equal terms with men.

2 Although the question of the admission of women to the Diplomatic Service was always considered in relation to their admission to the Consular Service, as well, for reasons of expediency the discussion in this chapter is confined to the Diplomatic Service as this was the area which received the most debate and the most publicity.

3 Apart from Brian Harrison's recent book *Prudent Revolutionaries: Portraits of British Feminists between the Wars* (Oxford: Clarendon Press, 1988), which focuses on domestic politics, though making mention of the fact that women directed much of their energy to work of an international character, the topic of women's international activities has been neglected by historians of the inter-war period.

4 See Denise Riley (1988), *'Am I that Name?' Feminism and the Category of 'Women' in History* (London: Macmillan, 1988) for discussion of 'women' as an unstable historical category.

5 I have borrowed this concept of political space – to denote a particular area within the political sphere – from Brian Harrison's discussion on the segregation of women in the House of Commons. In Brian Harrison, 'Women in a men's house, the women MPs, 1919–1945', *Historical Journal* (Vol. 29, No. 3, 1986).

6 I have avoided the term equal rights in order to stay clear of the equal rights versus protective legislation debate which divided the women's movement during the inter-war period.

7 Egon F. Ranshofen-Wertheimer, *The International Secretariat: A Great Experiment in International Administration* (Washington: Carnegie Endowment for International Peace, 1945), p. 369. The data listed above are also taken from a survey of the Secretariat Staff List Index held at the League of Nations Archives, Geneva, and the Staff Lists of the Secretariat found in *Official Journal of the League of Nations*: June 1921; September 1922; October 1923; January 1925; January 1926; January 1927; January 1928; November 1928; October 1929; October 1930; October 1931; October 1932; October 1933 (Part II); October 1934 (Part II); October 1935; October 1936; October 1937; October 1938; November–December 1939 (Part I).

8 Mrs Ogilvie Gordon, President of the Council for the Representation of Women in the League of Nations, to Sir Eric Drummond, Secretary General, 17 November 1926, in L[eague] of N[ations] A[rchives], R1458, 'Equality for Women in the Secretariat', 29/18166/x.

9 Dame Rachel Crowdy to Mrs C. Hoster, marked confidential, 26 April 1926. LNA, S157, 'Outgoing Letters April 1926'.

10 L[eague] of N[ations] doc[ument]. A.16.1930, 28 June, 1930 'Report of the Committee'. Also, LoN doc. Com.13/P.V.1-Com.13/P.V.7, 1931.

11 Ranshofen-Wertheimer, *op. cit.*, p. 369. The status of French women during the inter-war years had not reached that enjoyed by British women and parliamentary suffrage for women in France was not won until 1944. It may have been that the status of women in the Secretariat decreased under French influence, although this question requires further exploration.

12 Harrison, 'Women in a Men's House', *op. cit.*, pp. 636–41. Harrison's conclusions are based on calculations concerning women's participation in parliamentary

debate. In the period between 1919 and 1945 the three main areas on women's debating contribution were: 49 per cent in the area of welfare issues (such as education, public health, housing, unemployment and labour relations); 14 per cent on foreign and defence policy; 13 per cent on questions specially affecting women (including equal pay, family allowance, family law reform, equal franchise and women's service).

13 D.M. Northcroft, *Women at Work in the League of Nations*, 4th edition (London: Wadsworth and Co., 1926). This pattern appears to have persisted throughout the inter-war years. Also, file on 'The Representation of Women – League Committees and Conferences', LNA, R5677.

14 See note 7.

15 *Westminster Gazette*, 11 October 1927.

16 Helena Maria Swanwick, *I Have Been Young* (London: Gollancz, 1935), p. 384.

17 *Ibid.*, p. 396.

18 *Ibid.*, pp. 397–8.

19 *Ibid.*, p. 398.

20 *Ibid.*.

21 The discussions initiated by the Disarmament Committee resulted in several further League documents: LoN doc. A.73.1931.IX. 'Co-operation of Women and of the Press in the Organisation of Peace', Report by the Third Committee to the Assembly, Geneva, 22 September 1931; LoN doc. Conf.D.75. 'Collaboration of Women in the Organization of Peace', Geneva, 12 February 1932; LoN doc. A.10.1932. 'Collaboration of Women in the Organization of Peace', Report by the Secretary General, Geneva, 25 August 1932; and LoN doc. A.49.1932.IV. 'Collaboration of Women in the Work of the League', Report submitted by the Sixth Committee to the Assembly, Geneva, 10 October 1932.

22 LoN doc. A.73.1931.IX.

23 The possibility of such an inquiry was discussed on several occasions during the 1930s although a committee was not formed until September 1937. The work of the committee was interrupted by the outbreak of war in 1939; nevertheless, it appears to have formed the basis for the creation of the Status of Women Section of the Economic and Social Council of the United Nations.

24 LoN doc. A/III/13.1931.IX. Third Committee discussions, Geneva, 21 September 1931.

25 *Ibid.*

26 *Ibid.*

27 I have found reference to at least 20 women's international organizations working in Geneva at this time, not to mention the dozens of national societies which sent deputations and which corresponded with the League. Of the international organizations, the best known include the Women's International League for Peace and Freedom, the World's Young Women's Christian Association, The International Council of Women, The International Woman Suffrage Alliance (later renamed The International Alliance of Women for Suffrage and Equal Citizenship), the International Cooperative Women's Guild and the International Federation of University Women.

28 Dame Rachel Crowdy to the Secretary General, 15 August 1923, LNA, R636, 12/11634x/4631. In a memo to the Secretary General from Princess Radziwill of the Information Section, she suggests that the exclusion of women on the Committee of Experts for education of children in the aims of the League would create a very bad impression amongst women's organizations. Memo 31 May 1926, Name Index File (Radziwill), LNA, 13/51801/48790. On another occasion, writing about the International Co-operative Women's Guild that '[c]ette

organisation est très importante et il vaut la peine de reserver nos biens avec elle':
Minute Page, 24 November 1930, LNA, R2184, 5A/2115/2115.

29 It is interesting to note that the Women's International League for Peace and
    Freedom often diverged from this pattern, concerning itself with economic
    questions and questions of international law; but it held less influence at the
    League than organizations like the International Council for Women which
    conformed to the trend.

30 *Westminster Gazette*, 25 August 1926.

31 Margery Corbett Ashby, *Council for the Representation of Women in the League
    of Nations Annual Report, 1929–1930.*

32 Letter to the editor in *The Times*, 4 October 1921.

33 Report of Gabrielle Radziwill of the Information Section on the Congress of the
    International Woman Suffrage Alliance in Paris 1928. LNA, R1013, 1926
    International Bureau, 13/48861x/27029.

34 *Daily Telegraph*, 26 August 1929.

35 Dame Rachel Crowdy to Mr W. Talter, 4 June 1927. LNA, S158, 'Outgoing
    Letters June 1927'.

36 Memo from Dame Rachel Crowdy to the Secretary General, 19 March 1926
    asking that all correspondence from women's organizations continue to be sent to
    her. LNA, R1013, 1926 International Bureau, 13/48861x/27029.

37 Dame Rachel Crowdy to Miss H. Forchhammer, 28 March 1929. LNA, S158
    'Outgoing Letters, March 1928'. Concerning the Child Welfare Committee, in
    1925 she told Miss Forchhammer that '[a]s for the principle of having a woman
    representative you may count on my support of this': Dame Rachel Crowdy to
    Miss H. Forchhammer, 24 February 1925. LNA, S157 'Outgoing Letters
    February 1925'.

38 *Woman's Leader*, 1 November 1929.

39 Swanwick, *op. cit.*, p. 414.

40 During the inter-war years the arguments put forward for improving the role of
    women at the level of international politics were only rarely infused with the idea
    that women had some innate qualities which made them especially well equipped
    for peace work or work of a humanitarian nature. Instead, there appears to have
    been an emphasis on the idea that the nature of women's work in 'bearing and
    rearing, teaching, nursing, amusing or otherwise serving' contributed towards the
    creation of a unique orientation to the world, and one which had specific political
    ramifications at the social and humanitarian level. Eleanor Rathbone, 'Changes in
    Public Life', in R. Strachey (ed.), *Our Freedom and its Results* (London: Hogarth
    Press, 1936), p. 75

41 At this time women were employed by the Foreign Office as typists and junior
    clerks but were barred from taking up posts outside the country.

42 In the interdepartmental inquiry on the admission of women to the Diplomatic
    and Consular Services carried out between 1934 and 1936, the possibility was
    raised of instituting an experimental period, a sort of trial run to the full admission
    of women. In a statement which reveals what women were up against, the official
    reply was:

    Admittedly, there can be no proof of this [that is, women's unsuitability] until
    the experiment is tried, but if the experiment were attempted and proved
    unsuccessful, His Majesty's Government consider that not only would it be
    difficult to close an avenue once opened to women, but considerable injustice
    might be caused to the individual women who had entered the service.

    P[arliamentary] P[apers], Accounts and Papers, 1935–36, xxvii, 'Documents relating to the Admission of Women to the Diplomatic and Consular Services, July 30, 1934–April 1936', Section 1, No. 4.

43 The doors of the Diplomatic Service were officially opened to women in March 1946 when a committee created by the Foreign Secretary reported that there was no longer any reason to exclude women since many women were already working in overseas posts and had proved themselves capable for such work. However, the marriage bar was retained for several decades. For information concerning the other fields which were open to women during the wars see Gail Braybon and Penny Summerfield, *Out of the Cage: Women's Experience in Two World Wars* (London: Pandora Press, 1987).

44 PP, Reports Commissioners, 1930–31x, Report of the Royal Commission on the Civil Service (Tomlin Commission).

45 Marginalia on memo by Sir John Rae, 14 November 1934. PRO T220/40. From my research it would appear that the government's decision against the admission of women was largely due to pressure from the Foreign Office. Others on the committee of inquiry who were not themselves representing the Foreign Office took the view that it was the Foreign Office which was responsible for the failure of the committee to come to a more favourable decision. See letter by Sir John Rae, 14 November 1934, PRO T220/40. In fact, when the question was reopened in 1945, this earlier committee was referred to in Treasury Minutes as a packed jury against the admission of women. Memo by Mr Winnifirth, 6 March 1945, PRO T220/40.

46 Comments of Sir Hubert Montgomery when speaking to the Royal Commission of the Civil Service, quoted in Hilda Martindale, *Women Servants of the State* (London: George Allen and Unwin, 1938), p. 190.

47 PP, Accounts and Papers, 1935–36, xxvii, *op. cit.*, Paragraph 23e.

48 See note 64.

49 *Ibid.*, Section 1, No. 2.

50 *Ibid.*, Section 1, No. 7.

51 The support for the admission of women to these services came from many MPs, most notably Nancy Astor, and from the dozens of women's organizations who queued to give evidence before the various committees of inquiry.

52 Letter to the editor from the principals of the Oxford and Cambridge women's colleges. *The Times*, 26 May 1936.

53 PP Reports Commissioners, 1930–31x, *op. cit.*, Appendix XVII to Minutes of Evidence, Part III.

54 *News Chronicle*, 22 January 1934.

55 This seems to have depended upon the particular Foreign Secretary in charge. MacDonald and Henderson were very supportive of its work, Henderson working unceasingly between 1929 and 1931 for disarmament, while Chamberlain was more cool towards the League.

56 Quoted in Harrison, 'Women in a men's house', *op. cit.*, p. 636.

57 *Ibid.*, p. 640.

58 The Peace Ballot was a private referendum organized in 1934–35 by the League of Nations Union.

59 *Daily Mail*, 6 April 1934.

60 *The Spectator*, 23 January 1942.

61 *Ibid.* Nicolson took the hardened view that women were inclined towards peace. In 1938 he expressed concern that he might have put the 'women's vote' against him by criticizing the Munich agreement: 'I expect that the historians of our decline and fall will say we were done the moment we gave the women the vote. The men see that I was right and the women feel sentimental about Chamberlain.'

Harold Nicolson, *Diaries and Letters*, 1930–1939, edited by Nigel Nicolson (London: Collins, 1966), entry for 8 October 1938, p. 376. See also entry for 13 October 1938, 376.

62 Article by Lady McKenna in *Weekly Dispatch*, 25 March 1938.

63 C. Howard Smith, 25 February 1932, Minutes Sheet, PRO FO371/16455 (W2143/1008/98).

64 Sir John Simon regarding disarmament efforts in the summer of 1932, quoted in C. Thorne, *The Limits of Foreign Policy: The West, the League and the Far Eastern Crisis of 1931–33* (London: Hamish Hamilton, 1972), p. 110. Literature on British diplomacy of the inter-war years suggests that there was a confused foreign policy during these years as a result of the hopes placed in the League but a wariness about its success. There was a divorce between the outward actions and the inner convictions of the government, especially by the 1932–36 period (the period of the central inquiry into the admission of women to the diplomatic service) when the government was gradually pursuing a policy of rearmament, but had to be wary of public opinion. Also, it is argued by Thorne and others that the Foreign Office had not given up old diplomacy and preferred negotiation between diplomats to the open diplomacy of the League. See K. Middlemas, *The Diplomacy of Illusion. The British Government and Germany, 1937–1939* (London: Weidenfeld and Nicolson, 1972), pp. 16–32, and P. Kennedy, *The Realities Behind Diplomacy: Background Influences on British External Policy, 1865–1980* (London: George Allen and Unwin, 1981), pp. 243–55.

65 PP, Accounts and Papers, 1935–36, xxviii, *op. cit.*, Addendum II to the Report, Part 2.

66 Draft version of a letter to Mrs Ogilvie Gordon, President of the Council for the Representation of Women on the League of Nations from the Foreign Secretary, Sir John Simon, 16 August 1932, Minutes Sheet, PRO FO 371/16455 (W8685/1008/98).

67 R.H. Campbell, 26 February 1925, Minutes Sheet, PRO FO371/11070 (W1547/300/98).

68 Council for the Representation of Women in the League of Nations *Annual Report*, 1932.

69 In reference to the social activities of the League, F.P. Walters writes that foreign ministers and diplomatists were apt to regard them with distrust: Sir Austen Chamberlain not infrequently suggested that they should guard against interfering in the national affairs of member states, in F. P. Walters, *History of the League of Nations* (London: Oxford University Press, 1960), p. 186.

70 'Report to Council', extract from *Official Journal of the League of Nations*, July 1926, found in PRO FO371/14945 (W5575/9/98).

71 Mr Wilson Harris to Mr Cadogan, 7 May 1930, PRO FO371/14945 (W5575/9/98).

72 A letter from the President of the Council for the Representation of Women in the League of Nations in 1932, to Princess Radziwill of the League Information Section, outlines the fact that the British League of Nations Union executive would only pass a memorandum on the fuller cooperation of women in the work of the League if women's claim to be diplomats and consuls was omitted. Ogilvie Gordon to Princess Radziwill, 9 July 1932, LNA, R3604.

73 *Observer*, 1 July 1962.

74 Quoted in Brian Harrison's 'Women in a men's house', *op. cit.*, p. 628.

7

Gender planning in the Third World: meeting practical and strategic needs

CAROLINE O. N. MOSER

The important role that women play in Third World development processes is now widely recognized. However, conceptual awareness of the issues of gender and development has not necessarily been translated into planning practice. Indeed, for many practitioners involved in different aspects of socio-economic development planning, the lack of adequate operational frameworks has been a particular problem. The purpose of this article is to contribute to the resolution of this problem. It describes the development of gender planning, a planning approach which, in taking account of the fact that women and men play different roles in Third World society and therefore often have different needs, provides both the conceptual and methodological tools for incorporating gender into planning.[1]

The article mentions briefly the background to such an approach before describing the underlying conceptual rationale of gender planning, which relates to the identification of women's triple role and the distinction between practical and strategic gender needs. It illustrates the capacity of different planning interventions to meet gender needs, with examples from such sectors as employment, housing and basic services. Finally, it provides a critique of a number of different policy approaches to women and development from the perspective of gender planning, and identifies the potential and limitations of each approach for meeting the needs of low income Third World women.

Background

The United Nations Decade for Women (1976–85) has played a crucial role in highlighting and publicizing the important but often previously invisible role of women in the economic and social development of their countries and communities, and the plight of low income women in Third World economies. In fact, during this decade there has been a considerable shift in approach on the part of both academic researchers and policy-makers. Researchers have moved away from a preoccupation with the role of women within the family toward an understanding of the complexities of women's employment. Research on both waged workers and those in the informal sector, in urban and rural areas, has assisted in identifying both the importance and the diversity of low income women's productive activities to Third World economies.[2] Policy-makers have begun to shift their focus from a universal concern with welfare-oriented, family-centred programmes which assumed motherhood as the most important role for women in the development process, to a diversity of approaches emphasizing the productive role of women. The so called Women in Development (WID) approach, adopted by the United States Agency for International Development (USAID), with its underlying rationale that women are an untapped resource that can provide an economic contribution to development, has had an important influence in popularizing income generating projects for women.[3]

More recently a further shift in approach, principally in academic writing, has recognized the limitations of focusing on women in isolation and has drawn attention to the need instead to look at gender and development. The focus on gender rather than women was originally developed by feminists concerned about the manner in which the problems of women were perceived in terms of their sex, i.e. their biological differences with men, rather than in terms of their gender, i.e. in terms of the social relationship between men and women, a relationship in which women have been systematically subordinated.[4] Gender-aware approaches are concerned with the manner in which such relationships are socially constructed; men and women play different roles in society, their gender differences being shaped by ideological, historical, religious, ethnic, economic and cultural determinants. These roles show similarities and differences between classes as well as societies, and since the way they are socially constructed is always temporarily and spatially specific, gender divisions cannot be read off on checklists.

As a result of these developments lip service is now payed to women and development at international, governmental and non-governmental levels. Despite the recognized limitations of focusing on women in isolation, ministries of women's affairs and WID units with predominantly female staff have proliferated throughout the world in countries as diverse as Japan, Zimbabwe and Belize.[5] This has not, however, necessarily meant that the issue of gender has been satisfactorily incorporated into the wide diversity of planning disciplines concerned with the lives of low income communities in Third World countries.

There are a number of reasons for this problem. First, most authorities responsible for development planning have only very reluctantly recognized gender as an important planning issue; decision making powers continue to remain not only male dominated but also gender blind in orientation. Second, the primary concern of much recent feminist writing has been to highlight the complexities of gender divisions in specific socio-economic contexts, rather than to show how such complexities can be simplified so that methodological tools may be developed enabling practitioners to translate gender awareness into practice. Last, for those involved in planning practice, it has proven remarkably difficult to graft gender on to existing planning disciplines. Personal experience of attempting to do so in a variety of development policy and planning training courses has led to the conviction that women will always be marginalized in planning theory and practice until theoretical feminist concerns are adequately incorporated into a gender planning framework, which is recognized in its own right as a specific planning approach.[6]

The rationale for gender planning

Can we plan for the needs of low income families generally or is it necessary to plan for the needs of women in their own right? Gender planning is based on the underlying conceptual rationale that because men and women play different roles in society, they often have different needs. Therefore, when identifying and implementing planning needs it is important to disaggregate households and families within communities on the basis of gender. To identify these different needs requires an examination of two planning stereotypes relating first to the structure of low income households and, second, to the division of labour within the household.

Despite an emphasis on planning for people, in current Western planning theory and practice concerned with low income communities there is an almost universal tendency to make two assumptions, regardless of the empirical reality of the particular planning context. First, that the household consists of a nuclear family of husband, wife and two or three children. Second, that within the household there is a clear sexual division of labour in which the man of the family, as the breadwinner, is primarily involved in productive work outside the home, while the woman as the housewife and homemaker takes overall responsibility for the reproductive and domestic work involved in the organization of the household. Implicit in this is also the assumption that within the household there is an equal control over resources and power of decision making between the man and the woman in matters affecting the household's livelihood. In most Third World societies this sexual division of labour is seen to reflect the natural order and is ideologically reinforced through such means as the legal and educational system, the media and family planning programmes, without recognition that within it the woman's position is subordinate to that of the man's.[7] However, this abstract stereotype model of society and the divisions of labour within it has severe limitations when applied to most Third World contexts, particularly in relation to the triple role of women and women-headed households.

The triple role of women[8]

In most low-income households, women's work includes not only the reproductive work (the childbearing and rearing responsibilities) required to guarantee the maintenance and reproduction of the labour force but also productive work, often as secondary income earners. In rural areas this usually takes the form of agricultural work, while in urban areas women frequently work in informal sector enterprises located either in the home (in subcontracting or piece rate work) or at the neighbourhood level.[9] In addition women are involved in community managing work undertaken at a local community settlement level in both urban and rural contexts. With the increasingly inadequate state provision of housing and basic services such as water and health, it is women who not only suffer most but who are also forced to take responsibility for the allocation of limited resources to ensure the survival of their households. Where there is open confrontation between community-level organizations and local authorities in attempts to put direct pressure on the state or non-governmental organizations for infrastructural provision, again it is women who, as an extension of their domestic role, frequently take primary responsibility for the formation, organization and success of local-level protest groups.[10] Women, within their gender-ascribed role of wives and mothers, struggle to manage their neighbourhoods. In performing this third role they implicitly accept the sexual division of labour and the nature of their gender subordination.

In most Third World societies the stereotype of the male breadwinner, i.e. the male as productive worker, predominates, even when it is not borne out in reality. Invariably when men perceive themselves to have a role within the household it is as the primary income earner. This occurs even in those contexts where male 'unemployment' is high and women's productive work actually provides the primary income. In addition, generally men do not have a clearly defined reproductive role, although this does not mean empirically that they do not play with their children or assist their women partners with domestic activities.

Men are also involved in community activities but in markedly different ways from women, reflecting a further sexual division of labour. The spatial division between the public world of men, and the private world of women (where the neighbourhood is an extension of the domestic arena) means that men and women undertake different community work. While women have a community managing role based on the provision of items of collective consumption, men have a community leadership role in which they organize at the formal political level generally within the framework of national politics.[11] In organizations in which these two activities overlap, especially in societies where men and women can work alongside each other, women most frequently make up the rank and file voluntary membership while men are only involved in positions of direct authority and work in a paid capacity.[12]

That women and men have different roles has important implications for policy-makers. Because the triple role of women is not recognized, the fact that women, unlike men, are severely constrained by the burden of simultaneously balancing these roles of reproductive, productive and community managing work is ignored. In addition, by virtue of its exchange value, only productive work is recognized as work. Reproductive and community managing work, because they are both seen as natural and non-productive, are not valued. This has serious consequences for women. It means that the majority, if not all, the work they do is made invisible and fails to be recognized as work either by men in the community or by those planners whose job it is to assess different needs within low income communities. In contrast, the majority of men's work is valued, either directly through paid remuneration or indirectly through status and political power. While the tendency is to see women's and men's needs as similar, the reality of their lives shows a very different situation.

Women-headed households

The second problem with this abstract stereotype model of Third World society is that it fails to recognize that low income households are not homogeneous in terms of family structure. Although nuclear families may be the dominant type a diversity of other structures also occurs. It is now widely recognized, for instance, that the extended family does not necessarily disappear with modernization or urbanization, where it remains vital for low income survival strategies in both rural and urban areas. However, the most important non-nuclear family household structure is the woman-headed household, of which there are two main types. First, there are *de jure* women-headed households, in which the male partner is permanently absent due to separation or death, and the woman is legally single, divorced or widowed; second, *de facto* women-headed households in which the male partner is temporarily absent, due for instance to long-term work migration or refugee status. Here the woman is not legally the head of household, and is often perceived as a dependant despite the fact that she may, for the majority of her adult life, have primary if not total responsibility for the financial as well as the organizational aspects of the household.

It is estimated that today one-third of the world's households are headed by women. In urban areas, especially in Latin America and parts of Africa, the figure reaches 50 per cent or more. In rural areas where men traditionally migrate it has always been high, while in refugee camps in areas of Africa and Central America it is nearer 80–90 per cent.[13] While there are considerable regional variations, globally the number of *de facto* women-headed households is increasing rather than declining. In many parts of the world this is not a new phenomenon, simply one that is now more openly acknowledged. The reasons for this recognition are twofold. First, attitudes within communities about the stigma of women living on their own have been changing. This is particularly evident in communities under conflict, where women forced to live on their own have themselves become more confident in confronting criticisms about their status.[14] Second, there has been a growing recognition by planners implementing projects, if not formulating policy, that they cannot ignore women heads of households if they are concerned with the successful completion of their work.

The economic conditions of women-headed households vary considerably, depending on such factors as the woman's marital status, the social context of female leadership, her access to productive resources and income and the composition of the household. Frequently, women-headed households have a high dependency ratio and limited access to employment and basic services. Consequently, all too often these households fall below the poverty line and are disproportionately represented among the poorest of the poor.[15] Although women who head households do not constitute a separate category, nevertheless their problem of the triple burden is exacerbated, which may have specific policy implications.

Identifying practical and strategic gender needs

When planners are blind to the triple role of women, and to the fact that women's needs are not always the same as men's, they fail to recognize the necessity of relating planning policy to women's specific requirements. In particular, development planning based on a sectoral approach does not provide the integrative strategies women require. Employment planning, for instance, is concerned primarily with individuals as paid workers and assumes a household support system, while women's participation in the labour force is constrained by their triple commitment. Social welfare planning which concentrates on the childrearing roles of women does not adequately take account of their income earning activities. For example, health facilities in low income areas are frequently undersubscribed because their opening hours are inappropriate for working mothers. The failure to make the necessary accommodation does not merely jeopardize the implementation of policy, with programmes frustrating rather than meeting basic needs, but may perversely worsen the position of women.

If planning is to succeed it has to be gender aware. It has to develop the capacity to differentiate not only on the basis of income, now commonly accepted, but also on the basis of gender. This requires modifications, particularly in local-level planning, to achieve a more integrative approach which takes account of women's particular requirements. It is important to emphasize that the rationale for gender planning does not ignore other important issues such as race, ethnicity and class, but focuses specifically on gender precisely because this tends to be subsumed within class in so much of policy and planning.[16] Having addressed the argument for gender planning it remains to clarify and expand upon the various elements of this approach.

Gender needs

Planning for low income women in the Third World must be based on their interests, in other words their prioritized concerns. By identifying the different interests women have it is possible then to translate them into planning needs, in other words the means by which their concerns may be satisfied. From this the requirements for gender policy and planning can be formulated and the tools and techniques for implementing them clarified. In the process of identification of interests it is useful to differentiate between 'women's interests', strategic gender interests and practical gender interests, following the threefold conceptualization made by Maxine Molyneux.[17] Translated into planning terms these then are identified as women's needs, strategic gender needs, and practical gender needs.[18]

At the outset, an important distinction must be made between women's interests and gender interests. The concept of women's interests assumes compatibility of interest based on biological similarities. In fact the position of women in society depends on a variety of different criteria, such as class and ethnicity as well as gender, and consequently the interests they have in common may be determined as much by their class position or their ethnic identity as by their biological similarity as women. Within the planning context women's needs also vary widely, determined not only by the specific socio-economic context but also by the particular class, ethnic and religious structures of individual societies. Consequently, although the category of women's needs is frequently referred to by planners in general policy terms, it is of limited utility when translated into specific planning interventions.

Women may have general interests in common but these should be called gender interests, to differentiate them from the false homogeneity imposed by the notion of women's interests. As Molyneux has argued:

> Gender interests are those that women (or men for that matter) may develop by virtue of their social positioning through gender attributes. Gender interests can be either strategic or practical each being derived in a different way and each involving differing implications for women's subjectivity.[19]

The distinction between strategic and practical gender interests is of critical importance, as is the distinction between strategic and practical gender needs. Frequently, different needs are confused, and clarification is essential if realistic parameters are to be identified as to what can be accomplished in the planning process, as well as the limitations of different policy interventions.

Strategic gender needs

Strategic gender needs are those needs which are formulated from the analysis of women's subordination to men, and deriving out of this the strategic gender interest identified for an alternative, more equal and satisfactory organization of society than that which exists at present, in terms of both the structure and nature of relationships between men and women.[20] The strategic gender needs identified to overcome women's subordination will vary depending on the particular cultural and socio-political context within which they are formulated. Strategic gender needs, as Molyneux has identified, may include all or some of the following:

> the abolition of the sexual division of labour; the alleviation of the burden of domestic labour and childcare; the removal of institutional- ised forms of discrimination such as rights to own land or property, or access to credit; the establishment of political equality; freedom of choice over childbearing; and the adoption of adequate measures against male violence and control over women.[21]

Strategic gender needs such as these are often identified as feminist, as is the level of consciousness required to struggle effectively for them. Historically it has been shown that the capacity to confront the nature of gender inequality and women's emancipation can only be fulfilled by the bottom up struggle of women's organizations. Despite a few optimistic examples, state intervention alone has not removed any of the persistent causes of gender inequality within society as a whole and thus has failed to fulfil the strategic gender needs which for feminists are women's real interests.[22]

Practical gender needs

In contrast, practical gender needs are those needs which are formulated from the concrete conditions women experience, in their engendered position within the sexual division of labour, and deriving out of this their practical gender interests for human survival. Unlike strategic gender needs they are formulated directly by women in these positions, rather than through external interventions. Practical needs therefore are usually a response to an immediate perceived necessity which is identified by women within a specific context. As Molyneux has written, 'they do not generally entail a strategic goal such as women's emancipation or gender equality . . . nor do they challenge the prevailing forms of subordination even though they arise directly out of them'.[23]

The sexual division of labour within the household gives women primary responsibility not only for domestic work involving childcare, family health and food provision but also for the community managing of housing and basic services, along with the capacity to earn an income through productive work. Therefore in planning terms, policies for meeting practical gender needs have to focus on the domestic arena, on income earning activities and also on community-level requirements of housing and basic services. In reality, basic needs such as food, shelter and water are required by all the family, particularly children, yet they are identified specifically as the practical gender needs of women not only by policy-makers concerned to achieve developmental objectives but also by women themselves. Both are therefore often responsible for preserving and reinforcing (even if unconsciously) the sexual division of labour. Since there is often a unity of purpose between the socio-economic development priorities of intervening agencies and practical gender needs identified at the local level, the two frequently and easily become conflated. This serves the purposes of planners who are then identified as meeting women's needs. At the same time, it can make it even more difficult for women themselves to recognize and formulate their strategic gender needs.

Meeting practical and strategic gender needs in policy and practice

It has become very popular for policy-makers and the media alike to label any policy or programme associated with women as 'feminist' or 'women's lib', terms used by many in such a derisory manner that they provoke a hostile and negative reaction from both female and male planners. Identification of the triple role of women and the differences between practical and strategic gender needs can assist practitioners to understand that planning for the needs of low income women is not necessarily feminist in content. Indeed the vast majority of policies, programmes and projects directed at women worldwide are concerned with women within their engendered position in the sexual division of labour, as wives and mothers, and are intended to meet their practical gender needs. Without denying the importance of such interventions, it is critical to recognize that practical gender needs only become feminist in content if and when they are transformed into strategic gender needs.

While the room for manoeuvre for addressing gender needs varies within each specific socio-political context, the distinction between practical and strategic gender needs and the identification of the triple role of women may provide useful methodological tools for planning. They may assist in diffusing the criticisms of those who find feminism unacceptable by showing them that working with women is most often not feminist. Alternatively, they may be helpful for policy-makers responsible for meeting the practical gender needs of women, in assisting their adoption of more challenging solutions. The following examples of a number of interventions, in such sectors as employment, housing and basic urban services, illustrate the potential and limitations of different planning practices to reach practical or strategic gender needs within specific planning contexts.

Gender needs in employment

With the lives of the majority of low income women dominated by the necessity to generate an income, one of the most fundamental problems faced is a lack of adequate skills. The provision of skill training, therefore, often meets an important practical gender need by allowing access to employment. How far it also reaches more strategic gender needs depends not only on whether it increases women's economic independence but also on the type of training. In many ex-British colonies, for instance, community development centres have, for decades, provided women's training courses in home economics, introducing a diversity of skills intended to assist women to become better provisioners within the household. Such training recognizes the reproductive role of women and can meet practical gender needs relating to basic health and nutrition; but it does not recognize women's productive role and the important practical gender need to earn an income.[24]

In contrast to this, skill training in such areas as primary school teaching, nursing and dressmaking often meets income generating needs. Probably the most common type of training is dressmaking, taught throughout the world, at a diversity of levels ranging from government programmes, located in purpose-built premises, through medium-sized non-governmental projects to small self-help groups. In diverse cultures and contexts the underlying rationale for the provision of dressmaking skills is similar: this is a skill women already know, or should know, and one they can use not only in the home but also to earn an income. Such training can meet a practical gender need, but because dressmaking is an area in which women traditionally work, this does not challenge the gender division of labour.[25]

The training of women in areas traditionally identified as men's work may not only widen employment opportunities for women, but may also break down existing occupational segregation, thereby fulfilling the strategic gender need to abolish the sexual division of labour. Women's training in house building skills such as masonry and carpentry provides one such example. Although in most societies women are traditionally involved in rural house building, the urban-based development of a formal skilled house construction sector has been accompanied by an occupational sex segregation, with construction now designated as men's work, other than in those contexts, such as India, where women still provide unskilled labour.[26] Skill training for women in the construction sector often meets with hostility and resistance precisely because it challenges the existing sexual division of labour. However, as case studies from Sri Lanka, Jamaica and Nicaragua show,[27] once trained and having gained the tacit acceptance of male colleagues, women construction workers tend to find work either in existing projects or in the construction sector more generally.[28]

Gender needs in human settlements and housing

In the planning of human settlements and housing the necessity to introduce a gender perspective is still not widely recognized, despite the fact that women, as wives and mothers, are primary users of space both in their houses and in the local community.[29] Although consultation with women about housing design would ensure that their spatial needs are recognized, this rarely occurs.

Examples of the detrimental effects of insensitive house design are wide-spread, particularly where modernization or developmentalism have resulted in radical design changes. This often affects Muslim women who, because their social life is almost entirely confined to the home, have special needs for internal space.[30] Zoning legislation that separates residential and business activities assumes the separation of productive and reproductive roles and is particularly problematic for women with children. Because of the necessity to balance roles, women are often involved in informal sector activities in or around their homes. Where zoning legislation prevents the making and selling of goods from their homes, the only solution is to do so illegally.[31] Gender-aware changes in zoning legislation to allow household enterprises can therefore meet the practical gender need of women to earn an income.

The fact that women are the principal users of housing does not necessarily mean that they become the owners of either house or land. Tenure is generally given to men as household heads, even where women *de facto* have primary household responsibilities. For women, tenure rights are a strategic gender need which ensures protection for themselves and their children in unstable or violent domestic situations. Without land rights women often cannot provide collateral to gain access to credit; since ownership of land represents a form of savings, women may end up without capital in the event of marital separation. Housing projects that provide for ownership regardless of the sex of the household head may be difficult to design in countries where women do not legally possess rights of ownership. However, in other contexts where women's lack of land tenure is a consequence of tradition there may be relatively simple means of making land ownership rights available to women.[32]

Gender needs in basic services

The planning of childcare facilities, such as a crèche or nursery, provides a good example of the way in which differences in location can result in different gender needs being met. If located at the woman's workplace it will certainly meet her practical gender need for adequate childcare facilities, essential for her to undertake waged employment. If located in the community this may encourage a sharing of responsibilities within the family, although if anyone other than the mother delivers the child it is likely to be another female member of the family. If, however, the nursery is located at the father's place of work, this provides the opportunity for meeting both practical and strategic gender needs since it involves the father in taking some of the responsibility for childcare, and thereby alleviates the burden of domestic labour on the woman.

In the transport sector one of the most critical problems faced by women is that transport services are organized to meet the needs of male workforce schedules, with buses running from the periphery to the centre during morning and evening peak periods.[33] Low income women often not only use public transport more than men but require it for multiple activities, such as school, shopping and health-related trips, in addition to work trips. While the provision of adequate off peak transport meets practical gender needs it cannot meet strategic gender needs since it does not alleviate women's burden of domestic labour and childcare. In addition, in many large cities the fear of male harassment prevents low income women from using public transport, particularly late at night. Where women only transport is introduced this meets the more strategic gender need of countering male violence.

The examples cited above show the limitations of individual sectoral interventions for low income women. Because of the need to balance their triple role, women require integrative strategies which cut across sectoral lines. The examples also reveal that the majority of planning interventions for women meet only practical gender needs, and do not seek to change existing divisions of labour or other forms of discrimination against women, and are therefore not feminist in content. In reality, practical gender needs remain the only specific policy target for most of those concerned with planning for women. The underlying reasons for this, and the extent to which shifts in policy have occurred during the past 30 years, can best be understood through the examination of different policy approaches to women.

Policy approaches to low income Third World women and gender planning

Throughout the Third World, particularly in the past decade, there has been a proliferation of policies, programmes and projects designed to assist low income women. Identification of the extent to which such planned interventions have been appropriate to the gender needs of women requires an examination of the conceptual rationale underlying different policy approaches from a gender planning perspective. Each approach can be evaluated in terms of which of women's triple roles it recognizes, and which practical or strategic gender needs it meets. Such analysis illustrates the utility of the methodological tools of gender planning evaluation.

Until recently there has been little systematic classification or categorization of the various policy initiatives to help low income women.[34] Concern for their needs coincided historically with a recognition of their important role in development. Since the 1950s a diversity of interventions has been formulated, not in isolation but reflecting changes in macro-level economic and social policy approaches to Third World development. Thus the shift in policy approach toward women, from 'welfare', to 'equity' to 'anti-poverty', as categorized by Buvinic,[35] to the two other approaches categorized here as 'efficiency' and 'empowerment', has mirrored general shifts in Third World development policies, from modernization policies of accelerated growth through basic needs strategies associated with redistribution to the more recent compensatory measures associated with structural adjustment policies.

While the different policy approaches are described chronologically it is recognized that the linear process implied is an oversimplification of reality. In practice many of the policies have appeared more or less simultaneously. Implementing agencies have not necessarily followed any ordered logic in changing their approach, most frequently jumping from welfare to efficiency without consideration of the other approaches. Different policies have particular appeal to different types of institutions. Policy-makers often favour combined policy approaches in order to meet the needs of different constituencies at the same time. Finally, shifts in policy approach often occur not only during the formulation stage, but also during the implementation process.[36] In order to examine the inter-relationship between different policy approaches and gender needs they are described here as ideal types.

The welfare approach

The welfare approach is the oldest and still the most popular social development policy for the Third World in general and women in particular. Its underlying rationale toward women reflects its origins, which are linked to the residual model of social welfare, first introduced by colonial authorities in many Third World countries. Their concern with law and order and the maintenance of stable conditions for trade, and agricultural and mineral expansion, meant that social welfare was a low priority. Echoing the nineteenth-century European Poor Laws with their inherent belief that social needs should be satisfied through individual effort in the marketplace, administrations dealt largely with crime, delinquency, prostitution and other forms of deviant behaviour, while voluntary charity organizations carried a large share of the burden of social welfare.[37] Since it was also compatible with the prevailing development paradigms of modernization, many post-independence governments continued this policy.[38] On the basis that 'social welfare institutions should come into play only when the normal structure of supply, the family and the market, break down',[39] the ministries of social welfare, created for the implementation of such residual measures for vulnerable groups, were invariably weak and underfinanced.

In fact it was First World welfare programmes, specifically targeted at vulnerable groups, which were among the first to identify women as the main beneficiaries. As Buvinic has noted, these were the emergency relief programmes widely initiated in Europe after the end of the Second World War, accompanying the economic assistance measures intended to ensure reconstruction. Relief aid was provided directly to low income women who, in their engendered roles as wives and mothers, were seen as those primarily concerned with their family's welfare. This relief distribution was undertaken by international private relief agencies and relied on the unpaid work of middle-class women volunteers for effective and cheap implementation.[40]

The creation of two parallel approaches to development assistance – on the one hand financial aid for economic growth, on the other hand relief aid for socially vulnerable groups – was then replicated in development policy toward Third World countries. This had critical implications for Third World women. It meant that the international economic aid which prioritized government support for capital-intensive industrial and agricultural production to accelerate growth focused on increasing the productive capacity of the male labour force. Welfare provision for the family was targeted at women who, along with the disabled and the sick, were identified as vulnerable groups, remaining the responsibility of the marginalized ministries of social welfare.[41] Further assistance was then provided by non-governmental organizations, such as the mothers' clubs created in many Third World countries and, to a lesser extent, by bilateral aid agencies with specific mandates for women and children, such as the United Nations Children's Fund (UNICEF).

The welfare approach is based on three assumptions. First, that women are passive recipients of development, rather than participants in the development process. Second, that motherhood is the most important role for women in society. Third, that childrearing is the most effective role for women in all aspects of economic development. While this approach sees itself as family centred in orientation, it focuses entirely on women in terms of their reproductive role, assumes men's role to be productive and identifies the mother–child dyad as the unit of concern. The main method of implementation is through top down hand-outs of free goods and services. When training is included it is for those skills deemed appropriate for non-working housewives and mothers. In their mothering roles, low income women have been the primary targets for improving family welfare, particularly of children, through an increasing diversity of programmes, reflecting a broadening of the mandate of welfare over the past decades. With their origins in relief work, the first, and still the most important concern of welfare programmes is family physical survival, through the direct provision of food aid to vulnerable groups. Generally this is provided on a short-term basis after such natural disasters as earthquakes or famines. However, it has increasingly become a longer-term need for refugees seeking protection, whose numbers have grown from 12 to 15 million in the past two decades. Although the majority of refugees in camps are women, left as heads of households to care and often provide for the children and elderly, they usually do not have refugee status in their own right but only as wives within the family.[42] Projects implemented by the United Nations High Commission for Refugees (UNHCR) and non-governmental organizations most often focus on these women in their reproductive role, with special attention given to those pregnant or lactating, identified as a vulnerable group in the same category as the elderly, orphans and handicapped.[43]

The second important type of welfare programme is the extensive international effort to combat Third World malnutrition not just through food but also through nutritional education targeting children under five years, and pregnant and nursing mothers. Since the 1960s, mother–child health programmes (MCH) have distributed cooked or rationed food along with nutrition education at feeding centres and health clinics.[44] In linking additional food for children and nutrition education for mothers, MCH focuses on the mother–child dyad and the reproductive role of women on the assumption that extra provisions will make them better mothers. Although by the early 1980s considerable criticism had been expressed about the use of food aid to guarantee nutritional improvement of children, the focus on women in their role as mothers was not seen as problematic.[45]

Most recently, especially since the 1970s, welfare policy toward women has been extended to include population control through family planning programmes. Thus development agencies responding to the world's population 'problem' identified women, in their reproductive role, as primarily responsible for limiting the size of families. Early programmes assumed that poverty could be reduced by simply limiting fertility, achieved through the widespread dissemination of contraceptive knowledge and technology to women. Only the obvious failure of this approach led population planners to recognize that variables relating to women's status, such as education and labour force participation, could affect fertility differentials and consequently needed to be taken into consideration.[46]

Although welfare programmes for women have widened their scope considerably over the past decades, the underlying assumption remains that motherhood is the most important role for women in Third World development, which means that the concern is to meet practical gender needs relating to women's reproductive role. Intrinsically, welfare programmes identify women rather than lack of resources as the problem, and place the solution to family welfare in their hands without questioning their natural role. Although the top down hand-out nature of so many welfare programmes tends to create dependency rather than to assist women to become more independent, they remain very popular precisely because they are politically safe, since they do not question the traditionally accepted role of women within the sexual division of labour. Such assumptions tend to result in the exclusion of women from development programmes operated by the mainstream development agencies that provide a significant proportion of development funds.[47] The fact is that the welfare approach is not concerned with meeting strategic gender needs, one of the most important of which, the right for women to have control over their own reproduction, was highlighted by a Third World women's group which wrote:

> Women know that childbearing is a social not purely personal phenomenon: nor do we deny that world population trends are likely to exert considerable pressure on resources and institutions by the end of the century. But our bodies have become a pawn in the struggles among states, religions, male heads of households, and private corporations. Programs that do not take the interests of women into account are unlikely to succeed.[48]

Although by the 1970s dissatisfaction with the welfare approach was widespread, criticism differed as to its limitations, coming from groups representing three very different positions. First, in the United States, a group of mainly female professionals and researchers were concerned with the increasing evidence that Third World development projects were negatively affecting women. Second, development economists and planners were concerned with the failure of modernization theory in the Third World. Third, the United Nations designated a Women's Decade, starting in 1976. This was a result of the 1975 International Women's Year Conference, which formally put women on the agenda and provided legitimacy for the proliferation of a wide diversity of Third World women's organizations.

During the 1970s, criticisms of such groups resulted in the development of a number of alternative approaches to women, namely equity, anti-poverty, efficiency and empowerment. The fact that these approaches share many common origins, were formulated during the same decade and are not entirely mutually exclusive, means that there has been a tendency not only to confuse them, but indeed to categorize them together as the Women in Development (WID) approach. With hindsight it is clear that there are significant differences among these approaches which it is important to clarify.[49]

The equity approach

By the 1970s, studies showed that although women were often the predominant contributors to the basic productivity of their communities, particularly in agriculture, their economic contribution was referred to neither in national statistics nor the planning and implementation of development projects.[50] At the same time new modernization projects, with innovative agricultural methods and sophisticated technologies, were negatively affecting women, displacing them from their traditional productive functions, and diminishing the income, status and power they had in traditional relations. Findings indicated that neocolonialism as much as colonialism was contributing to the decline in women's status in developing countries.[51]

On the basis of evidence such as this, the WID group in the United States challenged the prevailing assumption that modernization was equated with increasing gender equality, asserting that capitalist development models imposed on much of the Third World had exacerbated inequalities between men and women. Recognition of the damaging effects of ignoring women in United States Agency for International Development (USAID) projects during the First Development Decade made the WID group work to influence USAID policy. Lobbying of Congress and participation in Congressional hearings resulted in the 1973 Percy Amendment to the US Foreign Assistance Act, which mandated that US assistance help 'move women into their national economies' in order to improve women's status and assist the development process.[52]

The original WID approach was in fact the equity approach.[53] This approach recognizes that women are active participants in the development process, who through both their productive and reproductive roles provide a critical, if often unacknowledged, contribution to economic growth. The approach starts with the basic assumption that economic strategies have frequently had a negative impact on women, and acknowledges that they must be brought into the development process through access to employment and the marketplace. It therefore recognizes their practical gender need to earn a livelihood. However, the equity approach is also concerned with fundamental issues of equality which transcend the development field. As Buvinic has described, its primary concern is with inequality between men and women, in both public and private spheres of life and across socio-economic groups.[54] It identifies the origins of women's subordination as lying not only in the context of the family but also in relationships between men and women in the marketplace, and hence it places considerable emphasis on economic independence as being synonymous with equity.

In focusing particularly on reducing inequality between men and women, especially in the sexual division of labour, the equity approach meets an important strategic gender need. Equity programmes are identified as uniting notions of development and equality. The underlying logic is that women beneficiaries have lost ground to men in the development process. Therefore in a process of redistribution men have to share in a manner that entails women from all socio-economic classes gaining and men from all socio-economic classes losing, through positive discrimination policies if necessary. The rational consequence of this is seen to be greater equality with an accompanying increase in economic growth.[55]

In fact the theme selection for the 1975 International Women's Year (IWY) conference showed that the equity approach, despite its identification as developmental, was in many respects more concerned with reflecting First World feminist preoccupations with equality. Third World delegations, while acknowledging women's problems, identified development as their main concern, maintaining that this would increase women's status, with Second World delegates more concerned with peace, claiming that the capitalist system with its militarism was responsible for women's problems – hence the theme of equality, development and peace.[56]

Nevertheless, the World Plan of Action for the Implementation of the Objectives of IWY firmly reflected the equity approach, with its call for equality between men and women, its requirements that women should be given their fair share of the benefits of development, and its recognition of the need for changes in the traditional role of men as well as women.[57] The plan set the agenda for future action of both governments and development agencies for the Women's Decade, with the common goal of integrating women into the development process. In reality the interpretation of the agenda varied. This was reflected in the language used, which ranged from the definitely expressed aim to 'integrate', 'increase', 'improve' or 'upgrade' women's participation in development to the more tentatively worded desire to 'help create a more favourable climate for improving women's options in development'.[58]

Despite such rhetoric, equity programmes encountered problems from the outset. Methodologically, the lack of a single unified indicator of social status or progress of women and of baseline information about women's economic, social, and political status meant that there were no standards against which success could be measured.[59] Politically, the majority of development agencies were hostile to equity programmes precisely because of their intention of meeting not only practical gender needs but also strategic gender needs, whose very success depended on an implicit redistribution of power.[60] From the perspective of the aid agency this was identified as unacceptable interference with the receiving country's traditions. At the same time, recognition of equity as a policy principle did not guarantee its implementation in practice.[61]

Despite their endorsement of the Plan of Action, similar antipathy was felt by many Third World governments, legitimized by their belief in the irrelevance of Western-exported feminism to Third World women. In fact one of the outcomes of the 1975 conference was the labelling of feminism as ethnocentric and divisive to WID. Many Third World activists felt that to take 'feminism to a woman who has no water, no food and no home is to talk nonsense',[62] and labelled Third World socialists and feminists as bourgeois imperialist sympathizers. At the same time the fact that there was only one reference to women in the UN New International Economic Order showed that the importance of women was still identified in terms of their biological role by those formulating policies in the Third World.

In a climate of widespread antagonism to many of its underlying principles from the development agencies and Third World governments alike, the equity approach has been effectively dropped by the majority of implementing agencies. However, its official endorsement in 1975 ensured that it continues to provide an important framework for those working within government to improve the status of women through official legislation. Tinker and Jaquette, in reviewing the 1975–85 women's decade conference documents, noted that the goal of legal equality of women – including the rights of divorce, custody of children, property, credit, voting and other citizen rights – had been accepted as a minimum basis of consensus from which to begin the discussion of more controversial issues.[63]

Significant though the ratification of such legislation is, it is necessary to recognize that it meets potential rather than actual strategic gender needs. Property rights, arranged marriages, dowry and child custody rights provide much cited examples of the highly sensitive strategic gender needs which are often still curtailed by custom, even when amended by law. Even the incorporation of practical gender needs into the mainstream of development plans does not guarantee their implementation in practice. Mazumdar, for instance, noted that the incorporation of women's concerns into the framework of India's Six Year Plan indicted India's constitutional commitment to equality of opportunity.[64] However, such constitutional inclusions in no way ensured practical changes, which in her opinion would be largely a function of the strength of the political power base of organized women's groups. Ultimately the equity approach has been constructed to meet strategic gender needs through top down, legislative measures. The bottom up mobilization of women into political pressure groups to ensure policy becomes action is the mandate of the empowerment approach, developed by Third World women, and described below.

The anti-poverty approach

The anti-poverty approach to women can be identified as the second WID approach, in which economic inequality between women and men is linked not to subordination but to poverty, with the emphasis thus shifting from reducing inequality between men and women, to reducing income inequality. Here women's issues are separated from equity issues and linked with the particular concern for the majority of Third World women as the poorest of the poor. Buvinic has argued that this is a toned down version of the equity approach, arising out of the reluctance of development agencies to interfere with the manner in which relations between men and women are constructed in a given society.[65] However, this shift also coincided with the end of the unsuccessful First Development Decade and the formulation of alternative models of Third World economic and social development.

By the early 1970s it was widely recognized that modernization theory, with its accelerated growth strategies based on maximizing GNP, had failed either to redistribute income or solve the problems of Third World poverty and unemployment. Contrary to predictions about the positive welfare effects of rapid economic growth, financial benefits had not trickled down to the poor. An early initiative was the International Labour Organization's (ILO) world employment programme, in which employment became a major policy objective in its own right. The working poor were identified as the target group requiring particular attention and the informal sector with its assumed autonomous capacity to generate employment was seen as the solution.[66] In 1972 the World Bank officially shifted from a preoccupation with economic growth to a broader concern with the eradication of absolute poverty and the promotion of redistribution with growth. Integral to this was the basic needs strategy, with its primary purpose of meeting basic needs such as food, clothing, shelter and fuel, as well as social needs such as education, human rights and participation in social life through employment and political involvement.[67] Low income women were identified as one particular target group to be assisted in escaping absolute deprivation: first, because the failure of trickle down was partially attributed to the fact that women had been ignored in previous development plans and, second, because of the traditional importance of women in meeting many of the basic needs of the family.[68]

The anti-poverty policy approach to women focuses mainly on their productive role on the basis that poverty alleviation and the promotion of balanced economic growth requires the increased productivity of women in low income households. Underlying this approach is the assumption that the origins of women's poverty and inequality with men are attributable to their lack of access to private ownership of land and capital and to sexual discrimination in the labour market. Consequently, it aims to increase the employment and income-generating options of low income women through better access to productive resources. The preoccupation of basic needs strategies with population control also resulted in increasing recognition that education and employment programmes could simultaneously increase women's economic contribution and reduce fertility.

One of the principal criticisms of employment programmes for women is that since they have the potential to modify the sexual division of labour within the household they may also imply changes in the balance of power between men and women within the family. In anti-poverty programmes this redistribution of power is said to be reduced because the focus is specifically on low income women, and because of the tendency to encourage projects in sex-specific occupations in which women are concentrated, or projects which are particularly targeted at women who head households. Nevertheless, the fear that programmes for low income women may reduce the already insufficient amount of aid allocated to low income groups in general means that Third World governments have remained reluctant to allocate resources from national budgets to women. Frequently the preference is to allocate resources at the family or household level, despite the fact that they generally remain in the hands of the male head of household.[69]

While income generating projects for low income women have proliferated since the 1970s, they have tended to remain small in scale, to be developed by non-governmental organizations (most frequently all-women in composition), and to be assisted by grants, rather than loans, from international and bilateral agencies. Most frequently they aim to increase productivity in activities traditionally undertaken by women rather than to introduce them to new areas of work, with a preference for supporting rural-based production projects as opposed to those in the service and distribution sectors which are far more widespread in the urban areas of many developing countries.[70]

Considerable variation has been experienced in the capacity of such projects to assist low income women to generate income. While Buvinic (1986) has highlighted the problems experienced by anti-poverty projects in the implementation process, due to the preference to shift toward welfare-oriented projects, such projects also experience considerable constraints in the formulation stage.[71] In the design of projects, fundamental conditions to ensure viability are often ignored, including access to easily available raw materials, guaranteed markets and small-scale production capacity.[72] Despite widespread recognition of the limitations of the informal sector to generate employment and growth in an independent or evolutionary manner, income generating projects for women continue to be designed as though small-scale enterprises have the capacity for autonomous growth.[73]

Frequently ignored, in addition, are the particular constraints that women experience in their engendered role. These may include problems of perception in separating reproductive from productive work, as well as those associated with balancing productive work alongside domestic and childcare responsibilities. In many contexts there are cultural constraints that restrict women's ability to move freely outside the domestic arena and therefore to compete equally with men running similar enterprises.[74] Where men control household financial resources, women are unable to save unless special safe facilities are provided. Equally where women cannot obtain equal access to credit because of, for instance, a lack of collateral, they are often unable to expand their enterprises unless non-traditional forms of credit are available to them.[75] Finally, the tendency to distinguish between micro-enterprise projects for men and income generating projects for women is indicative of the prevailing attitude, even among many non-governmental organizations, that women's productive work is of less importance than men's, and undertaken as a secondary earner or for 'pocket money'.

Anti-poverty income generating projects may provide employment for women, and thereby meet practical gender needs to augment their income. But unless employment leads to greater autonomy it does not meet strategic gender needs. This is the essential difference between the equity and anti-poverty approach. In addition, the predominant focus on the productive role of women in the anti-poverty approach means that their reproductive role is often ignored. Income generating projects which assume that women have free time often only succeed by extending women's working day and increasing their triple burden. Unless an income-generating project also alleviates the burden of women's domestic labour and childcare through, for instance, the provision of adequate, socialized childcare, it may fail even to meet the practical gender need to earn an income.

The efficiency approach

While the shift from equity to anti-poverty has been well documented, the identification of WID as efficiency has passed almost unnoticed. Yet I would argue that the efficiency approach is now the predominant approach for those working within a WID framework – indeed, for many it may always have been so. In the efficiency approach the emphasis has shifted away from women and toward development, on the assumption that increased economic participation for Third World women is automatically linked with increased equity. This has allowed organizations such as USAID, the World Bank and the Organization for Economic Cooperation and Development (OECD) to propose that an increase in women's economic participation in development links efficiency and equity.

The assumption that economic participation increases women's status and is associated with equity has been widely criticized, as has the identification of such problems as lack of education and underproductive technologies as the predominant constraints affecting women's participation. Among others Maguire has argued that the shift from equity to efficiency has reflected a specific economic recognition of the fact that 50 per cent of the human resources available for development were being wasted or underutilised.[76] While the so called development industry realized that women were essential to the success of the total development effort, it did not necessarily follow, however, that development improved conditions for women.[77]

This shift toward efficiency coincided with a marked deterioration in the world economy, occurring from the mid-1970s onward, particularly in Latin America and Africa where the problems of recession were compounded by falling export prices, protectionism and the mounting burden of debt. To alleviate the situation, economic stabilization and adjustment policies designed by the International Monetary Fund (IMF) and the World Bank have been implemented by an increasing number of national governments. These policies, through both demand management and supply expansion, where designed to produce a reallocation of resources that would lead to the restoration of a balance of payments equilibrium, an increase in exports and a restoration in growth rates.

With increased efficiency and productivity being two of the main objectives of structural adjustment policies, it is no coincidence that efficiency is the policy approach toward women currently gaining popularity among international aid agencies and national governments alike. In reality this approach often simply means a shifting of costs from the paid to the unpaid economy, particularly through the use of women's unpaid time. While the emphasis is on women's increased economic participation, this has implications for women not only as reproducers but also increasingly as community managers. In the housing sector, for instance, one such example is provided by site and service and upgrading projects with self-help components, which now regularly include women in the implementation phase. This is a consequence of the need for greater efficiency: not only are women as mothers more reliable than men in repaying building loans, as workers they are equally capable of self-building alongside men, while as community managers they have shown far greater commitment than men in ensuring that services are maintained.[78]

Structural adjustment policies define economies only in terms of marketed goods and services and subsistence cash production and exclude women's reproductive work. This built-in gender bias concerning the process of the reproduction and maintenance of human resources allows economic resource reallocation policies to assume that women's unpaid labour is elastic in such activities as caring for children, gathering fuel, processing food, preparing meals and nursing the sick.[79] Disinvestments in human resources, made in the name of greater efficiency in IMF and World Bank conditionality policies have resulted in declines in income levels, severe social expenditure cuts in government health and education and reductions in food subsidies. These cuts in many of the practical gender needs of women are seen to be cushioned by the elasticity of women's labour in increasing self-production of food and changes in purchasing habits and consumption patterns.

Until recently structural adjustment has been seen as an economic issue, and evaluated in economic terms.[80] Although documentation regarding its social costs is still unsystematic, it does reveal a serious deterioration in living conditions of low income populations resulting from a decline in income levels. A gender-differentiated impact on intra-household resource distribution, with particularly detrimental effects on the lives of children and women, is also apparent.[81] Within the household a decline in consumption often affects women more than men, while the introduction of charges for education and health care can reduce access more severely for girls than for boys. The capacity of the household to shoulder the burden of adjustment can have detrimental effects in terms of human relationships, expressed in increased domestic violence, mental health disorders and increasing numbers of women-headed households resulting from the breakdown in nuclear family structures.[82]

UNICEF's widely publicized plea to devise adjustment policies 'with a human face' now challenges the efficiency basis of IMF and World Bank policy. It argues that women's concerns, both in the household and in the workplace, need consciously to be made part of the formulation of adjustment policies, which in turn will require the direct involvement of women in both the definition of development and the adjustments in its management.[83] On paper UNICEF's current recommendations to assist low income women would appear highly laudable. Yet optimism that an international agency has the capacity to effect policy measures designed to increase the independence of women must be treated with caution.

This point can be illustrated, for instance, through the appraisal of some of the recent compensatory policies endorsed by UNICEF. These are designed to protect the basic health and nutrition of the low income population during adjustment, before growth resumption enables them to meet their basic needs independently. In a diversity of nutrition interventions, such as targeted food subsidies and direct feeding for the most vulnerable, it is assumed that women in their community managing role will take responsibility for the efficient delivery of such services. For example, in Lima, Peru, the *Vaso de Leche* (glass of milk) direct feeding programme, which provides a free glass of milk to young children in the low-income areas of the city, is managed by women in their unpaid time. Similarly, the much acclaimed communal kitchen organizations, which receive targeted food subsidies, depend on the organizational and cooking ability of women to ensure that the cooked food reached families in the community.[84] While both programmes are aimed 'at improving the nutritional status of the population, especially the low-income groups',[85] this is achieved through reliance on women's unpaid time. These examples illustrate the fact that the efficiency approach relies heavily on the elasticity of women's labour in both their reproductive and community managing roles and only meets practical gender needs at the cost of longer working hours and increased unpaid work. In most cases this approach not only fails to reach any strategic gender needs, but also, because of the reduction in resource allocations, results in a serious reduction of the practical gender needs met.

The empowerment approach

The fifth policy approach to women is the empowerment approach, still neither widely recognized nor documented although its origins are by no means recent. Superficially it may appear synonymous with the equity approach, with references often made to a combined equity/empowerment approach. In many respects empowerment as an identified approach developed out of dissatisfaction with the original WID as equity, because of the latter's perceived co-optation into the anti-poverty and efficiency approaches. However, the empowerment approach differs from the equity approach not only in its origins but also in its identification of the causes, dynamics and structures of women's oppression and in terms of the strategies it proposes to change the position of Third World women.

The origins of the empowerment approach are derived less from the research of First World women and more from the emergent feminist writings and grassroots organization of Third World women. It recognizes that feminism is not simply a recent Western, urban, middle-class import. As Jayawardena has written, the women's movement was not imposed on women by the United Nations or Western feminists, but has an independent history.[86] Since the late nineteenth century Third World feminism has been an important force for change, but with women participating more often in nationalist and patriotic struggles, working-class agitation and peasant rebellions than in the formation of autonomous women's organizations. Although the empowerment approach acknowledges inequalities between men and women, and the origins of women's subordination in the family, it also emphasizes the fact that women experience oppression differently according to their race, class, colonial history and current position in the international economic order. It therefore maintains that women have to challenge oppressive structures and situations simultaneously at different levels.

The empowerment approach questions some of the fundamental assumptions concerning the inter-relationship between power and development that underlie previous approaches. While it acknowledges the importance for women of increasing their power, it seeks to identify power less in terms of domination over others (with its implicit assumption that a gain for women implies a loss for men), and more in terms of the capacity of women to increase their own self-reliance and internal strength. This is identified as the right to make choices in life and to influence the direction of change through the ability to gain control over crucial material and non-material resources. It places far less emphasis than the equity approach on increasing women's status relative to men but seeks to empower women through the redistribution of power within, as well as between, societies. It also questions two underlying assumptions in the equity approach: first, that development necessarily helps all men and second, that women want to be integrated into the mainstream of Western-designed development, in which they have no choice in defining the kind of society they want.[87]

One especially succinct articulation of the empowerment approach has been made by Development Alternatives with Women for a New Era (DAWN), a loose formation of individual women and women's groups set up prior to the 1985 World Conference of Women in Nairobi.[88] DAWN's purpose has been not only to analyse the conditions of the world's women, but also to formulate a vision of an alternative future society, which it identifies as follows:

> We want a world where inequality based on class, gender and race is absent from every country and from the relationships among countries. We want a world where basic needs become basic rights and where poverty and all forms of violence are eliminated. Each person will have the opportunity to develop her or his full potential and creativity, and women's values of nurturance and solidarity will characterise human relationships. In such a world women's reproductive role will be redefined: childcare will be shared by men, women, and society as a whole . . . only by sharpening the links between equality, development and peace, can we show that the 'basic rights' of the poor and the transformation of the institutions that subordinate women are inextricably linked. They can be achieved together through the self-empowerment of women.[89]

Using time as a basic parameter for change, DAWN distinguishes between long-term and short-term strategies. Long-term strategies are needed to break down the structures of inequality between genders, classes and nations. Fundamental requisites for this process include national liberation from colonial and neocolonial domination, shifts from export-led strategies in agriculture, and greater control over the activities of multinationals. Short-term strategies are identified as the necessity to provide ways of responding to current crises, with measures to assist women both in food production through the promotion of a diversified agricultural base, as well as in formal and informal sector employment.

Although short-term strategies correspond to practical gender needs, long-term strategies contain a far wider agenda than do strategic gender needs, with national liberation identified as a fundamental requisite for addressing them. In its description of this approach, however, DAWN does not identify the means of ensuring that once national liberation has been achieved, women's liberation will automatically follow. Recent liberation and socialist struggles in countries such as Cuba, Nicaragua and Zimbabwe have shown that this is not necessarily the case.[90] One of the reasons why the categorization of practical/strategic gender needs in this article avoids time as a determinant of change is because of the implicit underlying assumptions that short-term change leads to long-term transformation. In the same way it cannot be assumed that meeting practical gender needs will automatically result in the satisfaction of strategic gender needs.

The new era envisaged by DAWN also requires the transformation of the structures of subordination that have been so inimical to women. Changes in law, civil codes, systems of property rights, control over women's bodies, labour codes and the social and legal institutions that underwrite male control and privilege are essential if women are to attain justice in society. These strategic gender needs are similar to those identified by the equity approach. It is in the means of achieving such needs that the empowerment approach differs most fundamentally from previous approaches. Recognition of the limitations of top down government legislation to actually, rather than potentially, meet strategic gender needs has led adherents of the empowerment approach to acknowledge that their strategies will not be implemented without the sustained and systematic efforts of women's organizations and like minded groups. Important points of leverage identified by such organizations are therefore not only legal changes but also political mobilization, consciousness raising and popular education.

In its emphasis on women's organizations, the empowerment approach resembles the welfare approach, which also stresses the importance of women's organization, which leads some policy-makers to conflate the two approaches. However, whereas the welfare approach recognizes only the reproductive role of women and utilizes women's organizations as a top down means of delivering services, the empowerment approach recognizes the triple role of women and seeks through bottom up women's organization to raise women's consciousness to challenge their subordination. In fact, Third World women's organizations form a continuum from those whose purpose is direct political action, to those exchanging research and information, to the traditional service-oriented organizations with their class biases and limited scope for participatory action. While acknowledging the valuable function of different types of organizations, the empowerment approach seeks to assist the more traditional organizations to move toward a greater awareness of feminist issues.

An important distinction between the empowerment and equity approaches is the manner in which the former seeks to reach strategic gender needs indirectly through practical gender needs. The very limited success of the equity approach in directly confronting the nature of women's subordination through legislative changes have led the empowerment approach to avoid direct confrontation and to utilize practical gender needs as the basis on which to build secure support and a means through which more strategic needs may be reached. The following examples illustrate this.

In the Philippines, GABRIELA (an alliance of local and national women's organizations) ran a project which combined women's traditional task of sewing tapestry with a non-traditional activity, the discussion of women's legal rights and the constitution. A nation-wide educational tapestry making drive enabled the discussions of rights in communities, factories and schools, with the end product, a tapestry of women's rights seen to be a liberating instrument.[91]

A feminist group in Bombay, India, the Forum Against Oppression of Women, first started campaigning in 1979 on such issues as rape and bride burning. However, with 55 per cent of the low income population living in squatter settlements, the forum soon realized that housing was a much greater priority for local women and soon shifted its focus to this issue. In a context where women by tradition had no access to housing in their own right, homelessness, through breakdown of marriage or domestic violence, was an acute problem and the provision of women's hostels a critical practical gender need. Mobilization around homelessness, however, also raised consciousness of the patriarchal bias in inheritance legislation as well as in the interpretation of housing rights. In seeking to broaden the problem from a women's concern and to raise men's awareness, the forum has become part of a nation-wide alliance of non-governmental organizations, lobbying national government for a national housing charter. Through this alliance the forum has ensured that women's strategic gender needs relating to housing rights have been placed on the mainstream political agenda and have not remained simply the concern of women.

Conflicts often occur when empowered women's organizations succeed in challenging their subordination. One widely cited example, the Self-Employed Women's Association (SEWA) was started in Ahmedabad, India in 1972 by groups of self-employed women labourers. It initially struggled for higher wages and for the defence of members against police harassment and exploitation by middlemen. At first, with the assistance of the male-dominated Textile Labour Association (TLA), SEWA established a bank and provided support for low income women through skill training programmes, social security systems, production and marketing coperatives.[92] It has been said that the TLA expelled SEWA from its organization not only because the TLA leaders felt increasingly threatened by the women's advance toward independence, but also because their methods of struggle, in opposition to TLA policy of compromise and collaboration, provided a dangerous model to male workers.[93] In fact, SEWA has survived considerable setbacks in its development largely due to its widespread membership support and the fact that it has developed into a movement, making it increasingly difficult to eliminate. In addition, at various times the financial support SEWA received from international agencies assisted in giving the organization a level of independence within the local political context.

As highlighted by DAWN, 'empowering ourselves through organization' has been a slow global process, accelerating during and since the Women's Decade, in which diverse women's organizations, movements, networks and alliances have developed. These cover a multitude of issues and purposes, with common interests ranging from disarmament at the international level to mobilization around specific laws and codes at the national level. All share a similar commitment to empowering women and a concern to reject rigid bureaucratic structures in favour of non-hierarchical open structures, although these are not necessarily the most efficient organizational form. Experience to date has shown that the most effective organizations have been those which started around concrete practical gender needs relating to health, employment and basic services, but which have been able to utilize concerns like these as a means of reaching the specific strategic gender needs identified by women in particular socio-political contexts.

The potentially challenging nature of the empowerment approach has meant that it remains largely unsupported either by national governments or bilateral aid agencies. Despite the widespread growth of Third World groups and organizations whose approach to women is essentially one of empowerment, they remain underfunded, reliant on the use of voluntary and unpaid women's time, and dependent on the resources of those few international non-governmental agencies and First World governments prepared to support this approach to women and development.[94]

Conclusion

This chapter has outlined the essential components of a planning approach which, in incorporating gender into planning, challenges Western planning stereotypes. Its conceptual rationale is based on the identification of the triple role of women and the necessity of making a fundamental analytical distinction between practical and strategic gender needs. The methodological tools identified simplify complex theoretical feminist concerns relating both to the productive, reproductive and community managing roles of women, and to the nature of their gender subordination, so that they can be translated into specific interventions in planning practice. At the same time the examples illustrate how simplified methodological tools can assist planners in the appraisal and evaluation of complex planning interventions, and in the formulation of more gender-aware proposals at policy, programme or project level, within particular socio-economic and political contexts.

In order to provide a critique of different policy approaches to women from a gender planning perspective, it has proved necessary not only to evaluate the well documented welfare, equity and anti-poverty approaches, but also to classify more systematically the efficiency and empowerment approaches. This review shows that widescale confusions still exist concerning both the definition and use of different policy approaches, with many institutions at both national government and international agency level unclear in their policy approaches to women. Similarly, the ubiquitous WID approach has mystified rather than clarified conceptual categories and served to legitimize a diversity of approaches to women, which incorporate different underlying assumptions in relation to women's practical and strategic gender needs. Indeed it is precisely because of confusions such as these that is important to develop simple but rigorous tools to enable policy-makers and planners to understand with greater clarity the implications of their interventions, in terms of both their potential and their limitations in assisting Third World women.

From this policy review it is clear that room for manoeuvre still remains limited, with welfare and more recently, efficiency the predominant policy approaches endorsed by most governments and international agencies. With increasing political and ideological control in many contexts, severe difficulties continue to be encountered in shifting policy toward the anti-poverty, equity or empowerment approach. However, there are also individuals and groups involved in changing policy approaches. Among them are government and aid agency personnel who argue that the efficiency approach can also be the means, with a hidden agenda, of empowering women. Most important are the proliferating number of underfinanced, small-scale, Third World women's organizations, in which women, increasingly, are struggling not only to meet practical gender needs but also to raise consciousness about the struggle for strategic gender needs.

Notes

1 This chapter is the result of five years of research, developing the conceptual rationale for gender planning. The author acknowledges the collaborative work and support of Caren Levy, without which this would not have been written. She would also like to thank Maxine Molyneux, Linda Peake, Michael Safier, Marianne Schmink and Peter Sollis for their comments on various drafts, and to acknowledge the support of the Ford Foundation in the development of training courses and materials on gender planning. For earlier versions of some sections of this article, see C.O.N. Moser, 'Women's needs in the urban system: training strategies in gender aware planning', in J. Bruce, M. Kohn and M. Schmink, *Learning About Women and Urban Services in Latin America and the Caribbean* (New York: Population Council, 1986); and C.O.N. Moser and C. Levy, 'A theory and methodology of gender planning: meeting women's practical and strategic needs', *DPU Gender and Planning Working Paper No. 11* (London: Development Planning Unit, 1986).

2 Among the wide diversity of studies of Third World women's employment are D. Jain and N. Bannerjee (eds), *Tyranny of the Household* (New Delhi: Shakti, 1985); J. Nash and H. Safa (eds), *Women and Change in Latin America* (South Hadley, MA: Bergin and Garvey, 1986); N. Redclift and E. Mingione (eds), *Beyond Employment: Household, Gender and Subsistence* (Oxford, Basil Blackwell, 1985); and K. Young and C. Moser (eds), 'Women and the informal sector', *Institute of Development Studies Bulletin* (Vol. 12, No. 3, 1981).

3 The term WID was first coined in the early 1970s by the women's committee of the Washington, DC chapter of the Society for International Development, a network

of female development professionals, influenced by the work on Third World development undertaken by Ester Boserup and other 'new' anthropologists. See E. Boserup, *Women's Role in Economic Development* (New York: St Martin's Press, 1970); I. Tinker, *Gender Equity in Perspective: A Policy Perspective* (Washington, DC: Equity Policy Center, 1982); and P. Maguire, 'Women in development: an alternative analysis', mimeo (Amherst, MA: Center for International Education, 1984). USAID, with its Office of Women in Development, has been one of the most resolute supporters of the WID approach. Together with the Harvard Institute of International Development they have produced a case-study based methodology to identify how women have been left out of development on the grounds that 'women are key actors in the economic system, yet their neglect in development plans has left untapped a potentially large contribution': C. Overholt, M. Anderson, K. Cloud and J. Austin, *Gender Roles in Development* (West Hartford, CT: Kumarian Press, 1984), p. 3.

4 A summary of the distinction between sex and gender is provided by A. Oakley, *Sex, Gender and Society* (London: Temple Smith, 1972). A. Whitehead has highlighted the reasons for choosing the term subordination, rather than patriarchy, to refer to the general character of male/female relations, in A. Whitehead, 'Some preliminary notes on the subordination of women', *Institute of Development Studies Bulletin* (Vol. 10, No. 3, 1979).

5 S. Gordon (ed.), *Ladies in Limbo: The Fate of Women's Bureaux* (London: Commonwealth Secretariat, 1984).

6 From 1981 to 1986 the author taught at the Development Planning Unit, University College London, in training courses for Third World planners involved in such sectors as transport, housing, employment, land use and infrastructure. Efforts to make them gender aware by grafting gender on to their particular planning disciplines met with little success, and led to the recognition of the necessity to distinguish between gender-aware planning (in, say, transport) and gender planning, a specific planning approach in its own right. This was developed at the DPU in the training course, Planning with Women for Development (1983–86), in in-country workshops in Egypt (1987) and Peru (1988), and in gender planning workshops with British non-governmental organizations involved in Third World countries, such as Voluntary Service Overseas (VSO), Christian Aid and Oxfam UK (1987–88).

7 The gender division of labour and its ideological reinforcement is discussed historically by J. Scott and L. Tilly, 'Women's work and the family in 19th century Europe', in E. Whiting *et al.* (eds), *The Changing Experience of Women* (Oxford: Martin Robertson/Open University Press, 1982). M. Barrett, *Women's Oppression Today* (London: Verso, 1980) provides a contemporary account in advanced economies, while women's subordination in an international perspective is examined by O. Harris, 'Households as natural units' and M. Mackintosh, 'The sexual division of labour and the subordination of women', both in K. Young, C. Wolkowitz and R. McCullagh (eds), *Of Marriage and the Market* (London: CSE, 1981); D. Elson and R. Pearson, 'Nimble fingers make cheap workers: an analysis of women's employment in Third World export manufacturing', *Feminist Review* (Vol. 7, Spring 1981); and B. Rogers, *The Domestication of Women* (London: Kogan Page, 1980).

8 The term triple has already been used in relation to women in various contexts. Bronstein, for instance, discusses the three ways in which Third World peasant women suffer in terms of a triple struggle, 'as citizens of underdeveloped countries; as peasants, living in the most impoverished and disadvantaged areas of those countries; and as women in male-dominated societies': A. Bronstein, *The*

Triple Struggle (London: War on Want, 1982). In contrast to this, European feminists have used the term to refer to the increasing parental caretaking role of women: J. Finch and D. Groves (eds), *A Labour of Love: Women, Work and Caring* (London: Routledge and Kegan Paul, 1983) and G. Pascall, *Social Policy: A Feminist Analysis* (London: Tavistock, 1986).

9 In developing the conceptual rationale of gender planning, the term productive work is used to indicate work that has an exchange value, either actual or potential. This includes work in both the formal and the informal sectors, as well as in family enterprises. In this case it may not be perceived as work with an exchange value, since a salary is not given directly for work undertaken. It is critical, however, to acknowledge that reproductive work is also productive, but because of the production of use value under non-wage relations it is not identified as such. For further discussion of this debate see J. Gardiner, 'Women in the labor process and class structure', in A. Hunt (ed.), *Class and Class Structure* (London: Lawrence and Wishart, 1977); CSE, 'On the political economy of women', *Pamphlet No. 2* (London: Conference of Socialist Economists, 1976); and M. Barrett, *op. cit.* It is recognized, therefore, that the use of the term productive work as referring only to work with an exchange value is an over-simplification of reality, particularly in subsistence economies where the divisions are not always separated. In fact, it is recognition of the multiple forms of women's work that has highlighted the severe limitations of categories used principally to show the differences between men's productive work and women's reproductive work. The purpose of this simplification is not to undervalue or ignore the importance of production for use value, but is based on the necessity for the development of a conceptual rationale of gender planning which recognizes that women, unlike men, have a triple role as producers, reproducers and community managers.

10 The important role of women in local-level protest groups has been most widely documented in urban South America. See, for instance, the case studies by M. Barrig and A. Fort, 'La ciudad de las mujeres: Pobladoras y servicios. El caso de El Augustino', in C. Anderson and I. Baud (eds), *Women in Development Cooperation: Europe's Unfinished Business* (Antwerp: Centre for Development Studies, 1987); and C.O.N. Moser, 'Mobilization is women's work: struggles for infrastructure in Guyaquil, Ecuador', in C.O.N. Moser and L. Peake (eds), *Women, Human Settlements and Housing* (London: Tavistock, 1987). However, this phenomenon is neither uniquely South American nor urban. Recent examples that show the community managing role of women in rural environments and basic service struggles in Asia and Africa include J. Barrett, A. Dawber, B. Klugman, I. Obery, J. Shindler, J. Yawitch, *South African Women on the Move* (London: Zed, 1985); G. Omveldt, *Women in Popular Movements: India and Thailand during the Decade of Women* (Geneva: United Nations Research Institute for Social Development,1986); K. Sharma, B. Pandey and K. Nantiyal, 'The Chipko Movement in the Uttarkhand region, Uttar Pradesh, India' and S-Y. Yoon, 'Women and collective self-reliance: South Korea's new community movement', both in S. Muntemba (ed.), *Rural Development and Women: Lessons from the Field* (Geneva: ILO/DANIDA, 1985).

11 A recent unpublished random survey of Third World community-level organizations showed a consistent trend for political organizations to be run by men with mainly men members, and collective consumption groups to be in the hands of women. For instance, in Lima the *junta comunal* is most frequently led and controlled by men, while the Community Kitchen Associations are organized by women; in Manila the *baranguay* captain is generally a man, while the women's club is obviously led by a woman; in Bombay the National Slum Dwellers

Association local representative is a man, but the Mahila Mandal leader is a woman. C.O.N. Moser, 'Are there few women leaders or is it that the majority are invisible?', paper presented at a conference on local leaders and community development and participation (Cambridge: University of Cambridge, 1987).

12 The fact that men leaders are frequently paid for their work is legitimized by the fact that 'a man has to work', whereas women are expected to be selfless and 'pure', with their participation justified in terms of working to improve living conditions for their families: Moser, 'Mobilization is women's work'. An example of the gender division between paid men's work and unpaid women's voluntary work is provided by the UNICEF urban basic services programme in India, which was designed to provide paid employment for men in official positions but required the unpaid work of women in the community for its successful implementation. P. Mehta, 'Evaluation of the UNICEF Indian Urban Infrastructure Programme', unpublished report (London: Development Planning Unit, 1986).

13 Useful reviews of Third World women-headed households are provided by M. Buvinic and N. Youssef with B. Von Elm, *Women-Headed Households: The Ignored Factor in Development Planning*, report submitted to the Office of Women in Development, USAID (Washington, DC: International Center for Research on Women, 1978); and U. Lele, 'Women and structural transformation', mimeo (Washington, DC: World Bank, 1985). In many contexts it is difficult to assess their numbers accurately because discrimination and stigma against women-headed households makes officials reluctant to admit the scale of the problem. For instance, the author was informed by a senior Indian administrative official that in a metropolitan Indian city the figure was between 3 and 4 per cent. A woman social worker working in the slums in that same city put the figure at 70 per cent, thus demonstrating the differences both in definition and perception.

14 M. Weeda, 'The role of social planning and participation in the refugee context: a question of integration or marginalization?', MSc in social planning for developing countries dissertation (London: London School of Economics, 1987).

15 K. White, M. Otero, M. Lycette and M. Buvinic, *Integrating Women into Development Programs: A Guide for Implementation for Latin America and the Caribbean* (Washington, DC: International Center for Research on Women, 1986).

16 Different feminist approaches place varying emphasis on the relative importance of class and gender. While radical feminists utilizing the concept of a sex class stress that the sexual imbalance of power is biologically based, and see sexual politics as the central area of struggle (H. Hartmann, 'The unhappy marriage of Marxism and feminism: towards a more progressive union', in L. Sargent (ed.), *Women and Revolution* (Boston MA: South End Press, 1981)), Marxist feminists, in contrast, identify economic or class relations as the primary oppression, with capitalism particularly responsible for women's double oppression in productive work (Barrett, *op. cit.*). Finally, socialist feminists have emerged in part as an attempt to deal with the 'unhappy marriage' of Marxism and feminism, and seek to expose the pervasiveness and persistence of patriarchy within and across societies and classes even in socialist countries: Maguire, *op. cit.* and Sargent, *op. cit.*

17 M. Molyneux, 'Mobilization without emancipation? Women's interests, state and revolution in Nicaragua', *Feminist Studies* (Vol. 11, No. 2, 1985).

18 In fact, Molyneux (in *ibid.*) does not define interests as such, nor does she make the distinction between interests and needs. From a planning perspective this

separation is essential because of its focus on the process whereby an interest, defined as a prioritized concern, is translated into a need, defined as the means by which concerns are satisfied.

19 *Ibid.*, p. 232.

20 Following the definition of interests and needs made in this article, Molyneux's differentiation between practical and strategic gender interests provides a useful theoretical and methodological distinction when translated into practical and strategic gender needs. For example, if the strategic gender interest, i.e. the prioritized concern, is for a more equal society then a strategic gender need, i.e. the means by which the concern may be satisfied, could be identified as the abolition of the sexual division of labour. On the other hand, if the practical gender interest is for human survival, then a practical gender need could be the provision of water.

21 Molyneux, *op. cit.*, p. 233.

22 *Ibid.*, pp. 232–3.

23 *Ibid.*, p. 233.

24 In a recent example from Nigeria, the curriculum in a community development home economics course included new recipes such as angel cakes to be cooked in a Western-style oven. M.T. Erinle, 'Evaluation of a government income generating project for women in Kwara, Nigeria' in 'Planning with women for urban development, 1985 participants' report', *Gender and Planning Working Paper No. 9* (London: Development Planning Unit, 1986). In fact the majority of low income women dropped out of the programme, preferring to cook for sale traditional food such as *gari*. While the training recognized the reproductive role of women and might have met nutritional needs, assuming that angel cake had greater nutritional value than the traditional foods it substituted, it failed to recognize the productive role of women, which was a priority for the women themselves.

25 The capacity to earn an income from dressmaking varies from place to place, as the following three examples show. In Amman, Jordan, the urban Development Department implements an extensive programme in purpose-built premises, although there are considerable problems for Muslim women in working outside the home. Consequently, the majority attending sewing classes are young, unmarried women, for whom the class itself is an escape from the tedium of the home. For the few older women who for economic reasons try to put their newly acquired skill to practice, there are very limited job opportunities. In Madras, where medium-sized non-governmental organizations such as the Dom Bosco Society run extensive courses, one of the problems for newly trained dressmakers is the lack of demand for their skills in a context where the majority of women still wear the sari, and sewing of the *kurta* is still traditionally a man's occupation. In Recife, Brazil, where in one self-help mothers' group, *Tres Carneiros*, some 80 women received dressmaking training, problems relate to the oversupply of dressmakers in a low income slum community and the lack of resources for buying the sewing materials.

26 National Institute of Urban Affairs, *Women Construction Workers: With Particular Reference to Legal Security and Social Justice* (Delhi: NIUA, 1982).

27 M. Fernando, 'New skills for women: a community development project in Colombo, Sri Lanka', in Moser and Peake, *op. cit.*; M. Schmink, 'The working group approach to women and urban services', mimeo (Gainesville, FL: Center for Latin American Studies, University of Florida, 1984); I. Vance, 'More than bricks and mortar: women's participation in self-help housing in Managua, Nicaragua', in Moser and Peake, *op. cit.*

28 In a recent community-level project in Colombo, Sri Lanka, for instance, masonry

training was initially extended to women as a means of ensuring that those who headed households, but lacked both employment and housing, could get access to the project. Initially the women were hesitant to train, experiencing problems with the male trainer who had to be persuaded by the project officer to find room for them in his crowded training shed. But the demand for masonry skills grew so rapidly that the project was soon forced to absorb women straight into construction teams and provide on-the-job training: Fernando: *op. cit.*

29 For an extensive analysis of the consequences of household stereotypes for human settlements and housing policy, see C.O.N. Moser, 'Women, human settlements and housing: a conceptual framework for analysis and policy-making', in Moser and Peake, *op. cit.*

30 In Tunis, Tunisia, in two low income settlements, Mellassine, a squatter upgrading project, and Ibn Khalkoun, a planned community, women were dissatisfied with house design because of the small size of the inner courtyard. Pressure on land, insensitivity to women's needs and middle-class aspirations to European architecture had resulted in a reduction of inner courtyard area, in some cases leading to psychological depression, neuroses and even suicide among women. Resources for Action, *Women and Shelter in Tunisia: A Survey of the Shelter Needs of Women in Low-income Areas* (Washington, DC: USAID, Office of Housing, 1982).

31 At the Dandora site and service project, in Nairobi, Kenya, partially funded by the World Bank, restrictive zoning legislation was identified by women as the main cause of arrears in repaying building loans: P. Nimpuno-Parente, 'The struggle for shelter: women in a site and service project in Nairobi, Kenya', in Moser and Peake, *op. cit.*

32 In an upgrading project in Jordan, for instance, it was found that because a woman staff member happened to be in charge of handling the title deeds in the community development office, many men in the community allowed their wives to complete the relevant paperwork. As a result, title deeds ended up in the women's names, thus meeting, if unintentionally, their strategic gender need to own land.

33 A study of transport needs in Belo Horizonte, Brazil showed that the routeing of buses from the low income settlements to the industrial areas and then into the city meant that women spent twice as much on transport costs, with their daily average travel time three times longer than men's. M. Schmink, 'Women in the urban economy in Latin America', *Population Council Working Paper No. 1* (New York: The Population Council, 1982).

34 The most systematic classification of different policy approaches to women is the informative work of Buvinic, 'Women's issues', *op. cit.*; and 'Projects for women in the Third World: explaining their misbehavior', *World Development* (Vol. 14, No. 5, 1986), pp. 653–64.

35 Buvinic, 'Women's issues', *op. cit.*

36 Buvinic, 'Projects for women . . .', *op. cit.*

37 M. Hardiman and J. Midgley, *The Social Dimensions of Development* (London: Wiley, 1982).

38 S. Macpherson and J. Midgley, *Comparative Social Policy and the Third World* (Sussex: Wheatsheaf, 1987).

39 H. Wilensky and C. Lebaux, *Industrial Society and Social Welfare* (New York: Free Press, 1965).

40 Buvinic, 'Projects for women', *op. cit.*

41 In most countries the ministries of social welfare and the profession of social planning, frequently seen as their mandate, are dominated by women, particularly

at the lower levels. Consequently this is often identified as 'women's work', serving to reinforce social planning as soft edged and of lesser importance than the hard edged areas of economic and physical planning.

42 L. Bonnerjea, *Shaming the World: The Needs of Refugee Women* (London: World University Service, 1985).

43 Gender blindness on the part of those formulating refugee programmes has severe consequences. As Barbara Harrell-Bond has commented, 'The failure to recognize their pivotal position in the household economy, and the special needs and particular vulnerability of women in the refugee situation has led not just to women being disadvantaged, although this is obviously the case, but to whole programs going awry': B. E. Harrell-Bond, *Imposing Aid: Emergency Assistance to Refugees* (Oxford: Oxford University Press, 1986), p. 267. See also Weeda, *op. cit.*

44 T. Jackson and D. Eade, *Against the Grain: The Dilemma of Project Food Aid* (Oxford: OXFAM, 1982).

45 In their critique of food aid, Jackson and Eade (*ibid.*) argue that MCH programmes can have detrimental effects on participants. In support of this assertion they cite a survey in the Dominican Republic that found food aid to be encouraging malnutrition. Pre-school children who ate rations at a MCH centre and were weighed monthly were found not to gain weight noticeably except during the mango and avocado season and whenever food aid stopped. After questioning the mothers, the nutritionist concluded that when children received food aid mothers tended to overestimate the value of this foreign 'wonder food' and to feed them less local food. When the food aid failed to arrive, mothers would, as a matter of course, ensure that their children had food. This resulted in a weight gain. The experiment repeated elsewhere confirmed the same findings that with food aid there was not weight gain; without food aid weight increased. See L. Hilsum, 'Nutrition education and social change: a women's movement in the Dominican Republic', in D. Morley, J. Rhode and G. Williams (eds), *Practising Health for All* (Oxford: Oxford University Press, 1983).

46 By 1984, for instance, the World Bank *Development Report* (New York: Oxford University Press, 1984) identified reducing infant and child mortality, educating parents (especially women) and raising rural incomes, women's employment and legal and social status as key incentives to fertility decline. However, recognition of the links between women's autonomy over their own lives and fertility control is not widespread and women continue to be treated in an instrumental manner in population programmes. The lack of satisfactory birth control methods, and the introduction of more invasive techniques (such as IUDs and hormonal implants) is making birth control even more women centred. As DAWN has argued, this lets men off the hook in terms of their responsibility for birth control, while increasingly placing the burden on women, whose own ambivalence toward contraceptive technology will only be removed when the technology is better adapted to the social and health environments in which it is used: DAWN, *Development, Crisis, and Alternative Visions: Third World Women's Perspectives* (Delhi: DAWN, 1985).

47 A. Germaine, 'Poor rural women: a policy perspective', *Journal of International Affairs* (Vol. 30, 1977).

48 DAWN, *op. cit.*, p. 42.

49 The lack of definition of WID is widespread in the proliferating number of national-level WID ministries and bureaux, which implement a wide diversity of policies under the umbrella of the WID approach: Gordon, *op. cit.* UNICEF, in a policy review paper on the agency's response to women's concerns, also showed a

lack of clarity in defining its policy approach when it stated, 'There is a growing recognition within UNICEF of the multi-dimensional nature of women's roles and the need for increasing support to programs that are both women- and mother-centred and are based on a development rather than a welfare approach': UNICEF, 'Policy review: UNICEF response to women's concerns', E/ICEF/1985/ L.1 (New York: UNICEF, 1985). Although UNICEF distinguished between welfare and development, no further elaboration of the latter was provided.

50 Boserup, *op. cit.*

51 Tinker, in her documentation of development projects that have widened the gap between men and women, argued that development planners were 'unable to deal with the fact that women must perform two roles in society whereas men perform only one': I. Tinker, 'The adverse impact of development on women', in I. Tinker and M. Bramsen (eds), *Women and World Development* (Washington, DC: Overseas Development Council, 1976). She attributed the adverse impact of development on women to three types of planning error. First, errors of omission or failure to acknowledge and utilize women's productive role. Second, errors that reinforced values which restrict women to the household engaged in childbearing and childrearing activities. Third, errors of inappropriate application of Western values regarding women's work: I. Tinker, 'Introduction: the seminar on women in development', in Tinker and Bramsen, *op, cit.* Another extensive discussion of these issues is found in Maguire, *op. cit.*

52 Maguire, *op. cit.*; Tinker, *Gender Equity, op. cit.*

53 The *Oxford English Dictionary* defines 'equity' as 'fairness' and 'equality' as 'condition of being equal'. Despite her important analysis of policy approaches to women, Buvinic has never sought to qualify the semantic shift from equity to equality. In much of the literature the two terms are often used interchangeably, despite the definitional difference. See Buvinic, 'Projects for women' and 'Women's issues', *op. cit.*

54 Buvinic, 'Projects for women', *op. cit.*

55 Buvinic, 'Women's issues', *op. cit.*

56 C. Stephenson, 'Feminism, pacifism, nationalism and the United Nations Decade for Women', *Women's Studies International Forum* (Vol. 5, 1982).

57 United Nations, *Report of the World Conference of the International Women's Year* (New York: United Nations, 1976).

58 World Bank. *Women in Development* (Washington, DC: World Bank, 1980); Maguire, *op. cit.*

59 United States Agency for International Development, *Report on Women in Development:1978* (Washington, DC: USAID Office of Women in Development).

60 As Buvinic has commented, 'Productivity programs for women usually require some restructuring of the cultural fabric of society, and development agencies do not like to tamper with unknown and unfamiliar social variables. As a rule of thumb, they tend to believe in upholding social traditions and thus are reluctant to implement these programs': Buvinic, 'Women's issues', *op. cit.*

61 In Europe, the Organization for Economic Cooperation and Development, Development Assistance Committee (OECD/DAC) 'Guiding principles to aid agencies for supporting the role of women in development' identified integration as critical to policy on WID issues. In a review of European development assistance, Anderson and Baud argue,

at the most abstract level the concept points the way toward a society in which men and women have interchangeable social roles, so that gender will only be marginally a defining element in life choices. The policy statements of most donor countries are in general accord with this general abstract idea of equality. At the level of actual policy, integration has been mainly interpreted to mean an increasing number of women in existing policies and programs . . . implicit in such an approach is the idea that current development models are in principle favorable to women, and that they therefore do not need to take account of women's vision or priorities.

C. Andersen and I. Baud (eds), *Women in Development Cooperation: Europe's Unfinished Business* (Antwerp: Centre for Development Studies, 1987).

62 C. Bunch, 'Copenhagen and beyond: prospects for global feminism', *Quest* (Vol. 5, 1980).

63 I. Tinker and J. Jaquette, 'UN Decade for Women: its impact and legacy', *World Development* (Vol. 15, No. 3, 1987).

64 V. Mazumdar, 'From research to policy: rural women in India', *Studies in Family Planning* (Vol. 10, 1979).

65 Buvinic, 'Women's issues', *op. cit.*

66 C.O.N. Moser, 'The impact of structural adjustment on women: Concepts and issues', paper presented at the Institute for Africa Alternatives Conference (London: City University, 1987).

67 P. Streeten with S. J. Burki *et al.*, *First Things First: Meeting Basic Human Needs in Developing Countries* (Oxford: Oxford University Press, 1981); D. Ghai, 'Basic needs and its critics', *Institute of Development Studies Bulletin* (Vol. 9, No. 4, June 1978).

68 M. Buvinic, 'Has development assistance worked? Observations on programs for poor women in the Third World', paper presented at the annual meeting of the Society for International Development (Baltimore, MD: SID, 1982).

69 A typical example is that of loans provided to landless families in Bangladesh to assist household-level rice processing businesses by enabling the men to buy additional paddy. Although their wives then undertook additional production activities, men still 'sold the final product and controlled the earnings'. In contrast to this is a *gari* (processed cassava) processing project in Ghana, in which the introduction of improved technology enabled the women to considerably increase their output of *gari*. Here women controlled the marketing and were able to use their additional resources to buy a tractor to assist the men to put more land under cassava cultivation. In this case, 'involving women in the design of the new technology undoubtedly contributed to the success of the project': M. Carr, *Blacksmith, Baker, Roofing-sheet Maker . . . Employment for Rural Women in Developing Countries* (London: Intermediate Technology Publications, 1984).

70 While undertaking gender planning training workshops during 1987–88, the author reviewed documentation on a range of projects that had received financial assistance from such UK-based agencies as Oxfam and Christian Aid. Their support for women's income generating projects at that time included projects as diverse as handmills in Tanzania; fish processing in Sierra Leone; dressmaking in Brazil; foundry work in Bangladesh; rope making in Bangalore, India; *khadi* spinning in Tamil Nadu, India; and clay pot making in Indonesia. However, one largely unrecognized income generating activity for low income urban women was the street foods trade. Recent research has shown this as vital to urban survival strategies, with the widespread availability of low cost cooked food reducing the time women spend in food marketing and home preparation. See M. Cohen, 'Women and the urban street food trade: some implications for policy', *DPU Gender and Planning Working Paper No. 12* (London: Development

Planning Unit, 1986); UNICEF, *Urban Examples: Street Food Trade*, UE14 (New York: UNICEF, 1987).

71 Buvinic, 'Projects for women', *op. cit.*

72 H. Schmitz, 'Factory and domestic employment in Brazil: a study of the hammock industry and its implications for employment theory and practice', *Institute of Development Studies Discussion Paper No. 146* (Brighton: Institute of Development Studies, 1979); C.O.N. Moser, 'The informal sector reworked: viability and vulnerability in urban development', *Regional Development Dialogue* (Vol. 5, No. 2, 1984).

73 *Ibid.*

74 C.O.N. Moser, 'Surviving in the suburbios', *Institute of Development Studies Bulletin* (Vol. 12, No. 3, 1981).

75 J. Bruce, *Market Women's Cooperatives: Giving Women Credit* (New York: Population Council, 1980).

76 Maguire, *op. cit.*

77 The following quotations from international organizations illustrate not only that women are essential to the total development effort, but also suggest efficiency has always been a primary rationale for working with women.

> 'The experience of the past ten years tells us that the key issue underlying the women in development concept is ultimately an economic one': USAID, *AID Policy Paper: Women in Development* (Washington, DC: USAID Bureau for Program and Policy Coordination, 1982). '[L]eaving questions of justice and fairness aside, women's disproportionate lack of education with its consequences in low productivity, as well as for the nutrition and health of their families, has adverse effects on the economy at large': World Bank, *Recognizing the 'Invisible' Women in Development: The World Bank Experience* (Washington, DC: World Bank, 1979), p. 2. 'Substantial gains will only be achieved with the contribution of both sexes, for women play a vital role in contributing to the development of their countries. If women do not share fully in the development process, the broad objectives of development will not be attained': OECD, doc. 18241 (29 November 1983).

78 Fernando, *op. cit.*; Nimpuno-Parente, *op. cit.*

79 D. Elson, 'The impact of structural adjustment on women: concepts and issues', paper presented at the Institute for Africa Alternatives Conference (London: City University, 1987).

80 R. Jolly, 'Women's needs and adjustment policies in developing countries', address given to Women's Development Group, OECD (Paris: OECD, 1987).

81 G. Cornia, R. Jolly and F. Stewart, *Adjustment with a Human Face*, Vols 1 and 2 (Oxford: Oxford University Press, 1987, 1988).

82 UNICEF, *The Invisible Adjustment: Poor Women and the Economic Crisis* (Santiago: UNICEF Americas and the Caribbean Regional Office, n.d.).

83 Jolly, *op. cit.*

84 V. Sara-Lafosse, *Comedores Comunales: La Mujer Frente A La Crisis* (Lima: Grupo de Trabajo, Servicios Urbanos y Mujeres de Bajos Ingresos, 1984).

85 Cornia *et al.*, *op. cit.*

86 K. Jayawardena, *Feminism and Nationalism in the Third World* (London: Zed, 1986).

87 United Nations Asian and Pacific Centre for Women and Development, *Feminist Ideologies and Structures in the First Half of the Decade for Women*, report from the Bangkok Workshop (Bangkok: UNAPCWD, 1979).

88 The project Development Alternatives with Women for a New Era (DAWN) grew

'from small seeds planted in Bangalore, India in August, 1984': DAWN, *Development, Crisis, and Alternative Visions: Third World Women's Perspectives* (New Delhi: DAWN, 1985). In 1985, collaborating institutions included the African Association of Women for Research and Development (AAWORD), Dakar, Senegal; the Women and Development Unit of the University of the West Indies (WAND), Barbados; the Asian and Pacific Development Centre (APDC), Malaysia; and the Chr. Michelson Institute (CMI), Norway, with support provided by the Ford Foundation, the Populations Council and the Norwegian Agency for International Development (NORAD). Research organizations and funding institutions such as these have all played a critical role in supporting the development of the empowerment approach.

89 DAWN placed great importance on the relationship between international structures of domination, warfare and technology and the subordinate position of Third World women. Thus they state: *op. cit,* pp. 73–5:

> We want a world where the massive resources now used in the production of the means of destruction will be diverted to areas where they will help to relieve oppression both inside and outside the home. This technological revolution will eliminate disease and hunger, and will give women means for safe control of her fertility.

90 M. Molyneux, 'Women's emancipation under socialism: a model for the Third World?', *World Development* (Vol. 9, Nos 9/10, 1981).

91 M. Gomez, 'Development of women's organizations in the Philippines', in *Women, Struggles and Strategies: Third World Perspectives, Women's Journal* No. 6 (Rome: ISIS International, 1986).

92 J. Sebsted, *Struggle and Development among Self-Employed Women, A Report for SEWA* (Washington, DC: USAID, 1982).

93 M. Karl, 'Women and rural development', in *Women in Development: A Resource Guide* (Geneva: ISIS Collective, 1983).

94 Evidence suggests that considerable support has come from the governments of such countries as Canada, Denmark, Netherlands, Norway and Sweden. The Netherlands government, in its development cooperation policy, has probably gone furthest in questioning the WID approach and identifying the importance of what is termed an autonomy approach: M. Boesveld, C. Helleman, E. Postel-Coster and J. Schrijvers, *Towards Autonomy for Women: Research and Action to Support a Development Process,* Working Paper No. 1 (The Hague: RAWOO, 1986). A 1986 summary of their overseas development assistance objectives include 'stimulating structural improvements in the position of women ... increasing women's control over their own lives ... strengthening women's organizations'. It is recognized that a stimulus for the shift in approach was the appointment of a feminist as minister for development cooperation from 1982 until 1986: See M. Berden and A. Papma, 'The Netherlands', in Anderson and Baud (eds), *op. cit.*

8

From transnational relationships to international relations: Women in Development and the International Decade for Women

KATHLEEN NEWLAND

> . . . the shift in thought that has taken place is characterized by a shift from the state and its power as the unit of analysis, to the identity group to which the individual owes allegiance.
>
> John Burton[1]

Study of the role of women in development fits neatly within the world society paradigm in international relations. The model is itself a relatively recent development in international relations whose hallmark is the change of perspective described by John Burton above. The Women in Development (WID) movement as it emerged in the 1970s and 1980s was built upon a strong sense of solidarity among women across national boundaries. Their interactions form a part of the dense web of transnational relationships that comprise world society. What follows is an attempt to sketch out the emergence of the WID movement as a transnational phenomenon and point to the tensions within it, to illustrate how it moved into the sphere of international (that is to say, inter-state) relations through the inter-governmental machinery of the United Nations and to assess the impact that the shift had on the orientation of the movement.

The emergence of the Women in Development movement

It is somewhat arbitrary to set a starting point for something as amorphous and diverse as the WID movement. The attempt to do so is certainly not meant to suggest that concern for women's roles in development and the impact of development on women originated in this period. Particularly in revolutionary settings and in wars of national liberation, women's roles had been re-examined, owing in large part to their active participation in the struggle. In some cases, notably China, traditional restrictions on women were identified with the oppressiveness of the past order. In almost all cases the value of their contribution to liberation and the need for their participation in reconstruction was acknowledged. But these reassessments took place largely within the national context. It was not until the 1970s that a sufficient number of women in a sufficient number of countries came to share a sense of common purpose strong enough to characterize their interaction as a movement for the equal participation of women in the development efforts of their countries, both as contributors and beneficiaries.

The WID movement emerged into a receptive policy environment. In the 1970s development planners, funders and practitioners were facing the fact that the development projects and plans of the 1950s and 1960s had failed, in the aggregate, to make a substantial and lasting impact on the living standards of the poor majority. Though food production and gross national product had risen, in many areas so had malnutrition and pauperization. Sparked by Ester Boserup's landmark book, *Women's Role in Economic Development*,[2] awareness gradually dawned that one key, perhaps *the* key, to understanding and possibly resolving these contradictions was the previously overlooked role of women as producers. The inclination to look more broadly into the circumstances of women's lives was at the same time given impetus by a growing sense of alarm at the high rate of population growth in the developing world. At last the voices of Third World women found a receptive ear.

The growing realization of the practical importance of women's role in development coincided with the rising tide of feminism in Europe and North America. One of its most influential pioneers, Simone de Beauvoir, was a dedicated Marxist and anti-colonialist. Her 1949 masterpiece, *The Second Sex*,[3] promulgated a structuralist view of the oppression of women which made it easier for women everywhere to recognize the common roots of the disadvantages under which they laboured, no matter how disparate their circumstances. Under the influence of de Beauvoir and other feminist writers such as Betty Friedan[4] and Germaine Greer,[5] the long standing women's movement in the West – which had long struggled for legal rights, enfranchisement, education and so forth – took a distinct feminist turn.

Added to the demand for women's rights was a deeper analysis of the psychological, social, sexual and cultural roots of discrimination. Many women found the vocabulary and analytical framework learned in leftist movements equally applicable to the position of women. Another ism, sexism, took its place alongside racism, neocolonialism and class-based oppression. This development had great resonance for women in the Third

World, for whom formal, juridical equality – while a desirable goal – held very little promise of fundamentally changing women's lot.

Out of the meeting of these two forces – the search for practical solutions to the failures of development and the growth of feminism based on a more systematic assessment of the roots of disadvantage – Women in Development was born as a transnational movement. The pragmatic strain justified the commitment of resources from the international development community, for which feminists (male and female) lobbied effectively. In 1973 the US law that established the US Agency of International Development was amended to require that a proportion of agency funds be used for activities specifically benefiting women. A Women in Development office was established in USAID. Many other bilateral aid agencies took similar steps. In 1975 the United Nations added to its existing women's departments an Institute for Training and Research for the Advancement of Women (INSTRAW) and later a Fund for Women and Development which became UNIFEM.

Virtually all of the specialized agencies of the United Nations system devised programmes directed to women. In 1977 the World Bank created the post of adviser on women and its president pledged an effort to monitor the impact of Bank activities on women and ensure that account was taken of women's role in development. Virtually all of the major foundations that were active in international development, from giants like Ford and Rockefeller to much smaller institutions, had active women's programmes by the end of the 1970s.

Though the funds allocated were relatively small and the programmes marginal to the mainstream work of the sponsoring organizations, they made possible the formation of an active, transnational coalition of women (for the WID programmes were overwhelmingly staffed by women) working on development from a female, if not always a feminist, perspective. The resources that were made available funded development projects designed to address women's problems specifically; equally importantly, they supported an outpouring of research on women which illuminated the previously obscure nature and dimensions of the obstacles to their advancement.

It would be misleading to portray the Women in Development movement as either powerful (other than in spirit and commitment) or unified. Those active in it remained, for the most part, marginalized within their own societies and institutions, unable to command adequate resources or redirect development policy. This marginality had, however, two positive aspects. First, it encouraged the formation of coalitions with like minded people in other countries, thereby strengthening the transnational character of the movement. Second, it put a brake on the cooptation of WID activists into development establishments still dominated by men and male priorities, which had for decades ignored the interests and needs of women.

The transnational solidarity of women has been subject to the same strains as have women's movements within countries, but magnified by the diversity of political systems, ideologies, economic level and cultural background. The disagreements on ideological grounds were substantive and often bitter, but the movement was broad and loose enough to accommodate the entire political spectrum except for the extreme right. More threatening divisions opened up in four distinct areas: feminism, cultural sensitivity, priorities for the women's movement and anti-feminist backlash against development.

One of the most fundamental divisions concerned the compatibility of feminism with Third World values and identity. As put by Kumari Jayawardena,

> The concept of feminism has been the cause of much confusion in Third World countries. It has variously been alleged by traditionalists, political conservatives and even certain leftists, that feminism is a product of 'decadent' Western capitalism; that it is based on a foreign culture of no relevance to women in the Third World; that it is the ideology of women of the local bourgeoisie; and that it alienates and diverts women, from their culture, religion and family responsibilities on the one hand, and from the revolutionary struggles for national liberation and socialism on the other. In the West, too, there is a Euro-centric view that the movement for women's liberation is not indigenous to Asia or Africa, but has been a purely West European and North American phenomenon.[6]

The debate on feminism within the movement took place against a more generalized background of cultural misunderstanding, which gave rise to considerable resentment among Third World women, primarily directed toward First World women. Women from the Second World, the industrialised socialist countries, were relatively passive participants in these discussions. They were content for the most part to point to the accomplishments of their own states, identify women's oppression with capitalist systems and express verbal solidarity with Third World women. But First World women plunged into feminist analyses of the oppression of Third World women.

The genuine, though initially sometimes not very well informed, interest of Western feminists in Third World women's problems was seen by some of the latter as patronizing. Western attempts to redefine male–female relationships in a certain way were perceived as intrusive and inappropriate, and the emphasis in the West on sexual liberation was seen as offensive by some. There was considerable resentment against researchers who flew into a developing country with a foundation grant and a tape recorder, and then flew back to relative comfort and security to earn degrees and build careers on the basis of their findings, while making no tangible contributions to the welfare of the people and communities they had studied. Efforts to deal with the oppression and exploitation of women within the family were felt as painful intrusions into the most intimate realms of private life.

Furthermore, there was a perception, or fear, that criticism of the traditional role of women in a given society was part of a general predilection to denigrate and insult indigenous culture and religion. It is undoubtedly true that customs or institutions such as polygamy, veiling, purdah, unilateral divorce, dowry, brideprice and child marriage were readily condemned as barbarous by outsiders with little knowledge of the setting and circumstances in which they took place, and little understanding of the sensitivity with which such issues must be approached. Even if citizens of the country in question were campaigning against some of these practices, it did little good to have strident condemnations blasting in from foreign observers. First, it engendered a defensive reaction even among reformers; second, it played into the hands of reactionaries who could use it to argue that domestic reformers were acting as agents of a kind of neocolonialism. Still, in some cases outside intervention, however much resented, drew attention and action to some issues that were extremely difficult to raise in the domestic context and might otherwise have continued to be ignored.[7]

The appropriate priorities for women's movements was another point of contention among women activists. The division was between those who felt that women's movements should give priorities to problems specifically affecting women, as opposed to problems affecting society as a whole, and those who felt that they should be vehicles for women's participation in broader struggles. The latter view was prevalent especially in countries still engaged in struggles for the achievement or consolidation of national liberation. The position of the Women's Association of Nicaragua (AMNLAE), described by Hermione Harris, was representative:

> The transformation of relationships between men and women is not AMNLAE's priority. Discussions continue but AMNLAE's publicly-declared aim is to involve women in reconstructing the country. The Association's leaders concur with the FSLN Directorate which identifies the liberation of women with the revolutionary project as a whole. 'We find that western feminists are somewhat intolerant of our definition of priorities', commented one AMNLAE ex-president, 'because these priorities are integrated into the national reconstruction plan. It is essential for us firstly to improve the basic conditions for the survival of all women, which means improving general social and economic conditions'.[8]

Finally, there were those both within and outside of the movement who came to question whether, under prevailing circumstances, development was good for women. Opening employment opportunities and income generating activities for women, in the near universal absence of domestic role sharing, doubled their workloads.[9] Much of what women saw of development had not brought benefits but had, indeed, introduced new stresses while removing old sources of security. In this view, the role of women in development as it had evolved was to perform all of their traditional functions and many new ones under ever more difficult circumstances – in other words to do more work with less help and less protection. One response to this was to insist that the sex role issues be enjoined and action taken to equalize workloads; but another was wholesale rejection of the ideas both of development and social change. The negative effects of development had set the stage for an anti-WID backlash.

These fissures in the WID movement were not irreparable, for the partners in the transnational coalition retained a willingness and a capacity to listen and to learn rapidly from each other. By the mid-1970s the movement was strong enough to command the attention of, and demand a response from, even reluctant governments. But the fissures could be and were exploited by the male-dominated establishment to exert control over the movement. At least one valuable lesson had been learned from the colonial experience: divide and rule. The next section will show how this impulse worked through the United Nations.

International Women's Year and the Decade for Women

Designation by the United Nations General Assembly of the year 1975 as International Women's Year (IWY) was a milestone for the transnational women's movement. It signalled public acknowledgement by governments, at the international level, of the importance of women's issues. It provided an umbrella of legitimacy for women's groups and for work on women's issues. It prompted a number of governments to revise parts of their legal codes, pass new legislation or establish departments or subdepartments to attend to women's issues. It triggered a huge statistical endeavour to uncover the facts of women's existence, which had the effect of revolutionizing perceptions of the problem. Perhaps the most powerful slogan of the following decade emerged from this statistical effort. It pointed out that women constitute half of the world's population, fill two-thirds of its work hours, receive one-tenth of its income and own less than one-hundredth of its property. It became difficult for anyone to deny the existence of a problem.

The successes of International Women's Year, and demands from women activists, prompted the United Nations to declare an International Decade for Women in the ten years following IWY (1976–85). The key events of the eleven-year period were the IWY conference in Mexico City in 1975, the mid-Decade conference in Copenhagen in 1980 and the end-of-Decade conference in Nairobi in 1985. The outpouring of research, data collection and publicity continued throughout the Decade and had an unmistakable consciousness raising effect. It continued to strengthen the Women in Development movement in particular, by demonstrating over and over again the high economic and human costs of discrimination.

There was, however, another powerful effect of the extension of the United Nations umbrella over the women's movement. The transnational movement was a loose coalition of women's groups, academics, marginalized national and international civil servants, foundation staff, trade union women, peasant organizations, urban cooperatives and so forth. It had no hierarchy and it was too diverse for any one approach to dominate. But the United Nations is an inter-governmental organization and to the extent that the movement came under UN auspices it moved away from the transnational, world society web of relationships and into the cold realist light of international, inter-state relations.

The three UN conferences were meetings of official delegations of the member governments – though in each case parallel meetings were held which were open to all comers. The conference agendas, the position papers, the statements of delegations were the products of intra- or inter-governmental processes. Not surprisingly, the feminist, and even the female, content of the official proceedings dwindled over the course of the Decade and the conference debates came more and more to resemble any other General Assembly debate. A number of the First World delegations, which were always at a disadvantage in General Assembly debates, tried, for a while, to keep the focus on women's issues. But they too finally succumbed to cynicism and entered the political fray.

Lip service was paid to the Decade's touchstones of equality, development and peace but the different priorities of the member governments dominated. At the 1975 conference, the major topic was the New International Economic Order; in 1985 it was Middle Eastern politics. The major obstacles to equality for women in the Draft Programme of Action debated at the 1980 conference were listed as imperialism, racism, colonialism and so forth; there was no mention of sexism or anything like it. It took an extended and acrimonious debate on the floor of the conference to win the insertion of 'discrimination based on sex' to this list, with a footnote adding 'which in a group of countries is called sexism'.[10] The argument was reminiscent of the disagreements within the women's movement on the priority to be assigned to women's rights versus national liberation; but in the inter-governmental context it stifled virtually all discussion of the oppression of women as an issue in its own right.

The final conference, in 1985, reached an impasse on the contentious political issues, but at the eleventh hour a truce was negotiated which allowed the delegations to adopt a 350-item Forward-Looking Plan of Action, which was in fact devoted primarily to the needs, rights and responsibilities of women. It had been drafted by the WID bureaucrats in the UN, the fifth column of the transnational women's movement within the halls of the inter-governmental forum. Since so much of the debating time had been taken up with the political issues, the draft was passed virtually unaltered.

The Decade for Women has been widely branded as a failure because of the diversion of attention from women's problems to more general political issues. Some of the women who participated in the diversion, as delegates of governmental or quasi-governmental delegations to the conferences, naturally rejected that conclusion. They point to the importance of a forum which allowed women's voices to be heard on matters of global importance that affect the lives of women, such as apartheid, Zionism and the international division of labour. But there remain many who question whether the conferences really allowed women's voices to be heard or whether they just allowed women to be used as mouthpieces for positions determined by non-feminist, or even anti-feminist, political establishments. What can scarcely be doubted, however, is that the Decade shifted the gears of the international women's movement in a direction that many WID activists regarded as reverse – away from the needs and interests of women as an identity group, in Burton's terms, back to a focus on 'the state and its power as a unit of analysis'.

Equally damaging, perhaps, were the tactics used in the conference processes to achieve the shift of gears: an attack on feminism as incompatible with Third World values, a polarization of the debate on priorities, a fanning of cultural misunderstandings and a degree of encouragement to the anti-feminist backlash. In short, fissures in the women's movement were exploited and widened. The next section will look at the lasting effect of all this on the orientation of the Women in Development movement.

WID after the Decade for Women

Since the Decade for Women ended in 1985 there has been a great deal of reflection on its impact. The worldwide attention and legitimacy associated with the declaration of International Women's Year and the Decade for Women brought many people and some money into the women's movement. It forced governments to address themselves, however superficially, to the issues. Laws were changed, an international convention on sex discrimination was adopted and signed by 116 states,[11] national machinery was established, commitments were made. Some degree of leverage for women was achieved. But the quality of life for most women has been little changed.

The Women in Development movement evolved during the Decade. It benefited from the increase in resources and attention given to women's issues. It gained in sophistication as a result of the tremendous explosion of knowledge and data that it helped to create. As a result of trial and error it gained most of all from the communication among women from different countries, who were willing to listen to and teach each other even through the periods of greatest tension.

But the movement also suffered from the bruising encounters of the Decade, experienced largely in the inter-governmental setting. The negative side of the learning experience brought a certain defensiveness into the movement: WID practitioners – those who were actually involved in designing, funding, implementing and evaluating programmes – learned how easily divisions within their ranks could be exploited. They learned that the tensions were most acute on cultural matters, particularly those having to do with relations between women and men. Maxine Molyneux has made a distinction between what she calls the practical and the strategic interests of women.[12] The latter are the substance of the feminist agenda and have proved to be by far the most controversial, for they question women's roles rather than simply helping women to perform better in those roles assigned them. These are the kind of issues that the WID movement has learned that it is easier to avoid.

It is easy to speculate on the reasons for this reluctance to tackle the fundamentals of women's rights as individuals and relations between the sexes. Development policies are set within male-dominated institutions which still see WID as an instrument rather than a goal in itself: a means for lower population growth, higher economic growth or more successful political mobilization. The international WID bureaucracies and pro-grammes exist on sufferance; like the women's associations in many countries, they cannot afford to alienate their bosses.

Still more important than the bureaucratic–political reasons for avoiding the most controversial issues is a recognition that a successful formula for dealing with them at the transnational level has not been discovered. Many WID practitioners have found themselves having to make painful trade offs between short-term and long-term goals. No matter how great their conviction that a fundamental redefinition of sex roles is needed before women can realize their full potential, they know that conflict and suffering are inevitable in the process of change – and that success is far from guaranteed. They know that male privilege is deeply entrenched and strongly defended by virtually all the institutions of society. Their purpose is to improve women's lives, not throw them into a maelstrom. So they back away from confronting sexism, and work within the constraints of purdah, machismo, unequal division of labour, restrictive interpretations of religious teaching and so forth. Within these constraints, they make what progress they can.

The understandable reluctance to confront sexism, the contradiction-laden attempt to empower women without challenging men, has led WID programmes into two particular channels, one accommodationist, one separatist. The accommodationists focus on the practical needs of families for which women are the key providers. The emphasis is on such issues as food production for home consumption, water, fuel, income generation and child health. A project supported by the United Nations Development Fund for Women (UNIFEM) in Gambia is characteristic.[13] It has supplied milling machines to village communities to grind millet, a task which previously took women working by hand an average of four hours a day. The laborious task of pounding millet was part of a sixteen-hour-a-day routine that also included cultivation of the crop, threshing, cooking, wood gathering and water collecting as well as general housework and child care. Most of the beneficiaries of the mills were putting the energy released from pounding into additional food cultivation, giving their families a better diet and many of the women a cash income for the first time from the marketing of the surplus. The project has genuinely improved the quality of life for its participants and raised the standard of living in their communities and done so without in any way threatening the sexual division of labour. Indeed, it has probably reinforced it by reducing the strain imposed on women by their heavy workload.

A second way of working for women in development while avoiding the contentious issues of relations between the sexes is to work with women outside traditional family structures, that is to say with women-headed households, female migrants, women left behind by male migrants or abandoned women. As a development priority this choice is unassailable, for women-headed households make up 25–50 per cent of all households in many regions and they are the poorest of the poor. The independence of these women, which is often involuntary, is a prior fact and helping them to achieve a higher standard of living in self-sufficiency is no threat to the establishment. By dealing with women in isolation from men, however, it leaves unchallenged the roots of their disadvantages.

Conclusion

The transnational Women in Development movement has survived integration into inter-governmental relations but has altered its character. The feminist analysis of women's subordination set in motion by Simone de Beauvoir and others, which laid the basis for worldwide solidarity among women as it bared the common origin of their dilemmas, has gone out of fashion. A coalition of women (and some men) has survived but it is weaker for turning its back on its theoretical roots. A confrontational approach to men is not required; what *is* needed is a clear sense of women's practical and strategic interests (to use Molyneux's terms). The WID movement has yet to find a way of dealing with the basic structures of subordination. Women within their own societies are, in many cases, doing so. No one doubts that it will be a slow and painful process. Perhaps the role of a transnational coalition in this most sensitive endeavour can be no more than to offer a framework of encouragement and support – while doing as much as possible within existing constraints to improve the material conditions of women's daily lives.

Notes

1 J. W. Burton, 'World society and human needs' in M. Light and A.J.R. Groom (eds), *International Relations: A Handbook of Current Theory* (London: Frances Pinter, 1985), p. 47.
2 E. Boserup, *Women's Role in Economic Development* (London: Allen and Unwin, 1970).
3 S. de Beauvoir, *The Second Sex* (New York: Alfred A. Knopf, 1952).
4 B. Friedan, *The Feminine Mystique* (New York: W.W. Norton, 1963).
5 Germaine Greer, *The Female Eunuch* (London: Granada Publishing, 1971).
6 K. Jayawardena, *Feminism and Nationalism in the Third World* (London: Zed Books, 1986).

7 Female circumcision is one such issue that was the subject of a fiercely resented campaign by Western women. After the rejection of that campaign, women from the affected countries took up the issue themselves. See *Female Circumcision, Excision and Infibulation: Facts and Proposals for Change* (Minority Rights Group Report No. 47, 2nd edition, 1985).

8 H. Harris, 'War and reconstruction: women in Nicaragua', in Olivia Harris (ed.), *Latin American Women* (Minority Rights Group Report No. 57, 1983).

9 K. Newland, *Women, Men and the Division of Labour* (Worldwatch Paper 37, Worldwatch Institute, 1980).

10 US State Department, quoted in J. S. Bernard, *The Female World from a Global Perspective* (Bloomington, IN: Indiana University Press, 1987), p. 168.

11 The Convention on the Elimination of All Forms of Discrimination Against Women. The 30-article treaty, drafted by the UN Commission on the Status of Women, was approved by the General Assembly in 1979 and entered into force in 1981. Of the 116 signatory states, 94 have ratified or acceded to the Convention. See C.G. Patton, 'NGO Report' in *International Studies Newsletter*, Vol. 15, No. 6, August 1988.

12 M. Molyneux, 'Mobilization without Emancipation: Women's Interests, State and Revolution in Nicaragua', *Feminist Studies* (Vol. 11, No. 2, 1958); see also C.O.N. Moser, 'Gender planning in the Third World: meeting practical and strategic needs' in this volume.

13 J. Madely, 'Making time for Africa's food' in *The Financial Times*, 1 September, 1988.

9

Feminism and the claim to know: contradictions in feminist approaches to women in development

ANNE MARIE GOETZ

Women have occupied inferior positions in all spheres of life, across most societies. The experience has provided the historical identity upon which feminist scholarship and politics has been based. This sense of common identity has been expressed most explicitly in the feminist concern over the effects of modernization upon subordinated, low income women in developing societies. It has taken on a political purpose and assumed its most prominent practical form with the policy proposals for the 'equitable integration' of women in economic development emanating from the United Nations Decade for Women (1976–85). Yet these policies have unfolded in the context of a dominant, western discourse about development that has reserved for itself the authority to define and name its epistemological categories: 'progress', 'modernization'; and its objects: 'third world', and 'third world women'.[1]

A chorus of objections has been raised by certain third world women, who link western feminism's dominant representations to imperialism.[2] They suggest that western feminists have been guilty of extrapolating from and projecting a privileged identity as a referent for the rest of the world. More tellingly, the Decade's generally barren record of ineffectual, social welfarist and separatist projects was a product of that same failure of nerve at the roots of the policy of integration. It attests to the analytical poverty of the assumption that all people of the same gender, across classes and cultures, are somehow socially constituted as a homogeneous group and form an automatic international constituency. The urgent problems of survival faced by women in the third world have made a feminist involvement in the question of women in development imperative. At the same time this involvement has snagged itself on the vast diversity of women's experience. Contradictions, between a feminist theory that questions oppressive categories of social organization and a politics predicated on the totalizing unity of a category labelled 'women', have been thrown into sharp relief.

This chapter will consider the implications for a feminist epistemology of women's experience of the Decade's development approaches – for those 'claims to know' upon which feminist practice bases its authority to intervene. The diversity of experience – or difference[3] – among women has thrown feminist politics into crisis. Lately, it has reinvigorated a feminist exploration of theories of knowledge despite the trend away from epistemology and foundationalism in modern social theory.[4] I will be discussing here two current models of a feminist theory of knowledge, which have evolved as responses to the challenge of difference. One adopts a culturally relativist position. Different female subjectivities are seen to be innate, and to valorize experience to such an extent that different women are entrenched in their particularities. The other, which participates in the post-modernist project of dismantling the claims of western normative universalism, poses as a fundamental problem the epistemological basis upon which feminists justify their project of transforming women's lives in contemporary cultures. In this second approach, the coherence, and even existence, of the single category 'women' is being undermined; in so doing, it discredits the idea of an epistemologically significant subjectivity in the name of which women can act in the world.

These alternatives are paralysing and inadequate in the face of the imperative to act posed by the survival problems of women in the third world. Critiques of liberal feminism have been timely and necessary, in so far as liberal feminism borrowed from the totalizing assumptions and methods of modern normative theory and based its claim to know about the lives of other women upon a white and western model. But we cannot replace the question 'What must be done?' with 'Who am I?', or with the retreating statement 'I cannot claim to know, and so can do nothing.' This chapter will conclude by trying to propose ways of thinking beyond this dichotomy.

Feminism and women in development

Feminist interest in women in development has been motivated by evidence from the third world of the absolute decline in women's status in developing societies. Progressively denied access to land and other resources, women have lost control over their own labour and its rewards. Their workloads have intensified, and female illiteracy and the poor nutritional status of their children have shown a stubborn persistence.[5] Feminist research on women in development (WID) has documented their declining status worldwide. It has also emphasized the differential impact of modernization upon men and women. In demonstrating the implications of this differentiation for successful development, the feminist approach has exhibited considerable explanatory power. Research on women in development is specifically feminist in that, as a part of a feminist critique of social organization, it has been concerned to illuminate those structures of exclusion embedded in standard development practice which served to marginalize women's interests and relegate them to the periphery of planned intervention. Feminist theory has argued that the theoretical and practical exclusion of women evident in their invisibility in development planning is no mere mistake or unintended consequence of planning.

Feminist perspectives on the locus of subordination have varied with ideological positions. Different models of development implicitly or explicitly inform analyses of the effects of capitalist accumulation and class formation on rural societies and gender relations. They lead to different understandings of the significance of persistent non-capitalist relations of production, processes of differentiation among rural households, and the impact of such processes upon the internal dynamics of the household and the structure of gender relations. The importance for policy of different feminist perspectives lies in the varying degrees to which women's loss of control over productive resources is seen to result from the intersection of class relations (in production) and gender relations (in reproduction). Practical consequences flow from various analytical assumptions about the nature of connections between patterns of social and economic transformation on the one hand and changes in the sexual division of labour on the other.

The subtleties distinguishing these approaches, however, have tended in the practice of policy formulation and project implementation to give way to the imperatives of the language, activities and procedures of technical development agencies. The resulting approaches to women in development follow dominant paradigms in development theory. Although approaches to women in development are broadly shaped by feminist assumptions (about the locus of gender subordination, the nature of the concept 'women', and the identity of 'woman'), the process of modifying women's projects to fit the blueprints for standard development projects has distorted their original objectives. In the end, they represent no threat to the existing power structures and budget allocations within the development establishment (understood to include the mainstream of development: the governments and agencies of developing countries, multilateral and bilateral development agencies and the larger non-governmental organizations). To the extent that this is so, the dominant approaches to women in development cannot be said to represent an identifiably feminist strategy.

On the other hand, much policy formulation for women has partaken of a liberal feminist faith in the efficacy of the modernization project. Hence the injunction, for example, to integrate women into a development process of which their own prior experience constituted a profound critique. The International Women's Year's World Plan of Action of 1975, which became the guiding document of the Decade for Women (1976–85), was addressed to governments for internal application. Women were presented as citizens needing legal redress and as clients needing services or as victims needing protection. With misogyny seen as an analytical mistake or an institutional oversight, the liberal feminist approach translated directly into the administrative, managerial and technical processes of the development establishment. Very typical of this approach was the injunction to governments, which drew a worldwide response, to set up ministries of women's affairs. These numerous tiny ministries, underfunded and staffed with weak political appointees, running handicrafts projects and largely uninvolved with the broader affairs of government and development, represent precisely the sorts of token gestures that many states can trumpet while neglecting to do anything further to involve women in their agricultural, industrial, service and social sector development plans.

There was in effect, if not actually, collusion between the restrictive nature of assumptions made by the Decade's policy-makers about the source of women's oppression and the limiting language of development practice; to a large extent, neither allows for an analysis of how the state itself, as well as the general direction of modernization, might systematically obstruct the inclusion of women's concerns. Both, too, are practices embedded in a western understanding of modernization. They have therefore tended to forbid the innovation, experimentation and continuous social learning which the consideration of women in development has to involve. The disjunctions experienced by the third world women who are the objects of policy interventions can be said to stem from these two inter-related processes: one relating to assumptions about gender and the locus of subordination, the other regarding the limiting implementation frameworks of technical development agencies.

A simple and typical example of how these two processes work together to constrain the possibilities of development projects for women is the history of a UNIFEM/FAO project in Guinea for women fish-smokers. The feminist assumptions informing the project grouped together women of different classes and creeds from the city of Conakry in a large cooperative. It fairly quickly fell apart owing to the divided allegiances of the women involved; they could not work well as a group by virtue merely of a shared biological characteristic. Also, traditionally the gender division of labour in the coastal fishing and fish preserving industry was such that the fishermen husbands of the women often guaranteed a supply of fish for their wives to purchase and process. The project, however, required the women, as a group, to purchase fish from the open market, making the activity much less profitable. The local gender division of labour was ruptured, with no viable alternative offered. Equally, the project was undermined by a number of aspects of formal project design and organization, including the fact that it required the women to attend project activities during regular daytime working hours. Fish smoking, especially in Conakry, is an activity women normally do at night. The fish smoke slowly overnight and the day is left free for other forms of employment such as trading. The effect of the project, therefore, was to leave the women collectively worse off.[6]

The burden of responsibility for the shortcomings of development projects for women, in misspecifying or ignoring important details of the sexual division of labour in different contexts, is an important matter for debate. My interest here in the implications of women's experience of development for a feminist theory of knowledge obliges me to limit my focus to the issue of the feminist assumptions informing policy.[7] In so doing I will be looking at feminist epistemology writ large as it emerges from several decades of project implementation for women, while stressing that it lags behind advances in the feminist approach to WID in research.

Approaches to WID: from welfare to empowerment

Before exploring the epistemological knots into which feminist theory has worked itself in its engagement with women in development, I will briefly review the history of WID. Since the publication in 1970 of Ester Boserup's work,[8] which documented the decline in women's social and economic status that came with the commoditization of subsistence economies in the developing world, a considerable body of literature has focused on the role of women in economic development. Research suggested that the exclusion of women from rural development programmes would undermine the effectiveness of these projects.[9] Similarly, as mediators to the household of such factors of social development as health, education and fertility awareness, women were recognized as being of critical importance to the satisfaction of basic needs.[10] Part of the reason for women's invisibility in development planning was traced to the conceptual and methodological biases in accounting for women's work, which of itself is indicative of the systematic undervaluation of women's unpaid subsistence and domestic labour.[11] This has suggested a link between the invisibility of women's labour, ideologies of their inferior status and their deteriorating position in the third world. That this link sometimes has fatal consequences is evident in the worsening gender survival differentials in certain countries.[12] This last connection has informed policy directed at providing external sources of income for women in order to improve their bargaining position within the household.[13]

Within the development establishment, policy for women has followed several broad approaches. Until the mid-1970s the consideration of women in planning and practice was guided by a rhetoric and model of female domesticity and male responsibility. This domestic female model – sculpted in a heavy hand along the lines of the biological mother in western familial ideology – structured welfare-oriented activities which limited economic intervention for women to activities centred on their functions as childbearers, rearers and homemakers. It is still typical of most UNICEF programmes whose focus remains upon the mother–child dyad to the exclusion both of women's productive roles and of the whole issue of the fathers' responsibilities for reproduction.

A specifically feminist policy interest in WID began to be expressed in the context and spirit of the concern with poverty and basic needs espoused by the development establishment during the 1970s. The observation was made that the new distributional focus of policy had failed to recognize the effects of gender inequality above and beyond those of class membership.[14] Policy was focused on rural women, who were seen to be at the heart of the crisis in simple commodity production. They were recognized as the victims of a development practice which had in many settings resulted in stagnating food production, nutritional decline, and a breakdown of rural communities which produced massive rural to urban migration. During the course of the UN Decade for Women a feminization of agriculture thesis was elaborated according to which the sexual division of labour in third world countries was seen to have shifted as a result of male migration in such a way as to consign subsistence agriculture almost exclusively to women. This obliged them to exploit themselves and their physical environments to the limit of endurance.[15]

The idea that the practice of development failed women by ignoring the importance of their productive roles and their role in mediating social change (as well as disregarding their particular vulnerabilities) led to the UN Decade for Women's strategy of integrating women into the development process. Although informed by a critique of the development process, this strategy is based on an ongoing faith in the benefits of modernization. (Boserup's work is typical of this.) The strategy of equitable integration reveals important contradictions and inequities in the development process, but it leaves unquestioned assumptions about both women and development which limit the effectiveness of planned change. An example is the suspect and misleading strategy of integrating women into a process in which they already fully participate, and of which their (mostly unremunerated) labour is an essential part. Integration strategy has been reluctant to establish systemic connections between such contradictions or to uncover their sources.

The case for the allocation of resources to women's projects was presented either as a human rights issue that also made sense in terms of economic development or in terms of the concern with poverty and uneven distribution. Mayra Buvinic has broadly labelled the two distinct approaches equity and poverty oriented.[16] The equity approach stresses the negative impact of economic growth for women and links this with women's subordination. In action, this strategy established a conceptual link between greater equality and justice for women on the one hand, and increased productivity on the other. It often seeks to engage women in non-agricultural wage labour as one means of breaking the nexus of subordination in the context of rural subsistence households. Poverty oriented approaches emphasize that a majority of the world's poor are women and argue that gender inequality promotes economic inefficiencies and perpetuates poverty. Often this approach focuses on aiding poor rural women to increase their productivity in the context of their subsistence activities.

Caroline Moser has added two further approaches to Buvinic's list: efficiency and empowerment.[17] The efficiency approach is a response to the hardships caused by global recession and the implementation of severe stabilization measures in developing countries. It parallels the current shift in dominant development paradigms towards structural adjustment policies. In its focus on the productive roles of women it reflects an economic recognition of women as an underutilized 'resource' for development. The focus is on increasing women's labour productivity and also on making use of women's unpaid time in, for example, an intensification of their nurturing roles in participatory community programmes such as health delivery systems.

The empowerment approach has developed largely independently of the development establishment in reaction to the perception that women's needs and goals were and are being subsumed to the imperatives of technical development agencies. This approach informs some of the more successful examples of women's development projects, which are based on the grassroots experiences of third world women and respond to their contextually defined needs. They put a high premium on autonomy; foreign assistance has often been refused. One group that gives theoretical expression to this approach is the network of third world activists, researchers and policy-makers participating in the Development Alternatives with Women for a New Era (DAWN) project.[18] DAWN addresses broader power issues in stressing the importance of the different sources of oppression that limit women's possibilities in development – stemming not only from gender but from conflicts of class, culture, race and nation. In its openness to such considerations of power, this approach challenges the social and cultural inequalities at the root of sexual hierarchies.

Contradictions: integration as separation

The liberal feminist strategy of integrating women in development shared with development institutions a general reluctance to situate the problems of women within a general context of social relations and systemic change. As a result integration came to mean small and separate projects for women, compartmentalized within development programmes, and the continued absence of women from priority development projects. Separate women's projects have provided planners with alibis to prove their commitment to basic needs without having to deal with the implications of treating women as equal agents in development. Women are still absent from the higher levels of planning. Restricted to a separate realm of women's projects, women's perspectives are kept from being heard at other levels of development. Abstracted from the situated, local level, women's concerns in development seem to evaporate.

An evaluation undertaken in 1987 of the United Nations Development Programme's mainstream (i.e., not specifically women-focused) projects illustrates this.[19] The report reviewed project evaluations undertaken in 1985–86, ten years after the beginning of the UN Decade for Women, with a view to assessing the way project evaluations address issues of women in development. Forty per cent of the sample did mention women in relation to income generating projects, but most often in relation to their traditional activities at the local level; no evaluation suggested improving the economic status of women in a way that would not reinforce the traditional division of labour. Sixty per cent of the sample remained silent about women. What was particularly striking about that group of projects was that all involved planning activities, such as creating and strengthening institutional mechanisms for project identification, policy formulation, implementation and monitoring. In other words, they were projects designed to strengthen the capacities of a country to determine the overall direction of its development. Women were completely absent from the process of setting national developmental priorities in national and sectoral development plans. This is the level at which crucial decisions about resource allocations are made, which fundamentally affect the impact of development upon people's lives.

Ironically, from the beginning, the liberal feminist language of integration has been based upon a separating out from the context of development of the category 'women' as a self-contained identity. This has lent itself to the bureaucratic process of labelling women reductively as a special and often undifferentiated category, isolating their concerns from the mainstream of development activities. Henrietta Moore has suggested that the failure of development policy for women has stemmed from this initial segregation, from seeing women as separate from men. The effect has been to ignore the importance of relations between men and women, as well as women's varying identities and development interests as farmers, labourers, householders, factory workers, merchants and so on.[20] Projects structured on the basis of oppositional constructs demand excessive deference to the cross-cultural relevance of women as a sociological category, with the result that women, seen as separate rather than central, have been added into the process of development at the margin.

This restrictive labelling of women isolates their concerns and compromises their development prospects, while providing inaccurate descriptions of their needs. Florence McCarthy's study of a rural development strategy in Bangladesh illustrates this process. The images of the target group, women, projected by the development establishment contrasted with the actual social situation of women in Bangladesh. In this setting, targeting women as a homogeneous group needing special treatment also excluded women from mainstream development activities. Worse, it provoked conflict, suspicion and jealousy between rural women and men, thereby eliminating the possibility of constructive project implementation.[21]

Contradictions: the limits of women

The analytical priority given to the category women – a category modelled on a white, western feminist experience and divorced from the social contexts and relations of class, ethnicity and race in which women are situated – has the epistemological effect of constraining the possibility of knowing. Third world women have suggested that the confrontational categories in which the western feminist project places questions of the relations between the sexes are not necessarily intelligible outside western contexts. Asoka Bandarage suggests that 'it must be recognised that the conjugal role relationship is not the central relationship for women in many of these [non-western, non-white] communities', and concludes that these women 'may be psychologically freer from men, especially their spouses, than their Western, middle-class counterparts'.[22]

This suggests that there has been a tendency in western feminism to employ oppositional categories in culturally disjunctive ways. Theorizing the sexual division of labour as a simple opposition of male and female interests presupposes a degree of sexual individuation that may not necessarily apply in different societies. Chandra Mohanty, in her discussion of the colonizing elements of western feminist scholarship, shows how this tendency to analyse 'sexual difference' in the form of a cross-culturally singular, monolithic notion of patriarchy or male dominance produces a reductive understanding of how gender subordination comes about in different contexts.[23] Like post-modernist feminists, third world feminists are questioning the oppositional logic at the root of a schism between women and men. They see as a problem the binary thinking that dictates western knowledge of sexual difference and the nature of gender identity. Politically, however, the positions of western postmodernist feminists and third world feminists are very different. Third world women have dismantled the fictive totality of the woman of western feminist discourse to reveal its rootedness in the specific identity of white western women. As Trinh T. Minh-ha points out:

> Just as *man* provides an example of how the part played by women has been ignored, undervalued, distorted, or omitted through the use of terminology presumed to be generic, *woman* more often than not reflects the subtle power of linguistic exclusion, for its set of referents rarely includes those relevant to Third World female persons.[24]

From this perspective, the application of feminism to development is merely another misleading humanism, projecting through its practice the experience of women's subordination and gendered identity in the West. As Lorraine Code shows, such epistemological assumptions have far reaching effects in precluding possibilities of adequately accounting for women's social experiences. They represent what she calls 'epistemic indolence'.[25] The problem is pinpointed by Gayatri Chakravorti Spivak when she suggests that 'in order to learn . . . about Third World women . . . the immense heterogeneity of the field must be appreciated, and the First World feminist must learn to stop feeling privileged *as a woman*'.[26]

Some of the difficulties with the analytical certainties and assumptions of western feminism as applied to women in development are evident in the implications of the use of the feminization of agriculture thesis, mentioned earlier. In the context of the crisis in simple commodity production in many LDCs, and particularly in Africa, this thesis has been seized upon by many women's organizations and women's bureaux within development agencies as a tidy way of conceptualizing both the urgency of the crisis in subsistence agriculture and the instrumentality of policy intervention for women. But use of this thesis tends to replicate by a simple inversion those habits of thought that may have helped produce the invisibility of women farmers and their exclusion from policy in the first place. Again, oppositional logic is invoked which depends for its coherence upon the homogeneity of an already constituted group (women), whose experience of oppression is understood to stem from gender difference. Power divisions are then characterized as fundamental, undifferentiated and unilateral: there are oppressors who oppress victims. This produces as limiting and rigid a picture of the oppressor as it does of the victim. It thus loses such essential distinctions for politics as those between individual and structure, ideas and actions. Women are constituted as a group via dependency relations on men who as a group are implicitly and permanently held responsible for these relationships. This precludes an analysis of specific historical circumstances that structure oppressive differences.

An emphasis on the feminization of agriculture imposes a gender definition on a problem which is not necessarily gender related, thus obscuring the need for structural change and scrutiny of the role of, for example, the state in inhibiting the emergence of a more dynamic agricultural sector. The exclusive identification of the work of women with subsistence and reproduction has the effect, at least within development agencies, of associating women with low productivity, backward attitudes – even fatalism – just as it associates men with the parasitic urban sector. This derides the importance of the many means women and men have devised of coping with their survival problems. It also obscures the extent to which women have become involved in other sectors of the economy. Moreover, positing so radical a schism in the sexual division of labour tends, as noted earlier, to set the interests of men and women in stark opposition. At the resource allocation level of development agencies, the perception that the resources devoted to women must be subtracted from men constrains planners to make zero-sum choices. It sets up an artificial competition between women and men in an area where their interests are inextricably intertwined: the common concern of structuring the household in such a way as to ensure survival and subsistence. Further, in abstracting women's agricultural activities from the household, this assumption produces a misleading idea of the range of decision making open to women.

Difference: the contemporary feminist response

Third world women have accused first world and western-trained feminists of exercising a certain cultural colonialism, of misrepresenting different women by homogenizing the experiences and conditions of western women across time and culture. Chakravorty Spivak has shown that western women are 'complicitous' in contributing to the continued 'degradation' of third world women whose micrology they interpret without having access to it.[27] Monica Lazreg, exploring 'the perils of writing as a woman on women in Algeria' suggests that third world women have been *produced* as a field of knowledge, essentializing their difference in a process that represents a 'caricature of the feminist project'.[28] Black feminists have accused white feminists of adding on difference at the margin 'without leaving the comforts of home' so as to support 'the seeming homogeneity, stability, and self-evidence of its experience-based epistemology'.[29] Trinh T. Minh-ha identifies this neutralized difference as 'the very kind of colonised-anthropo-logised difference the master has always granted his subordinates'.[30] Audre Lorde's response to the universalized picture of oppression in Mary Daly's *Gyn/Ecology* reproaches her for failing

> to recognise that, as women . . . differences expose all women to various forms and degrees of patriarchal oppression, some of which we share, some of which we do not . . . The oppression of women knows no ethnic nor racial boundaries, true, but that does not mean that it is identical within those boundaries . . . to imply . . . that all women suffer the same oppression simply because we are women is to lose sight of the many varied tools of patriarchy. It is to ignore how these tools are used by women without awareness against each other.[31]

These statements amount to descriptions of an epistemologically totalizing and culturally disruptive feminism. And to the extent that feminist theory's claim to relevance is based upon its claim to represent the meaning of women's social experience in all its heterogeneity, these critiques point to some fundamental problems. The original consciousness raising approach of traditional feminism – what Catherine MacKinnon has called its critical method[32] – involved a project of theorizing the collective expression of women's experiences and understanding the meaning of those experiences of subordination as expressions of the social constitution of sexed identities. This was informed by a political understanding that gender was not an inalienable description of human reality; an understanding derived from the insights of a traditional feminist ideology whose analysis of the political meaning of experience was concerned with deconstructing the legitimating surface of women's oppression.

Theorizing the social construction of subjectivity produced an understand-ing of the mechanisms of sexist oppression. In practice, and as seen above, particularly in the context of WID practice, that collective critical reconstitution of women's experiences in traditional feminist movements has tended to reproduce the situational consciousness of the white, bourgeois, heterosexual feminist, developing a set of certainties structured around that specific subjectivity. Such certainties in liberal or Marxist feminist ideologies tended to inform the cross-cultural investigations of sexual subordination, producing a certain myopia with respect to the details of sexual subordination in different societies. The failure to guide practice with reference to the processes that shape human perceptions and norms promoted the disintegration of feminist pronouncements on women in development into a norm setting activity by a counter-elite.

If feminism is to have any impact as a political strategy, it must be able to find appropriate ways of knowing women's experiences and the structures that shape them; further, it must develop theoretical accounts of knowledge which retain continuity with those experiences. The experience and status of women in development is an issue for feminism internationally. At the same time, the disjunctions resulting from western feminist assumptions about the nature of women and the source of their oppression represent a serious challenge for feminism.

The issue of difference among women has changed the traditional feminist preoccupation with the differences between men and women. The earlier politics tended to be in tension over the issue of equality – involving both the elevation of women to the material and cultural status of men and fundamental change in the foundational social structures from which sexual asymmetry emerges in order to eradicate the male–female difference. The tension between the two roughly coincides with the political concerns of the ideological poles – liberal or Marxist – within feminism.

'Difference' has introduced a new tension upon which the contemporary feminist response cannot be mapped in any simple way. Broadly, though, this crucial question of the status that different women's experiences are to have in theory is answered along two lines. One group of feminists, sometimes called cultural feminists, take a position of respectful diversity; all women's experiences are affirmed and valorized in a new identity politics. The other group, often represented by, but not at all limited to, French feminists, emphasize the radical historical specificity, hence contestability, of every claim to knowledge stemming from particular experiences or identities.[33] Politically, the first approach often results in an ineffectual essentialism and separatism. The other produces an equally ineffectual position of endless deferral of epistemic responsibility, with a deconstructionist degendering of ontology which renders the need and even the possibility of a feminist politics problematic. The difficulty the movement has had in effectively accommodating diversity has left those feminist activists who are concerned to take action against oppression bereft of guidance which might help them avoid a reversion to universalizing assumptions.

Culturally essentialized knowledge: political separatism

If so much power lay in naming, then feminists set out to claim for themselves the capacity to name. In a sense, the identity politics of cultural feminism takes the consciousness raising project to a logical conclusion, deeply into the field of self-analysis and individualization. But this focus upon consolidating and expressing a personal and group identity resulted in the building of political refuges. These may have been islands of validation and self-affirmation, but they were islands all the same. They were separated by the seas of a newly individualized politics which tended to strand analyses concerned to uncover the interconnecting channels of power systems to which a feminist activism must be addressed. In effect, the political has come to be reduced to the personal, instead of being distilled from the personal towards a critical understanding of how structures of power construct difference. In other words, if the process of generalizing beyond the particular is made secondary to the valorization of personal experience, then the project of understanding how oppression is constituted as a system, and of locating the place where oppressions interconnect, and of facing our own implication in certain systems of oppression, is abandoned. Oppression comes to be seen as a dynamic between individuals. In the end, no politically useful under-standing of how difference is constructed emerges.

From this perspective, feminine subjectivities are held to be somehow innate. Consciousness raising, at its extreme, comes to a halt at each separate female identity, engaging in a process of revision only to include new subjectivities, essentializing difference and producing a highly relativist view of knowledge.[34] This respect for diversity also requires that all experiences of oppression be weighted equally. But an equalized notion of oppression leaves us without a way of thinking about justice or politics that can be applied to specific contexts. It leaves no core around which to act politically as feminists, in coalitions that might traverse national boundaries and limited identities. An example of what I mean by this is the dilemma faced by non-Israeli Jewish feminists upon the invasion of Lebanon by Israel in 1982. Was there a feminist position to be taken on the dispossession of the Palestinians which would not be seen as a threat to Jewish identity? Jenny Bourne, in her sensitive discussion of this issue, shows how identity politics in this case demanded an equality of positioning, an equating of the oppressions of anti-Semitism and imperialist racism, resulting in fragmentation in the women's movement and a muffling of critical inquiry.[35] The links between oppressions were ignored. According to Bourne, non-Zionist Jewish feminists such as Elly Bulkin could support both the Palestinian and the Jewish national movements, without considering that one was produced by the other, that one exists to oppose the other.[36] The same issues apply to western feminists in relation to the imperialist adventures of their own governments, their discriminatory trade practices, their environmentally unsound industrial practices, or the fact that in the west, women consumers help sustain sweatshop production lines from

Mexico to the Pacific Rim. The protective cloak of identity provides a way of denying connection.

Cultural feminists posit relatively unproblematic identities or subjectivities; but in so doing they cannot penetrate those mechanisms of oppressive power that sustain the perceived autonomy of the subject. So women are mystified within sealed categories of difference in a process that prevents questions being asked about the power dimensions of domination, exploitation, or marginalization. This purely experiential epistemology posits the existence of a more or less unproblematic reality – which is what feminist ideology has traditionally denied in refusing to grant undue authority to cultural traditions that sustain sexist oppression. Predicated on the understanding that experience may not necessarily reveal the truth of social relations, feminist ideology has always argued that the fact that women may accept oppression does not make oppression acceptable if women have little choice of roles in a male universe.

'Relativism', says Donna Haraway in her brilliant essay on the politics of location, 'is a way of saying nothing while claiming to be everywhere equally'.[37] The epistemological position of the cultural feminists is expressed politically in a permissive heterogeneity which sanctions a sterile separatism. In practice, it retreats from providing feminism with any viable claim with which to challenge the domination of male values in the world. What it produces instead, on the basis of the irreducible diversity of women, is a rigid differentiation of outlooks between authenticated female viewpoints. This limits the possibility of pursuing the intellectual challenge posed by feminism to existing models of social organization, and by third world and other subaltern groups of women to established feminist theory. In practice it is expressed as a weak pluralism, what Michele Barrett has called 'the lowest common denominator of feminism', which 'does not necessarily strengthen feminism in relation to the world in general'.[38] This is the spirit of the approach which came to dominate the international conferences of the United Nations Decade for Women, to quiet the competing claims of different feminisms.[39] Can this sort of pluralism ever seriously challenge those development practices which disproportionately disadvantage women? There is a fine divide between diversity and fragmentation, and it is a divide that can be widened by development planners who feel unwilling to accommodate women's concerns. The apparatus of domination has always been able to benefit from maximum differentiation. It can accommodate – and has done, as the history of WID has shown – separate spaces for potentially divisive differences much more easily than it can stomach a genuine inclusion of difference.

The impossibility of knowledge: political paralysis

Cultural feminists have been grappling with a contradiction inherent to feminism. On the one hand they have a theoretical project that identifies concepts and categories as problems in order to dismantle the certainties of western universalist thought, and on the other a political project which must assume unified terms (such as a coherent category of women) in order to justify action. In providing a reminder of this in-built contradiction, deconstruction warns against a feminism that re-invokes the monolithic knowledge and the power mechanisms of oppression. There is no post-modernist or deconstructive feminism as such. The positions taken by feminists who have borrowed techniques from deconstruction, in particular, vary and conflict.[40] Some of these feminists, such as Julia Kristeva, Jane Flax or Gayatri Chakravorty Spivak, have followed Jacques Derrida in applying the post-structuralist insight as to the positional (as opposed to absolute) construction of meaning to the dismantling of the claims of western foundationalist thought. This approach, when applied to the feminist concern to theorize the socially constructed meaning of women's experiences, reminds us that knowledge is always mediated by the knower's location in a determinate socio-political formation. Every account of truth, then, is idiosyncratic. Every claim to know privileges the ethnocentric and confirms the prejudices that give advantage to the knower. Every person claiming the capacity rationally to know is thus engaging in a self-flattering delusion; the possibility of knowing is infinitely postponed in a plural play of difference. Because of this, every account of the world is a construct, a narration, a fiction and hence each account is as worthy or true as its critique.

When the female subject – a product of humanist discourses of culture and ideology beyond individual control – is dismantled, female identity is revealed as a shifting social construct, with no epistemologically significant ontology. With neither sexuality nor social identity a biological given, the very possibility of female identity, which is romanticized in cultural feminism, is rendered problematical by the deconstruction of both the concept 'women' and the oppositional logic from which it is constructed. Inevitably, this process moves from the deconstruction of the category 'women' as opposed to men to a deconstruction of the identity of woman. Unhampered by a falsely unified idea of gender identity formulated either by patriarchy or cultural feminism, the identity of woman dissolves into a plurality of differences.

But if the category 'woman' is a fiction, the progressive peeling away of ideological and cultural veneers ultimately reduces the subject to a blank space, devoid of intentionality, making a feminist consciousness a constructed self-indulgence. Woman is caught in an abyss of negativity, deconstructing herself into a void. As Kristeva writes of the sign 'woman':

> A woman cannot be; it is something which does not even belong in the order of being. It follows that a feminist practice can only be negative, at odds with what already exists so that we may say 'that is not it', and 'that is still not it'. . . . In 'woman' I see something that cannot be represented.[41]

If the category 'woman' is fundamentally indeterminate, no positive conception of it is immune to deconstruction. This negation of the authority of the female subject renders futile any feminist theory with ambitions either to refute the distortions of androcentrism or to posit the rational availability of an alternative world order less oppressive to women (and men) because it is based on a more positive conception of female identity. In other words, if gender or race or class are constructs with no essential core to liberate they are incapable of validating conceptions of justice or alternative truths. Therefore, feminists must abandon any claim to know better constructed out of an understanding of the meaning of female experience. Not only that, they must abandon any claim to know at all, except in the most immediate and provisional of senses.

The positing of alternatives presupposes the ability to think outside our inherited structures of thought and consciousness, something which is impossible in deconstruction:

> The movements of deconstruction do not destroy structures from the outside . . . Operating necessarily from the inside, borrowing all the strategic and economic resources of subversion from the old structure, borrowing them structurally, that is to say, without being able to isolate their elements and atoms, the enterprise of deconstruction always, in a certain way, falls prey to its own work.[42]

In order to propose alternatives, one must employ the oppositional logic that denigrates alternatives; the very thinking that deconstructs structures of oppression reconstitutes them. Since there is no way to avoid this, the critic is required to do the next best thing: to engage in a process of continuous, interminable and essentially non-progressive dismantling of oppressive structures from a non-committal position of indeterminacy. The constraints of theorizing within existing structures have, as we have seen, been a problem for feminism. It has found itself replaying that same old story where dominating generalizations masquerade as neutrals. The roots of feminism's humanist heritage run very deep. The seductions of authenticity, essential truths and universals are such that one meta-narrative more often than not gets replaced with another.

The Derridean undermining of metaphysics through a textual strategy guided by the critic's indeterminacy evades the 'metaphysical nature of taking a yes-or-no position' by writing itself into an abyss of infinite deferral.[43] For feminists concerned with the political issues and imperatives for action created by the urgent problems of women in development, it is unacceptable, even irresponsible, to postpone the authority of the investigating subject in an infinite regression of backpedalling disclaimers. Feminists writing from the perspective of third world women, such as Lazreg, have claimed that such a position betrays a morally suspect conservatism: 'To subscribe to the notion that the metaphysics of difference-as-misrepresentation is inescapable is self-defeating and betrays resistance to changing the intellectual status quo', allowing feminists to dispense with 'an ethics of responsibility when writing about "different" women'.[44] It also indefinitely postpones the possibility of communication, of learning to see and know from a different perspective.

Biddy Martin and Chandra Talpade Mohanty suggest that the privilege of the critic's indeterminacy masks self-paralysing guilt or defensiveness, which are the wrong reasons for wishing to avoid implication in a (totalizing, culturally imperious) 'bad feminism'. They go on to maintain that while the feminist anti-humanist critique of 'man' and absolute knowledge must be pursued,

> it is equally important to point out the political limitations of an insistence on 'indeterminacy' which implicitly, when not explicitly, denies the critic's own situatedness in the social, and in effect refuses to acknowledge the critic's own institutional home.[45]

The post-modernist refusal to validate the subjective experience of specificity not only cripples the capacity to analyse change or theorize resistance; it also indicates a disingenuous reluctance to acknowledge that it is impossible for a specific, situated critic to be indeterminate. Likewise, the reduction of the world to text – of life to language – allows us to forget that, for feminists, some accounts are more vitally true than others. Are we to treat a battered wife's story as the moral equivalent to that of her husband? Or is the woman from Burkina Faso's claim to be largely responsible for food production on her family farm no more valid than the FAO policy document which targets agricultural inputs to men on the assumption that all farmers are men? Feminist politics must establish some minimalist, but objective, grounds on which to distinguish between the truth and falsity of divergent interpretations of the world.

Partial knowing: the politics of location and coalition

How can we start to see, responsibly and respectfully, from another's point of view, and yet at the same time find answers for an active feminism determined to make a difference? Political action requires that we find more stable ground for our assertions, which will not be lost every time we make an ideologically correct leap of faith. The question remains *how* do we know what we claim to know?

This question has been closely explored by feminists in relation to knowledge claims in the hard and objective world of science. Sandra Harding outlines three models for a feminist theory of knowledge as they surface in contemporary feminist practice: feminist empiricism, feminist standpoint theories and feminist post-modernism.[46] They can be seen to parallel, loosely, the feminist discussions in relation to difference as I have outlined them. Loosely, then, the feminist empiricist who accepts the tenets of philosophical realism and maintains that sexism is an identifiable, excisable, individual or institutional bias, parallels the liberal feminist's faith that legal and institutional reform will open up more space for women in the dominant project of western culture. The feminist standpoint theory is more attuned to the ideological dimensions of knowledge and to the social construction of each knower. Yet it claims that there is a distinct women's perspective to be discovered under the thick carapace of constructivism, offering a truth superior to men's truth. This shares in the perspective of cultural feminists who celebrate a proliferation of standpoints. It is also the perspective of radical feminists who champion women's superior access to truth, stemming from some innate identity and experience common to all women. Harding sees this perspective as the foundation for a 'successor science' of an alternative, better knowledge. Post-modernist feminism, as seen above, is sceptical of the very notion of truth, and casts doubt on the concept of an integral knower, or truth telling agent.

The empiricist position, as seen in relation to the liberal feminist project of integrating women in development, is committed to untenable beliefs about the process of knowing, basing it upon untested standards of objectivity. The standpoint and post-modern positions are in contradiction, yet both are attractive. We all feel drawn to common sense versions of identity, of home, of making personal meaning out of our experiences. At the same time our feminist commitment compels us to unpick the seamless fabric of the dominant paradigms that oppress us – but in a process that ultimately disrupts the firmness of our own identities. Harding, unsatisfactorily, resolves the tension by recommending that feminists simply reconcile themselves to this contradiction and pursue both projects in tandem, for each requires the success of the other:

> for an adequate successor science will have to be grounded on the resources provided by differences in women's social experiences and emancipatory political projects; and an effective deconstruction of our culture's powerful science requires an equally powerful solidarity *against* regressive and mystifying modernist forces.[47]

In this the radicalism of the feminist critique is attenuated with depoliticizing theoretical paradigms. It does not give us enough ground to stand on. We need to think beyond these tensions. Perhaps in the process of finding a new metaphor we would do well to remember that the field is defined by an urgent political project, not by a method or a stance. Bernice Johnson Reagan, in her discussion of the future of feminist politics, identifies precisely this urgency as the basis for cross-cultural coalitions. The reason to learn from another's perspective arises from the need to survive, not from a commiseration in oppression or a flaccid, fragmented notion of sisterhood.[48]

Successful coalitions are built upon both the strength of numbers – where one of the potential strengths of women has always resided – and on the fact that members always have some home beyond the coalition from which to draw self-affirming sustenance. The transition from the closed version of 'women' to the open exchange with other versions requires that we self-consciously place in the foreground those locations from which we claim to know, remaining all the while acutely aware of our partiality. It is not enough for us to choose our own names which others cannot pronounce. We have to agree to a process of mutual naming, a process which will forbid the romanticization of partial perspectives, and which may help some of us see where we collude in the oppression of other women. The liberal feminist experience with development policy has taught that differences cannot be codified through the naturalization of a single category of women taken to have cross-cultural validity; this form of dominance politics has fragmented women's symbolic environments without offering a culturally meaningful alternative.

Coalition building inevitably draws us into compromise. It can mean the temporary subsuming of one oppression in the interests of addressing a greater need elsewhere. This does not have to mean a loss of identity, though it does mean that the importance of difference will have to vary according to its source; oppressions cannot continue to be equated across the board. But how to gauge the urgency and truth for feminism of competing claims? First, there is a need for a more rigorously materialist analysis to point to the consequences and inter-relations of different sites of oppression: class, race, nation and sexuality. Second, each claim to knowledge must be recognized, and must recognize itself, as partial, situated and local. At the same time each must be open to revision. In this sort of context, it will be impossible to claim an abstract objectivity for knowledge; each claim will be understood to be embodied, to represent a partial knowing in which the knower consciously takes responsibility for her claims and her enabling practices. Embodied objectivity opens itself up to continual testing in relation to other knowing positions. And it is precisely because of the knower's partiality that she will be able to see with others without claiming to be them, or forcing them to see her way. This sounds like an impossibly unstable concept of feminist consciousness – as a self-contradictory and continually shifting, re-anchoring identity. But it is a process necessary to the project of reshaping what and how we know. As Zillah Eisenstein has asserted, it is precisely through this continually shifting, uncentred approach that feminism can most deeply challenge existing structures.[49]

Identity, recognized always as a construction, provides a point of departure for a political theory premised on the material identity of the theorist. Linda Alcoff shows, borrowing from the deconstructive emphasis on placement, that this identity is relational. Awareness of this positionality allows women to make the feminist transition from understanding their position as a locus of determined values, to using their specific perspective – with its awareness and interplay of difference – to interpret and construct values. The epistemological claims that emerge are contextually elaborated.[50] Coalition politics of this sort struggles to eliminate the elements of centre, unity and totality that organize structures into hierarchical oppositions. It also allows for the fact that women experience simultaneously many oppressions and must engage in a multitude of struggles that conflict and supplement each other. Thus while certain issues of sexist oppression may unite women cross-culturally, women of different nations within these broad alliances may be involved in struggles for racial justice or national liberation in which they will have to confront women from oppressor nations. Or third world women may struggle for freedom from personal oppression within the family while at the same time engaging in a common project with their menfolk to protect the integrity of their traditional economies.

In order for power-aware conversations which build coalitions to take place at all, we need to develop a meaning for objectivity that can encompass mutuality and exchange, rather than the logic of a dominant, single namer. Our partial perspectives require that we respect all objects of knowledge as agents and participants in the production of knowledge. Objectivity can no longer be the exercise of switching on a spotlight to flood a pre-chosen object in a singular light. Rather, it is a risky mutual engagement with the unknown, in which participants themselves stand to be changed. Agency in the creation of knowledge includes all of life; the environment too is an active, interacting, knowledge creating subject, not a resource to be colonized. The project of partial knowing entails an activation of categories of knowledge previously ignored or forced into submission: categories at the far end of distinctions such as reason/desire, male/female, culture/nature, centre/periphery.

The vision of diffused feminist struggles in which the complexity of oppression wins out over the dichotomy of victims and oppressors is being expressed in the emergent strategies of some third world feminists. Both the empowerment approach to WID and the theorizing of this approach by the DAWN collective address the multiple oppressions with which women must engage by virtue of their different positions in sexist, racist and imperialist conflicts. Those structures of power must be confronted with alternative values. The crises of survival these women face call for yes or no positions, to challenge the power structures within which they are caught while acknow-ledging the contextual and subjective specificity of those positions. This perspective has not yet been fully theorized. It is not entirely clear that it will not in practice revert to the multiple essentialisms of cultural feminism. One problem is that in its emphasis on the importance of self-reliance and its rejection of the IMF's conditionality clauses, DAWN does not bring itself to address fully the difficult development choices that face countries in radical financial crises and deepening resource constraints. There is an uncritical tendency to assume that women can deliver ecologically sound and fair development, with no analysis of the constraints that cramp all development initiatives, or of the power dimensions of change.

The position of the DAWN group does, however, offer a more culturally meaningful approach to the questions of difference in feminism. It suggests that if feminist theory is to avoid the epistemologically destructive attempt to understand the experience of women in development in terms of western models, this investigation must be scrupulously self-critical. The analysis of women's experience of development must also be used to reveal the presuppositions of western feminist thought. To engage with difference without diminishing it, we need to insist on a commitment to inclusiveness. We need to submit to a continual questioning of our own positions and claims. And we need to be guided in our coalitions by the questions of survival which women face at various historical moments according to the meanings that are attached to gender, race, class, sexuality, creed and nation. It *is* a relief to have torn off the heavily tinted lenses that gave us such a monochromatic picture of patriarchy and women's oppression, and to see them now in a plural play of light. We are more attuned now to nuance, but this advantage should not require us to sacrifice the possibility of knowing better about women's lived realities.

Notes

A series of conversations with Teresa Brennan wove themselves in and around the process of writing this, and I am grateful to her for her inspiration, as well as her valued advice on an earlier draft. Special thanks to Charles Turner for generosity with his time, his patience in reading the draft, and his careful comments. Also to Janet McCay, for those conversations in and on solidarity.

1 My use of descriptive terms such as 'third world women' or 'western women' is essentially inadequate, because these categories fail to contest and indeed, reinforce, reductive similarities between and among women from countries labelled industrialized or less developed, and also leave undisturbed the discursive and political stability of the First/Third World divide. They are used for lack of an adequate alternative, but at the least I will be dropping the capital letters – to suggest a questioning of the validity of these terms; they are used critically throughout. These terms have come, in the literature on women in development (WID), to be labels that obscure too much. Chandra Mohanty, in 'Under Western eyes: feminist scholarship and colonial discourses', *Feminist Review* (No. 30, Autumn 1988) provides a thorough critique of the way in which white western academic feminists have discursively colonized the material and historical heterogeneities of the lives of women in the third world, thereby producing/ reproducing through the term 'Third World women' a composite, singular, oppressed, object for analysis.

2 See Jessica Bernard's discussion of the reaction of third world women to approaches to women in development as expressed in the international forum of the UN Decade for Women, in *The Female World from a Global Perspective* (Bloomington, IN: Indiana University Press, 1987), Chapter 6. See also Nawal el Saadawi, Fatima Mernissi and Mallica Vajarathon's 'A critical look at the Wellesley Conference', in *Quest* (Vol. 4, No. 2, Winter 1978). For some critiques from third world and non-white women of the western feminist scholarship in relation to women in development see Gita Sen and Caren Grown, *Development, Crises, and Alternative Visions* (New York: Monthly Review Press, 1987); Asoka Bandarage, 'Third World women: more than mere statistics', in *Women's Review of Books* (November 1983); Monica Lazreg, 'Feminism and difference: the perils of writing as a woman on women in Algeria', in *Feminist Studies* (Vol. 14, No. 1, Spring 1988).

3 I am using the term 'difference' here as it bears upon issues of race, class, ethnic, national and cultural difference *between* women, and will also be addressing the

question of difference *within* the concept of 'woman'. I will not be looking at this issue as it has been dealt with by feminist psychoanalysis in addressing questions of sexual difference and differentiation – although it also bears importantly upon the issue of women in development as regards the debate over gender constitution. Representative texts on sexual differentiation in this area are Juliet Mitchell, *Psychoanalysis and Feminism* (Harmondsworth: Penguin, 1974); and Nancy Chodrow, *The Reproduction of Mothering: Psychoanalysis and the Sociology of Gender* (Berkeley, CA: University of California Press, 1978). The works of Jacques Lacan and Julia Kristeva have dominated this field in the 1980s.

4 The disjunctions consequent on the impositions of western feminist epistemological assumptions on non-western contexts are not the only reasons feminist theorists are re-exploring epistemological issues. Others stem from, for example, the need to defend feminist scholarship from marginalization in the dominant academic disciplines, or from the ongoing need to demonstrate the distinction between knowledge and prejudice in the rooting out of pervasive androcentrism in the definition of intellectual problems, and so on. See Mary E. Hawkesworth's careful discussion of the revival of feminist interest in epistemology in 'Knowers, knowing, known: feminist theory and claims of truth', in *Signs: Journal of Women in Culture and Society* (Spring 1989).

5 Development Dialogue, *Another Development with Women*, Special Issue, 1982.

6 For a more detailed description and analysis of this project's implementation history, see A.M. Goetz, 'Fish-smokers in Guinea: directions for a feminist critique of development policy formulation for women', paper presented to the Canadian Annual Africa Scholars Meeting, Kingston, Ontario, May 1988.

7 Kathleen Staudt, 'Bureaucratic resistance to women's programmes: the case of women in development', in E. Bonepath (ed.), *Women, Power and Politics* (New York: Pergamon Press, 1982) takes this question much further in examining how power structures in policy making within bureaucracies filter out the sophistications of research. Her point is taken further in her in-depth discussion of the fate of WID policy within the US Agency for International Development in Kathleen Staudt, *Women, Foreign Assistance, and Advocacy Administration* (New York: Praeger Special Studies, 1985).

8 Ester Boserup, *Women's Role in Economic Development* (London: George Allen and Unwin, 1970). Following Boserup, a great deal of research now documents the sexual division of labour in different production contexts, and the differential effect of modernization upon women and men. Some examples of work in this area include: Mona Etienne and Elanore Leacock (eds), *Women and Colonisation* (New York: Praeger, 1980); the essays collected in Wellesley Editorial Committee, *Women in National Development* (Chicago, IL: University of Chicago Press, 1977); Irene Palmer, 'Rural women and the basic needs approach to development', in *International Labour Review* (Vol. 115, No. 1, Jan.–Feb. 1977).

9 Examples include T.A. Abdullah and S.A. Zeidenstein, *Village Women of Bangladesh: Prospects for change* (Oxford: Pergamon Press, 1982); Irene Palmer, 'Women and green revolutions', paper presented at the conference on the Continuing Subordination of Women and the Development Process, Sussex, IDS, 1978.

10 Examples include G. Cochrane, *The Cultural Appraisal of Development Projects* (New York: Praeger, 1979); Guy Standing, *Labour Force Participation in Development* (Geneva: ILO, 1978); Meena Acharya and Lyn Bennett, *Women and the Subsistence Sector: Economic Participation and Household Decision Making*

in Nepal (Washington, DC: World Bank, 1982); Barbara Wolfe and Jere Behreman, 'Is income overrated in determining adequate nutrition?', in *Economic Development and Cultural Change* (Vol. 31, No. 3, 1983).

11 Examples include Bina Agarwal, *Agricultural Modernisation and Third World Women: Pointers from the Literature and an Empirical Analysis* (Geneva: ILO, 1981); Lourdes Beneria, 'Conceptualising the labour force: the underestimation of women's economic activities', in Nicky Nelson (ed.), *African Women in the Development Process* (London: Frank Cass, 1981); L. Goldschmidt-Clermont, *Unpaid Work in the Household: A Review of Economic Valuation Methods* (Geneva: ILO, 1982); ILO, *Women in the Economic Activities of the World: A Statistical Analysis* (Geneva: ILO, 1980).

12 Examples include Tim Dyson and Mick Moore, 'On kinship structure, female autonomy, and demographic behaviour in India', in *Population and Development Review* (Vol. 9, No. 1, 1983); P. Bardhan, 'On life and death questions', in *Economic and Political Weekly* (Vol. 9, Special Number, 1974); Amartya K. Sen and Joselyn Kynch, 'Indian women, well-being and survival', in *Cambridge Journal of Economics* (Vol. 7, 1983); Amartya K. Sen and S. Sengupta, 'Malnutrition of rural children and the sex bias', in *Economic and Political Weekly* (Vol. 18, Annual Number, 1983).

13 A clear exposition of the bargaining approach to resolving cooperative conflicts within the household is provided by Amartya K. Sen in Essay 16, 'Economics and the family' in Sen, *Resources, Values, and Development* (Oxford: Basil Blackwell, 1984); and also in Sen, *Women, Technology, and Sexual Divisions* (New York: UNTCD and INSTRAW, 1985).

14 See Palmer, *op. cit.*

15 The feminization of agriculture thesis is outlined in, among others: Irene Tinker, *New Technologies for Food Chain Activities: The Imperative of Equity for Women* (Washington, DC, Office of Women in Development: USAID, 1979); and S. Mautemba, 'Women as food producers and suppliers in the twentieth century: the case of Zambia', in *Development Dialogue* (1982).

16 Mayra Buvinic, Margaret Lycette and William McGreevy, *Women and Poverty in the Third World* (Baltimore, MD: Johns Hopkins University Press, 1983).

17 See Caroline Moser, Chapter 7 in this volume.

18 Gita Sen and Caren Grown present the perspectives and approaches of the DAWN collective in *Development, Crises, and Alternative Visions, op. cit.*

19 UNDP, *Women in UNDP-Supported Projects: A Review of how UNDP Evaluations deal with Gender Issues* (New York: UNDP Central Evaluation Office, 1987).

20 Henrietta Moore, 'Women and development issues', Lecture in the Women and Society series, Social and Political Sciences Committee, Cambridge University, February 1988.

21 Florence McCarthy, 'The target group: women in rural Bangladesh', in E. Clay and B. Schaffer (eds), *Room for Manoeuvre: An Exploration of Public Policy for Rural Development* (London: Heinemann and Grower, 1984).

22 Asoka Bandarage, 'Toward international feminism', in *Brandeis Review* (Vol. 3, Summer 1983), pp. 8–9.

23 Mohanty, *op. cit.*

24 Trinh T. Minh-ha, 'Difference: a special Third World issue', in *Feminist Review* (No. 25, March 1987), p. 16.

25 Lorraine Code, 'Experience, knowledge, and responsibility', in Morwenna Griffiths and Margaret Whitford (eds), *Feminist Perspectives in Philosophy* (London: Macmillan Press, 1988), p. 191.

26 Gayatri Chakravorty Spivak, 'French feminism in an international frame', in Spivak, *In Other Worlds* (New York: Methuen, 1987), p.136.

27 Gayatri Chakravorty Spivak, quoted in Lazreg, *op. cit.*, p. 89.

28 Lazreg, *op. cit.*, pp. 85–6, 97.

29 Biddy Martin and Chandra Talpade Mohanty, 'Feminist politics: what's home got to do with it?', in Teresa de Lauretis (ed.), *Feminist Studies/Critical Studies* (London: Macmillan Press, 1986), p. 193.

30 Minh-ha, *op. cit.*, p. 19.

31 Audre Lorde, 'An open letter to Mary Daly', in Cherrie Moraga and Gloria Anzaldua (eds), *This Bridge Called my Back – Writings by Radical Women of Colour* (New York: Kitchen Table, 1983), pp. 95, 97. Other writings which critique an essentialism based on the essence of a white, heterosexual, western women's experience include the three essays in: Ely Bulkin, Minnie Bruce Pratt, Barbara Smith, *Yours in Struggle: Three Feminist Perspectives on Anti-Semitism and Racism* (New York: Long Haul Press, 1984).

32 Catherine MacKinnon, 'Feminism, Marxism, method and the state: an agenda for theory', in *Signs: Journal of Women in Culture and Society* (Vol. 7, No. 3, 1982).

33 Examples of cultural feminists might include the feminists listed in n. 31. French feminists include Julia Kristeva, Helene Cixous and Luce Irigary. But this post-modernist approach certainly extends beyond that nation, and other examples would include Jane Flax or Gayatri Chakravorty Spivak.

34 For a critique of this aspect of cultural feminism, see Alice Echols, 'The new feminism of yin and yang', in Ann Snitow, Christine Stansell and Sharon Thompson (eds), *Powers of Desire: The Politics of Sexuality* (New York: Monthly Review Press, 1983).

35 Jenny Bourne, 'Homelands of the mind: Jewish feminism and identity politics', in *Race and Class* (Vol. 29, No. 1, Summer 1987).

36 *Ibid.*, p. 8.

37 Donna Haraway, 'Situated knowledges: the science question in feminism and the privilege of partial perspective', in *Feminist Studies* (Vol. 14, No. 3, Fall 1988), p. 584.

38 Michele Barrett, 'The concept of "difference"', in *Feminist Review* (No. 26, July 1987), p. 32.

39 Irene Tinker and Jane Jaquette, 'UN Decade for Women: its impact and legacy', in *World Development* (Vol. 5, No. 3, 1987).

40 Analyses of the uses and limitations of deconstruction and poststructuralism for feminist theory and politics include Teresa de Lauretis, *Alice Doesn't: Feminism, Semiotics and Cinema* (Bloomington, IN: Indiana University Press, 1984); Biddy Martin, 'Feminism, criticism and Foucault', in *New German Critique* (No. 22, Fall 1982); Alice Jardine, *Gynesis: Configurations of Woman and Modernity* (Ithaca, NY: Cornell University Press, 1985). I have not found it helpful to explore the French feminist school in this essay as I will be concentrating less on deconstruction's recuperative project than on its approach to demystifying western metaphysics. French feminists have focused on the semiotic and linguistic elements of Derridean analytic strategies to try to reconstitute that 'in-between' mode of speech which Derrida describes as *feminine* discourse; that which might have come before the dominant male symbolic economy. This quest for origins, developing a language of the female body, encourages a politically problematic biologism and essentialism. It is also a dead end street for analysis as the presumption of an authoritative grasp of reality through the body, or a female intuition, results in a theoretical monism that admits of no further elaboration or explication – there are no standards beyond the body upon which to weigh claims.

Gayatri Chakravorty Spivak, in her essay 'French feminism in an international frame' (in Spivak, *op. cit.*) discusses the implications of this approach with respect to some of the questions at issue here in her critique of Julia Kristeva's *About Chinese Women*, translated by Anita Baroows (London: Marion Boyars, 1977).

41 Julia Kristeva, 'Woman can never be defined', in Elaine Marks and Isabelle de Courtivron (eds), *New French Feminisms* (New York: Schocken, 1981), p. 137.
42 J. Derrida, 'The double session', in *Dissemination*, translated by Barbara Johnson (Chicago, IL: University of Chicago Press, 1981), p. 265.
43 Derrida, *op. cit.*, p. 24.
44 Lazreg, *op. cit.*, pp. 96, 99.
45 Martin and Mohanty, *op. cit.*, pp. 193–5.
46 Sandra Harding, *The Science Question in Feminism* (Milton Keynes: Open University Press, 1986). See also the work of Evelyn Fox Keller, Helen Longino and Donna Haraway.
47 *Ibid.*, p. 246.
48 Bernice Johnson Reagan, 'Coalition politics: turning the century', in Barbara Smith, *Home Girls: A Black Feminist Anthology* (New York: Kitchen Table, 1983). For other feminist discussions of coalition politics see in particular the essays collected by de Lauretis, *op. cit.*
49 Zillah Eisenstein, 'Developing a theory of capitalist patriarchy and socialist feminism', in Eisenstein (ed.), *Capitalist Patriarchy and Socialist Feminism* (New York: Monthly Review Press, 1979).
50 Linda Alcoff, 'Cultural feminism vs post-structuralism: the identity crisis in feminist theory', *Signs: Journal of Women in Culture and Society* (Vol. 13, No. 3, Spring 1988), p. 434.

10

Hidden from international relations: women and the international arena

FRED HALLIDAY

The silences of international relations

Over the last two decades questions of gender, and particularly those concerning the place and role of women, have acquired much greater importance within the social sciences as a whole. In response to the rise of a women's movement, and to the production of a growing body of analytic literature pertaining to women's position, there has been a marked development in the agenda and concepts studied in a range of academic disciplines. If this has been especially noticeable in history and sociology, it has also been evident in political science, economics and anthropology, and has acquired great importance in the most ideologically constitutive of the humanities, literature. There has, however, been one outstanding exception to this growing awareness of gender issues, namely international relations.

A survey of the articles published in and books reviewed by the main British and American journals of international relations will reveal little if anything on gender questions until very recently, and little that reflects an awareness of the expansion of interest in related areas of the social sciences.[1] If one looks at the contents of standard introductory courses on international relations, at the major textbooks, at the relevant shelves of academic bookshops, a similar absence is evident. In the flood of books published on nuclear strategy, terrorism, third world debt and the other preoccupations of the 1980s, there appeared to be nothing, not a single book, devoted to this question. To borrow from the image popularized in Sheila Rowbotham's study of women and history, women have been hidden from international relations.[2] It is as if the issues raised by feminism are not relevant to the international sphere and need not form part of the academic agenda for the study of international relations.

To overcome the invisibility of women requires analysis of why the concealment takes place and of the several reasons that combine to enforce this occultation. One explanation is institutional inertia. As long as a virtually complete silence on the issue exists, those concerned with it are either discouraged from working on it or choose to do so in other, more receptive academic disciplines – or in extra-academic contexts. A second factor is the selective insulation of international relations from developments in other social sciences. International relations is in some respects an enthusiastic importer, one might even at times suggest *comprador*, of concepts from other disciplines. However, there are large areas of social science theory that appear to be unrecognized within international relations. The growth of women's studies is one of them.

Finally, there is the conventional definition of what constitutes the subject-matter of international relations, namely high politics: issues of state policy, especially those concerning security and macroeconomic management. Gender issues have little apparent place in this hierarchy. Even the broadening of international relations to encompass more transnational questions, those distinct from security and not necessarily mediated through states, has done little to rectify the situation. The literature on transnationalism and world society has been almost as silent on gender issues as has the high politics alternative. Academic reserve is compounded by the fact that the domain of international practice – in foreign ministries, ministries of defence and related policy bodies – is itself an especially male-dominated reserve, beyond even the norms prevalent in policy making bodies as a whole (as the meagre number of women foreign ministers or ambassadors the world over indicates). In conventional ideology, women are not suited for such responsibilities and cannot be relied on in matters of security and crisis. Nothing could, it appears, be further from the traditional realm of women's concerns than international security and other global issues.[3]

There is, however, a more fundamental reason for the gender blindness of most of the field of international relations, namely an assumption of separation between the two spheres of gender and international relations. On the one hand it is presumed that international relations as such are little if at all affected by issues pertaining to women. To put it in simplistic terms, the assumption is that one can study the course of relations between states without reference to questions of gender. On the other hand, by neglecting the dimension of gender, international relations implicitly supports the thesis that international processes themselves are gender neutral; that is, that they have no effect on the position and role of women in society, and on the relative placement of women and men.

The fact is that, in common with other social practices, international processes do have gendered effects – from military and economic ones to the formation and diffusion of images of women and fashions of feminism. The language of international politics also suggests a strong conventional masculine and often homophobic content, with its emphasis on toughness and competition. It is insulting to be called a Pollyanna, a wimp or limp-wristed. The saying 'All's fair in love and war' should suggest a connection between these two Hobbesian domains.

The emergence of women's issues within international relations involves a dual challenge to any assumed separation of the two domains. One aspect of the challenge is to reveal how gender issues and values could and do play a role within international relations; the second aspect is to analyse the gender-specific consequences of international processes, be these military, economic, political or ideological. The latter modification has broad implications for the study of international relations as a whole, since it rests upon the argument that international relations should study the consequences of international processes within societies, and the resulting impact of these internal changes on international relations, as well as analysing the sphere of international processes *tout court*.

An emerging concern

Twenty years after the emergence of feminism within the social sciences, some awareness within international relations of the relevance of this topic has become evident. It may be valuable to identify the factors that have prompted the change. There has been some measure of interaction between international relations and other social sciences on questions of gender, so that questions and concepts raised in cognate disciplines can be seen as relevant to the international domain.

In the first place the growth of a feminist current within political and social theory has produced analyses with evident implications for international relations theory.[4] These include critiques of power and its symbolization in gender terms, as well as discussions of specifically gendered definitions of security, rights and authority. Human rights, for example, have become much more important issues in international relations and, in so far as they have acquired a gender dimension, it is directly relevant to analysis of the role of states and other actors in promoting or denying rights to women. This is so in the broader political arena, as well as in contested areas such as marriage and family law, contraception and abortion, policies on female employment, and responses to rape and other forms of violence against women. Discussions surrounding the problems associated with a concept of national interest have made its often partisan and group-specific character more evident. While much of the critique of national interest focuses on differences involving social groups, bureaucratic interests or ethnic and religious groups, this critique could evidently be extended to question whether definitions of national interest are gender specific and benefit men more than women under particular circumstances. The least that can be said is that different policies, be these military or economic, may have variant effects on men and women, and that any assumption of gender neutrality is debatable.

The second dimension of interaction between women and the international sphere is the extent to which international policies and processes, far from being gender neutral, in practice play an important role in determining women's place in society and in structuring economic, social and political relations between the sexes. This is perhaps most obvious in economics: international economic processes have strongly affected women in both developed and less developed countries in recent decades. The newly industrialized countries have seen mass recruitment of women into high technology industries.[5] In other third world countries, changes in agricultural employment, as well as high levels of male out-migration to richer third world states or to more developed countries have had great impact on the roles and responsibilities of women. The structural adjustment policies pursued by a number of third world governments in the 1980s, often at the behest of the IMF and World Bank, have had gender-specific consequences: as wage levels deteriorate, women are often compelled to work in the least remunerated areas while publicly financed services on which women and children are particularly dependent deteriorate. Thus women bear a disproportionate burden in debt repayment strategies. In the developed countries industrial change has promoted the employment of women in some areas and reduced it in others. The growth in some developed countries of an underclass, composed largely of women and children, is in part a product of new forms of international competition. In the political sphere, the entry of women into political life as voters and political subjects, an international phenomenon, has been one of the most marked changes of the twentieth century.

Even the most apparently insulated arena of all, family relations, has been affected in many ways by international changes in this century: by changes in medicine, especially with respect to contraception; by the spread of domestic technologies; by the diffusion of new role models and ideologies of male–female and parent–child relations. The constitution of women's position in society and economy, and of women's position in the home (for all that it is private and subject to national variations) owes much to changes and trends that are international and transnational.

There is no dimension of transnational relations more contentious and long running than the religious. It is not difficult to see how the changes in religious policy and fashion have, in recent years as earlier, had direct consequences for women. This is true for women in Islamic countries, where the rise of Islamicist movements in the 1970s and 1980s has affected many aspects of women's lives. It is also true within Catholic communities, where the reassertion of traditional doctrine on reproduction has provoked widespread resistance. At the cost of some exaggeration, it is possible to extend the slogan of the women's movement, that the personal is political, to assert that the personal is international, in the sense that inter-personal, micro-political relations are greatly influenced by transnational processes. If there are many ways in which this does not apply, there are far more ways in which it is true than conventional wisdom would have us believe. International processes often are not gender neutral, and gender relations, for all their autonomy, are not insulated from international factors.

Third, despite the subordination that women have and do experience, they have in recent years acquired much greater prominence as international actors. This has been true on issues of war and peace, in economic and social development, and in the growth of the women's movement itself which, in its concern to alter the position and thinking on a range of social and personal issues, has spread throughout the developed world and has had considerable resonance in the Third World as well.

The spread of women's organizations and campaigns across frontiers since the late 1960s is a striking example of transnationalism. Here is one of the clearest cases of *non-state* actors since, it can reliably be reported, women as a group do not hold state power in any of the 170 independent countries in the world. This development is marked by both the growing transnationalism of organization and debate on women's issues and by the combination of mobilization on women's questions with action on other, more conventionally international questions. As with many other aspects of transnationalism and feminism, this combination is less novel than is often supposed. One of the most striking transnational movements of modern times was the movement in support of women's suffrage in the first two decades of this century.

While questions of gender are seen as personal or single issues, they have long formed part of a broader political and ideological outlook, as is evident both in the campaigns to promote women's equality and in those that oppose it. The link between women's issues and political and international change was evident at the time of the French Revolution, in the writings of Mary Wollstonecraft among others. One of the originators of socialist internationalism in the 1840s was the feminist Flora Tristan. Similarly, opposition to women's equality may often correlate with certain attitudes to international issues. In the early 1980s one of the most active opponents of the Equal Rights Amendment to the US Constitution was Phyllis Schlafly, a right-wing leader who had also written three books on nuclear strategy in which she called for the US to have first-strike nuclear capability against the USSR and denounced Nixon and Kissinger as dupes of Moscow.

Many areas of foreign policy have a gender-specific component. Starting with the question of war, the conventional core of the subject, there is a wealth of discussion about the specific contribution of women to preventing war. There is often a conceptual ambiguity here since, as Ruth Roach Pierson has shown, there is a distinction between deriving a feminist position on peace from woman's role as mother, and arguing for such an approach because women are people normally separate from access to the means of warfare.[6] None the less, the argument on women and peace has a long militant and analytic tradition. If this connection was evident in the 1980s, in campaigns against nuclear weapons, it was equally a feature of the peace campaigns prior to and during the First World War.[7] In addition, there is substantial discussion of the role of women in war – as combatants in situations of resistance to occupation and as supporters of militaristic policies.[8] The spread within NATO countries of female recruitment to regular peacetime armies in recent years has prompted a wide ranging debate on how women can and do integrate themselves into military structures.[9] The dispute over the role of women on active duty in the US invasion of Panama served to underline how much resistance to change there is on this question by the military apparatus and the public.

If there is therefore a significant gender dimension to what is supposedly the core topic of international relations, comparable dimensions can be found in other areas of the subject. International institutions have come to devote much more attention to the position of women within societies as well as in relations among them, and the UN Decade for Women (1976–85) prompted widespread interest in issues of international law, development and national policies on women.[10] Both the UN and the EEC have produced a substantial body of policy and analysis on the position of women.[11] A great number of non-governmental organizations are active on women's issues, ranging from the general, such as for example the Gender and Development Unit at Oxfam, to the specific, such as the French-based Women Living under Muslim Law. The gender dimensions of international economic policy, be these in regard to employment, sexual divisions of labour, development or migration are also, as already noted, receiving much more attention. Foreign aid, one of the most prominent aspects of developed states' international economic policy, has acquired an overt gender component. A commitment to assisting women through development programmes has, since the mid-1970s, become wide-spread in OECD countries. A number of European countries, most notably Sweden, include benefit to women among the conditions of their aid programmes. The Percy Amendment, passed by the US Congress in 1973, stipulated that USAID programmes should spend at least $10 million annually on projects specifically designed to benefit women.

To sum up, there are at least four distinct ways in which issues pertaining to women and the international arena have, through a variety of processes, received greater recognition in recent years: through the encounter of feminism with international relations theory; through growing recognition of the gender-specific consequences of a range of international processes; through the emergence of women as distinct actors on the international scene; and through an increased awareness of the gender component of foreign policy issues.

States and women: nationalism and human rights

Many of the questions raised in these four broad aspects of the gender dimension of international relations can be illustrated by examining areas in which questions of gender intersect with established values and policies. One of the most contentious and relevant of all these topics is that of women and nationalism; another, equally difficult, is the place of women's rights in the formulation of inter-state relations. Both lead to what are, in conventional terms, unacceptable conclusions. This alone may suggest that they pose questions that are important in their own right, and also are relevant to the identification and discussion of the underlying assumptions of international relations as a whole.

If there is an assumption that national independence and national interest take precedence over the claims of any specific group within the nation, there has also been an assumption that, in general, the spread of nationalism is beneficial to women since they are a part of the nation. Nationalism mobilizes women into political life, exalts particular national traditions pertaining to women, and by granting them political rights as citizens provides a foundation for overcoming specific gender inequalities.[12] There is, however, another side to the story. Nationalist movements subordinate women in a particular definition of their role and place in society, enforce conformity to values that are often male defined and make it possible to delegitimize alternative policies on the grounds that these are alien. The use made of nationalist and anti-imperialist arguments to discredit and silence feminist movements in recent years is indication enough of this. States, not least newly independent states, exist to enforce hierarchies. Throughout the world, men have seen in the state and in the ideologies legitimating it – of which nationalism is the most potent – a means of enforcing their control over women.

Nationalism is far from being gender neutral. It seeks to mobilize women in support of its goals: independence and the consolidation of a specifically defined post-independence regime. Its effects for women are contradictory. How particular nationalisms have affected women in the countries concerned is an important topic for research and analysis; so is the broader theoretical question of how far an awareness of the position of women can lead to a questioning of the predominant values in international relations, namely state sovereignty and the primacy of national independence.

One possible way of approaching the broader question is by way of what one may term a feminist Luxemburgism. Rosa Luxemburg argued that the independence of nations should be seen as conditional upon how far it advanced the interests of the working class; in the case of pre-1914 Poland, she argued that Poland should, on these grounds, remain part of the broader Russian state.[13] A comparable argument could be raised with respect to women and national independence, namely that the independence of specific states should be judged by a range of criteria, including how far that independence has advanced the position of women.

In one sense Luxemburgist arguments are no longer relevant: a world of independent states has been created and the question of support, qualified or not, for their creation no longer applies. None the less, it is conceivable that in cases where national and national–religious ideologies subordinate women even more than was the case under foreign domination, the authority of the independent states and their officially sanctioned cultures should not be taken as self-evident. In countries such as Ireland and Malta, where divorce is still banned, the identification of nation with clerical authority has especially pernicious effects.

As in the case of the original Luxemburgist argument, there are many obvious counter-arguments: that women's position as members of a nation takes precedence over their position as members of a subordinate gender; that national independence as such is a superior goal to that of the rights of individual members of a nation; that it is not possible to overcome sectoral inequalities of class, ethnicity or gender within a nation until independence has been achieved. These are all strong arguments and would probably carry the day in any context. However, the feminist critique of nationalism and national sovereignty would, at least, open these issues up for discussion in a way that an assumption of the automatic primacy of national independence and sovereignty does not permit. In virtually all cases where nationalism has had deleterious consequences for women, discussion of the implications of this has been silenced or marginalized by appeal to supposedly higher values. Given the predominance of a nationalist framework for argument, women opposed to forms of oppression legitimated as traditional, authentic, popular and so forth have had to argue that such policies are not really those of the nation or are not historically justified. In this way the nationalists have forced the argument on to their terrain, denying the legitimacy of a discussion of the rights of women as such. It should be possible to reject, on universalist grounds, repugnant ideas and practices, be they traditional or otherwise. Similar nationalist distortion is, of course, evident with regard to other political issues, such as the rights of ethnic minorities, workers and intellectuals.[14]

There has, to date, been little discussion of an area in which gender could come to play a significant role in foreign policy, namely human rights. Yet the scope for such a modification is enormous. We have seen, in the 1980s especially, states make the future of their relations with other countries conditional upon their domestic performance with regard to some forms of human rights and impose, or threaten to impose, sanctions of various kinds if expectations are not met. Such demands have not, to date, encompassed the rights of women. But there is no reason in principle why comparable arguments should not be advanced. Countries with a commitment to gender equality could shape their foreign policies accordingly, and could try to mobilize coalitions in the UN, as they do on other issues, to put pressure upon delinquent states responsible for gendered apartheids.

There are, of course, many problems with this option, not least the dangers of backlash and retribution. These dangers, common to all human rights campaigns, should not conceal what is likely to be the most profound source of resistance to such campaigns, namely the belief that while some forms of human rights violation are proper subjects for foreign policy those pertaining to women are not. It is, in conventional terms, simply preposterous that questions of gender should play this kind of role in relations between sovereign states. There will, inevitably, be much talk of differing national traditions, and official spokesmen and spokeswomen will be produced from the countries concerned to denounce external interference in the internal affairs of the society in question. National and, where relevant, anti-imperialist sentiments will be mobilized to check any such external challenges to male domination, and to the state powers which reinforce and embody it. There are difficult issues here of both policy and theory: but the failure of such policies to emerge at all, and the probable response to them, illustrates clearly how important issues of women's subordination are in the overall constitution of national ideologies. It also shows how a commitment to gender equality, beyond any domestic or internal political consequences, does pose a challenge to prevailing conceptions of authority and sovereignty in international relations itself.[15]

Implications and problems

The scope of what is conventionally seen as the discipline of international relations has expanded considerably in recent years to encompass new thematic and conceptual areas. In the 1980s alone, the rise of international political economy has altered much of the academic content of teaching and research in international relations. In the case of women, it has been argued here that on the basis of four general considerations, the discipline can and should adjust to a set of issues that have, to date, received little attention. It is not as if consideration of gender will alter the teaching and research of international relations as a whole. It will, however, do more than just add another subject to the list of topics already considered, since in addition to the specific questions it raises and the alternatives to established values it suggests, the question of gender and international relations will reinforce a shift already present in much of the literature on transnationalism and international political economy. This involves asking not only how states and societies relate to each other, but also how international processes, be these inter-governmental or not, make themselves felt within societies. The force of the historical sociological literature lies in its demonstration of how the processes regarded as internal to states and economies are to a considerable degree products of international factors.[16] One of many potential contributions of a gender and international relations approach could be to show how gender relations in the economy, polity and family are shaped and changed by processes external to the society in question. This issue could therefore be part of a broader reorientation of international relations toward the study not only of inter-state behaviour but also of how states and societies interact.

That such a development will pose considerable difficulties in teaching and research is evident. The most general source of resistance will be reluctance to accept a general reorientation of international relations. But there are also more specific problems, and it may be worth identifying some of them in summary form. There is, first of all, the lack of adequate literature that is clearly within the field of international relations. Some materials are available in related areas – political science, sociology, development studies, history – and can be used as the bases for initial work. The production of a basic literature integrating these concerns with international relations is, however, an essential prerequisite for consolidation of research and teaching on this topic. Secondly, there is the question, recurrent in women's studies, of the balance between autonomy and integration. Should a distinct teaching and research programme be established, or should this work be integrated into the broader, established academic structure? A pragmatic initial response would seem to be that both approaches are needed, with specialist options and research reinforcing the inclusion of gender as a regular item in any comprehensive international relations course or textbook.

A third issue, equally recurrent, is that of title: the arguments for 'women and international relations' as against 'gender and international relations' have been well rehearsed, with the former suggesting a marginalization from the mainstream of the discipline and the latter committing the course to consideration of the constitution of gender beyond an examination of women themselves. In practice, there may be less difference in the course and research programmes of these two titles than at first sight appears. A programme entitled 'Women and International Relations' perhaps promises a less ambitious programme than a course claiming to encompass the broader range of questions raised by analysing gender.

Two other theoretical problems can be seen as relevant to this topic, and are well established points of debate in other areas of social science. One is the problem of cultural relativism – the claim that values pertaining to women and other social actors vary among societies and that it is therefore difficult or impossible to make general statements about what constitutes discrimination or domination in different societies. This has arisen directly in considerations of the position of women in national and religious contexts. For all the dangers of external misunderstanding, there may well have been rather too much concession to this, at the expense of assessing and criticizing ideologies and practices that, in the name of national traditions and authenticity, do oppress women. A similar tendency operates with other forms of power, along lines of race, class or age. While an awareness of relativity and difference is essential to an explanation of how and why systems of domination originate and are maintained, such a recognition need not necessarily lead, out of a misplaced anthropological generosity, to denying that forms of oppression do exist and recur in a wide range of societies and historical contexts.

The other theoretical problem is what might be termed precipitate totalization, that is the tendency, once connections between different levels of social and political practice have been established, to see all as the expression of a single mechanism or process. In this context, assertion of the relation between gender and international relations necessarily leads neither to the claim that gender issues constitute *the* core of international affairs and the key to understanding the international arena as a whole; nor does it lead to the argument that all aspects of women's location and experience can be derived from the international. To argue either of these would be to overstate the case. At the same time, enough has been done to show that, whatever distinctions prevail, issues pertaining to women do have a place in the study of international relations. Much of the resistance to this linkage stems not from a view of international relations in particular, but from a refusal to accept the validity of feminist concerns in general. As with other disputes on international relations and method, it may be best to shift discussion on to this general terrain rather than trying to resolve it in a necessarily restricted international relations context.

Without any overstatement, it would appear that there is a great deal of work to be done on women and international relations. It can only be hoped that this question will find recognition as an important and distinct topic within the overall research programme of the discipline, and that it will become an established element in its teaching agenda. Such a recognition is long overdue.

Notes

1 Among the rare exceptions of relevant discussion of international relations literature are Georgina Ashworth, 'The UN Women's Conference and international linkages in the women's movement' in Peter Willetts (ed.), *Pressure Groups in the Global System* (London: Frances Pinter, 1982) and Ellen Bonepath (ed.), *Women, Power and Policy* (New York and Oxford: Pergamon, 1982), Part 4.

2 Sheila Rowbotham, *Hidden from History: Thirty Years of Women's Oppression and the Fight Against It* (London: Pluto, 1973).

3 For discussion of this issue see Edward Crapol (ed.), *Women and American Foreign Policy* (Westport, CT: Greenwood Press, 1987). In the mid-1980s a Women's Foreign Policy Council was established by a group of US women, including Bella Abzug and Mim Kelber, calling for the location of a critical mass of women in senior foreign policy and defence positions.

4 See the chapters by Ann Tickner and Robert Keohane in this volume.

5 For an overview of literature on this see Ruth Pearson, 'Latin American women and the new international division of labour: a reassessment', *Bulletin of Latin American Research* (Vol. 5, No. 2, 1986), and, for an earlier analysis, Diane Elson and Ruth Pearson, 'The subordination of women and the internationalisation of factory production', in Kate Young, Carol Wolkowitz and Rosalyn McCullagh, *Of Marriage and the Market, Women's Subordination in International Perspective* (London: CSE Books, 1981).

6 For discussion of these issues see Sharon Macdonald, Pat Holden and Shirley Ardener (eds), *Images of Women in Peace and War* (London: Macmillan, 1987), especially the essay by Ruth Roach Pierson who develops the distinction between a feminist critique based upon ideas of motherhood and one deriving from women's separation from the means of warfare. An excellent discussion of issues

involved is Micaela di Leonardo 'Morals, mothers and militarism: anti-militarism and feminist theory', *Feminist Studies* (Vol. 11, No. 3, Fall 1985).

7 See Anne Wiltsher, *Most Dangerous Women, Feminist Peace Campaigners of the Great War* (London: Pandora, 1985), and Lela Costin in Judith Stiehm (ed.), *Women and Men's Wars* (Oxford: Pergamon, 1983). A fascinating study of the relationship between the suffragette movement, the trades union and the Irish independence movement on the eve of the First World War is given in George Dangerfield, *The Strange Death of Liberal England*. Dangerfield's thesis is that the combination of these three opposition forces was threatening to overthrow the British state, and that the challenge was only deflected by the outbreak of war.

8 Stiehm, *op. cit.*; Jean Bethke Elshtain, *Women and War* (New York: Basic Books, 1987). Elshtain's earlier work has been subject to considerable debate as in Judith Stacey, 'The new conservative feminism', *Feminist Studies* (Autumn 1983).

9 Judith Stiehm, *Bring Me Men and Women: Mandated Change at the US Air Force Academy* (Berkeley, CA: University of California, 1972); Cynthia Enloe, *Does Khaki Become You? The Militarisation of Women's Lives* (London: Pluto, 1983); Wendy Chapkis (ed.), *Loaded Questions: Women in the Military* (Amsterdam: Transnational Institute, 1981).

10 The main UN legal document is the *Convention on the Elimination of All Forms of Discrimination Against Women*, adopted by the General Assembly on 18 December 1979. It set up a 23-member Committee on the Elimination of Discrimination Against Women to monitor implementation. On the UN Decade for Women see Carolyn Stephenson in Stiehm, *op. cit.* The classic study of women and development remains Ester Boserup, *Women's Role in Economic Development* (London: Allen and Unwin, 1970). See also Gita Sen and Caren Grown, *Development, Crises and Alternative Visions: Third World Women's Perspectives* (New York: Monthly Review Press, 1987).

11 On women and the EEC see Catherine Hoskyns, 'Women, European law and transnational politics', *International Journal of the Sociology of Law* (Winter 1986) and 'The Community of Women', *Marxism Today* (January 1987).

12 For a comprehensive overview see Kumari Jayawardena, *Feminism and Nationalism in the Third World* (London: Zed Press, 1986).

13 Peter Nettl, *Rosa Luxemburg*, abridged edition (Oxford: Oxford University Press, 1969), pp. 500–19 and Horace B. Davis (ed.), *The National Question: Selected Writings by Rosa Luxemburg* (New York: Monthly Review Press, 1976).

14 These issues of women's rights and nationalist authenticity have been posed especially sharply in countries where religion constitutes the national position on women: Ireland, Algeria and Iran have all been cases of this. A searing critique of reverse ethnocentricity and the use of national–religious ideology to subordinate women in Iran is given by Azar Tabari, 'The women's movement in Iran: a hopeful prognosis', *Feminist Studies* (Vol. 12, No. 2, Summer 1986). Similar issues with regard to Iran are posed by Kate Millett in *Going to Iran* (New York: Coward, McCann and Geohegan, 1982). For a spirited debate on feminist orientalism see *New Left Review* (No. 170, July–August 1988).

15 Georgina Ashworth, 'A feminist foreign policy', talk given to LSE International Relations Department General Seminar, February 1987.

16 I have developed this further in 'State and society in international relations: a second agenda', *Millennium* (Vol. 16, No. 2, Summer 1987).

Index